FLEET'S HATCHET.

Severe Cross-Examina-
tion by Robinson.

IT WAS IN THE BOX
WITH OTHERS.

Contradiction of Yester-
day's Testimony.

Did Not Think at the Preliminary
This Hatchet Was Used
for the Murders.

LOOKING FOR A[...]

Unanimous Opinion at
New Bedford

That the Government
Case Is Lost,

WITHOUT A WORD FROM DEFENSE.

SOME STRONG TESTIMONY WILL BE
PRESENTED, HOWEVER,

In the Prisoner's Behalf.

Lizzie Seen Com[...]
from the Barn.

TIME FIXED BY S[...]
ERAL WITNESSE[...]

Medley Badly Knocked

THREE YOUNG BOYS EXAM[...]
THE BARN LOFT,

"WHAT IS THE DEFENSE? NOTHING, NOTHING, NOTHING.

Brilliant and Convincing Argument of District Attorne[...] Knowlton Brought To a Close at Noon.

"NOT GUILTY."

MISS BORDEN RETURNS

A Free and Vindicated
Woman.

Jury But an Hour and Six Minutes Reaching Its Conclusion.

PRISONER'S "I AM INNOCENT,"

NOT GUILTY OF MURDER.

Lizzie Borden Acquitted of the Crim[...] Charged Against Her.

The Jury Out In Deliberation On The Case Only a Li[...]
Over an Hour.

As The Verdict Was Announced, Lizzie Dropped Into [...]
Chair As Though Shot.

The  Sun.

EDGAR ALLAN POE AWARD-WINNING BOOKS
BY EDWARD D. RADIN:

12 Against Crime

12 Against the Law

LIZZIE BORDEN:

The Untold Story

by

Edward D. Radin

SIMON AND SCHUSTER

NEW YORK · 1961

FIRST PRINTING

LIBRARY OF CONGRESS CATALOG CARD NUMBER: 61–9597
MANUFACTURED IN THE UNITED STATES OF AMERICA
BY GEORGE MCKIBBIN & SON, INC., NEW YORK

To Beatrice, Vicki and Alice
in appreciation of their patience and encouragement

Acknowledgments

This book could not have been written had I not been able to consult the official court minutes of the trial of Lizzie Borden recorded by stenographer Frank H. Burt. I am deeply grateful to the Honorable Paul Cashman Reardon, Chief Justice of the Massachusetts Superior Court, for making this possible. I also wish to thank Mr. Edward J. Kelley, Executive Clerk to the Chief Justice, for his many courtesies. I am equally in debt to Mr. and Mrs. Dwight Waring, who permitted me to examine the only known copy of the official minutes of the Fall River District Court hearing.

Miss Constance S. Winslow, director of The Historical Society of Fall River, was extraordinarily generous when she allowed me to examine material and photographs gathered over the years about Lizzie Borden and the Borden family. Miss Winslow helped me even further when she verified information I had obtained in interviews.

I owe special thanks to Miss Margaret Enwright, Librarian, and her staff at the Fall River Public Library; to Mr. Philip A. Putnam, Assistant Librarian, Reference Department, Harvard Law School Library; and to Miss Mollie O'Meara, Butte Public Library, Butte, Montana.

I must acknowledge the friendly co-operation and the valuable suggestions made by the Honorable Benjamin Cook, Presiding Justice, Second District Court of Bristol, Fall River; the Honorable James J. Kelleher, Assistant Attorney Gen-

eral, Boston; the Honorable Edmund Dinis, District Attorney, Southern District, New Bedford; Mr. William P. Grant, Clerk, and Mrs. Estella Margarido, Head Clerk, Superior Court, Taunton; Mr. George F. Driscoll, Clerk, and Miss M. Martha Pellisier, Assistant Clerk, Second District Court, Fall River; Mr. I. Albert Matkov, Acting Librarian, Massachusetts State Library, and Mr. Howard L. Stebbins, Librarian, Social Law Library, Boston.

I was able to visit the famous murder scene through the courtesy of Mr. and Mrs. John McGinn, who now live in the Borden home.

Hours were spent on the telephone on my behalf by Jack Brennan, host of the Belmont Club, who arranged some interviews and smoothed so many paths for me during my stay in Fall River.

Some of those interviewed are named in the book; others requested that their names should not be published. To all of them I express my sincere thanks. The only statement I made to all of them was that I was writing a book about Lizzie Borden. I carefully avoided expressing any opinion concerning her guilt or innocence. I wanted, and believe I obtained, their judgments without influencing their opinions in any way.

EDWARD D. RADIN

Contents

LIST OF ILLUSTRATIONS

PICTURE SECTION
(*Following page 50*)

Lizzie Borden Prior to the Murders

The Borden House • Lizzie: Shortly after the Trial • The Handleless Hatchet

Andrew J. Borden • Mrs. Abbie D. Borden • District Attorney Hosea M. Knowlton • Defense Attorney George Robinson

Mr. Borden's Body • Mrs. Borden's Body

Miss Lizzie Borden: In Her Teens • In Her Twenties • About the Time of the Murders • In the Early 1900s

Stairway in the Borden House • Mrs. Adelaide B. Churchill • Miss Alice M. Russell

The Guest Room in Which Mrs. Borden's Body Was Found • Druggist Eli Bence • Assistant Marshal Fleet

Sketch of Lizzie Borden at the Trial • Bridget Sullivan, the Borden Maid • Maplecroft

The Legend

Lizzie Borden took an ax
And gave her mother forty whacks;
When she saw what she had done
She gave her father forty-one.

The legend of Lizzie Borden began on the sweltering hot morning of August 4, 1892, in Fall River, Massachusetts. On that day of steaming heat, it was later charged in court, Lizzie Borden quietly slipped into a second-floor guest bedroom where her stepmother was completing the final touches to making a bed. At that moment the two women were alone in the house; the family maid was outside washing the first-floor windows. In her hands Lizzie carried an ax or hatchet.

Nineteen times she flailed away in fury at the older woman, giving vent to long-suppressed hatred, hacking out a five-inch hole in the skull and chopping much of the head to ribbons. With her bloodletting lust satisfied at last, she let the body remain where it had fallen, quickly cleaned herself and the weapon, and then, for almost ninety minutes, calmly engaged in such homely chores as carrying up clothes from the cellar laundry, sewing a loop on a dress, ironing several handkerchiefs and leafing through a magazine. She was waiting.

When her elderly father arrived home, Lizzie greeted him with seeming serenity, told him Mrs. Borden had received a note and had gone out on a sick call, and, with disarming daughterly concern for his fragile health, urged him to rest against the enveloping heat, even assisting him to stretch out on his favorite sofa in the sitting room. Lizzie next tried to lure the maid into leaving the house by telling her of a sale of cheap cotton goods, but the servant, instead, went to her attic room, safely out of sight and sound. Soon after her father fell asleep, Lizzie returned to the sitting room, the same ax or hatchet in her hands.

Now the weapon of death descended ten times, once with sufficient force to slice through her father's cheekbone, sever an eye completely in half and continue on its path deep into his skull. As the weapon rose and fell in its rhythm of destruction, blood splashed onto the walls and even spattered the ceiling of the room. The bone-crushing blows may have snapped the handle of the weapon and ended the attack.

With the completion of the second murder, Lizzie dawdled no longer. In ten minutes or less she removed any and all traces of blood from her face, her hands, her hair; from her dress, her shoes, her stockings. And during that interval she also managed to scour the keen blade and the remaining stub of the handle so thoroughly that later scientific tests failed to show the slightest trace of blood even in hidden crevices. Confident that she was safe from detection, Lizzie Borden, who up to that first lethal moment had lived a blameless life, raised her voice to cry out the first alarm, her story all prepared.

Reports of the investigation that followed added substance to the legend. Lizzie Borden had shed no tears and had not shown any signs of visible grief even though she claimed she had found her father's body upon returning from a trip to the barn. In fact, as friends, neighbors, officials and others hurried into the charnel house, Lizzie easily was the least excited person there, coolly correcting an officer who referred to Mrs. Borden as her mother instead of stepmother.

The story of her laugh added a further touch of the macabre.

When her father arrived home, all the doors to the house were locked. While the maid was unbolting the front door to admit him, Lizzie, who was standing on the second-floor landing within a few feet of the open door to the guest room, suddenly laughed out loud. Whether it was the sight of the butchered body of her stepmother in a wide pool of coagulating blood or her pleased anticipation of the impending slaughter of her father that caused her glee, the legend leaves to the imagination.

Lizzie gave varying reasons for her trip to the barn. To police, she elaborated on her story. She had not visited just the barn, but had gone up into the hayloft, this on the hottest day of the year; she claimed she remained in that stifling atmosphere from twenty to thirty minutes while she searched through a small box for some lead she could use as sinkers, simple fishing equipment readily obtainable at a shop for only a few pennies. It was revealed in later testimony that as soon as an officer learned of her story, he visited the hayloft and saw no footprints in the heavy dust on the floor, although his own shoe impressions were clearly visible when he moved about.

Lizzie, by her own story, had to be in the house when her stepmother was murdered, yet she was unable to explain why she had neither seen nor heard anything. She simply said she thought Mrs. Borden had gone out in response to the note. No such note was ever found, no one ever saw it delivered, and public pleas and the offer of a large reward failed to produce anybody who wrote such a note or delivered it. The prosecutor stated flatly that there never had been a note, that it existed, along with her trip to the hayloft, only in Lizzie's imagination.

Further evidence quickly piled up. The very day before the murders Lizzie tried to buy the quickest-acting poison known; she was positively identified by the local druggist. That same night she visited a friend and, during the course of a strange conversation, dolefully predicted that "something" soon would happen at their home, a prediction which was fulfilled with remarkable speed. Three days after the murder Lizzie burned a dress in the kitchen stove, an act which did not become known until some time later. She gave police a silk dress and told them it was the garment she had been wearing the morning of the murders. Since no properly brought-up New England girl wears a silk dress in the morning while doing household chores, it obviously was not the one she had been wearing. And the burned dress, of course, was beyond recall. Her motive for the double murder was clear-cut: there had been a long smoldering feud with her stepmother over her father's fortune and Lizzie feared that he was rewriting his will against her.

It is little wonder, with a crime so gruesome, a suspect so unlikely, and a hatred so deep against her own father and the only woman she had ever known as a mother, that Lizzie Borden became a part of American folklore, a legend celebrated in verse, song, drama, ballet and literature.

Such is the familiar story of the legend. Since then countless thousands have chanted the four-line rhyme about the ax, which made its first appearance shortly after her arrest and long before her trial. Broadway has staged at least two dramas about her and she has been the central figure in a number of novels. Many essays have been written about the murders, and millions of television viewers watched a performance of an Agnes De Mille ballet based upon the legend, with a commentary offered by the late Joseph Welch, a distinguished member of the American bar. Just a few years ago Princess Margaret Rose of England delighted other people at a London gathering when she joined in singing the chorus of a song from a popular musical comedy —a song about Lizzie Borden. And every year now books appear in which Lizzie Borden's name is mentioned with no further identification thought necessary.

Yet even today Lizzie Borden remains little known as a person; it is the woman of the ninety-minute murders we see, hear and read about. Who was Lizzie Borden? What was she like? What kind of life did she lead? These and many more questions remain largely unanswered in the legend. And since Lizzie Borden was acquitted by a jury there is still another question: *Did she commit the murders?*

Her supporters said it was impossible for a well-bred woman to have been responsible for such atrocious murders and pointed to the absence of any bloodstains on her person as proof of her innocence. Some believers in her guilt suggested that the first observers at the scene had been too excited to notice traces of blood on her dress, the one she later destroyed. Others speculated that she could have removed her clothes and wielded the ax while naked. Meanwhile, neighbor quarreled with neighbor, friends disputed vehemently, and even members of families found themselves sharply divided as they debated the one and only question:

Did she or didn't she?

While the legend today seems to leave little doubt as to the answer, differences of opinion did exist then. Consider young Jim Kirby, a boy of twelve, a student at St. Mary's parochial school, which was on the same street as the Borden home. Young Jim knew Lizzie Borden and liked her. He had his personal reasons, reasons which will be given later, and he was one of her staunch supporters.

Recently, in a private club in Fall River, only a few minutes' walk from the original scene of the murders, James J. Kirby, now a silver-haired man of eighty, recalled those days when he was twelve. A retired executive, still physically vigorous and mentally alert, he carefully told me only what he knew from his own personal experiences with Lizzie Borden. When the last note had been taken, he was asked: "What do you think now? Was she innocent or guilty?"

The question obviously disturbed him. His youthful memories and dreams were suddenly fresh again and the dreams of our youth die hard. He moved a glass about on the table in front of him, studied the design on a familiar package of cigarettes, removed one, lit it, and took several puffs. The silence was unbroken, but the question remained to be answered and he was a courteous gentleman.

"Well," he said finally, "when I was twelve I was certain she was innocent. I believed it with all my heart and even had a few scraps with boys who sang that chant about the ax." He paused. "Since then, with all the stories I have heard and with everything I have read, I suppose I must in all honesty say that I think she was guilty."

Did she or didn't she?

Some years before the murders, while Charles Henry Putnam was a student at Brown University in Providence, he spent many weekends in nearby Fall River as the house guest of a fraternity brother. His young host was engaged to a local girl and she was very friendly with Lizzie Borden. As a result, Putnam frequently paired with Lizzie on those carefree weekends. Years later he discussed her with his son, James Putnam, a former book editor and today secretary of P.E.N., a world-wide writers' organization.

"Father died in 1949," said James Putnam. "The picture he gave me of Lizzie Borden is not the one you usually read. He described her as a nice girl, fond of outdoor activities, one who was fun to be with. He said she was a very pleasant companion and he enjoyed her company. I believe they went to church together on Sundays when he was visiting in Fall River. I got the impression from him that Lizzie was a gentle girl, well liked, highly respectable, and Father was certain that it was psychologically impossible for a person of Lizzie's character to have murdered those elderly people, particularly with an ax. Nothing he read or heard after that ever caused him to change his mind and he died still firm in his belief in her innocence."

Did she or didn't she?

Go to Fall River where Lizzie Borden was born, where she lived, where she died, and where she should be known best. The legend of Lizzie Borden is very much alive there. "When I was a kid going to school," a young insurance broker said, "I had to pass the murder house on my way. It may sound silly, but I used to hold my breath and run by it. Lots of us did. We were scared that something evil would come out and do us harm even though we knew Lizzie Borden no longer was connected with the house."

Did he know Lizzie Borden? No, he had caught occasional glimpses of her before her death when she rode around town in her chauffeur-driven limousine, but he had heard many stories. These stories, which make up the legend of Lizzie Borden, are repeated almost everywhere a stranger goes in Fall River. It is apparent that even in death Lizzie Borden is disliked or despised by many people in Fall River, and yet the city seems to take a perverse pride in her.

On exhibit at the Fall River Historical Society is an unpadded three-legged stool said to have been used by Lizzie Borden while she was held in the county jail awaiting trial. When the attendant is absent, children delight in climbing up on it. The card states that the stool was the only piece of movable furniture in her cell. Also on display is a large and cumbersome dinner pail with fitted compartments to hold various hot dishes. It still is the custom in many county jails for pre-trial prisoners to have the privilege of sending out for their own meals, and since Lizzie had the money to pay for these meals, her lunch pail traveled daily to the best hotel kitchen in Taunton.

The Historical Society issues a booklet of points of interest in Fall River. Included in the small list is the former Borden home, still standing, which is described as "the scene of the world-famous ax murder of Mr. and Mrs. Andrew J. Borden." The rest of the list is more prosaic, the most noteworthy item being a Cremonini mural decorating the ceiling of the Notre

Dame Church, the largest work by this artist on display in the United States. The title of the mural, interestingly, is the "Last Judgment."

Perhaps the last judgment has not yet been given in the Borden murders. At least one resident of Fall River has some doubt. Jack Brennan, owner-manager of the Belmont Club, was listening to patrons tell a visitor what they had heard about the case, the familiar stories of the legend being told again.

"How many of you have made a study of the case on your own?" he said suddenly. "I heard so much talk about the Borden murders when I was growing up here in town that I decided to find out the facts for myself. I read everything I could get including the old newspaper files in the library. You know, I'm not so sure Lizzie did it."

Did she or didn't she?

A jury of her peers said Lizzie Borden was not guilty and she was released. The legend maintains firmly that she was guilty.

In tracing down the legend, we are led repeatedly to one source, the works of the late Edmund Pearson. A noted librarian, the author of many scholarly books, he is recognized as the definitive historian of the Borden case. The facts of the Borden murders had been largely forgotten by 1924 when Pearson published his *Studies in Murder,* the first chapter of which was devoted to the Fall River crime. Since Lizzie Borden was still alive, Pearson delicately skirted the laws of libel but nonetheless indicated his belief that Lizzie had axed to death her father and stepmother.

The resurrection of the story by Pearson and the intriguing aspects of the case of a seemingly genteel woman who murdered with such efficient and appalling ferocity once again awakened world-wide interest in the case, an interest which has not slackened since then. Some years after her death, Pearson published his *Trial of Lizzie Borden,* the standard reference work on the case. He reproduced for the first time for modern readers parts of the actual trial testimony.

It is this book which is the source for most of what is now known about the crime and Lizzie Borden. Even in Fall River today you are referred to this book when trying to verify information. It contains a lengthy essay about the case, followed by a large section of the trial minutes, and it leaves most readers quite convinced that Lizzie Borden was guilty. Pearson openly states his belief in her guilt and the reader can only wonder why a court and jury refused to face overwhelming facts and allowed themselves to be swayed by sentimentality or guile.

Pearson certainly can be called the father of the literature on Lizzie Borden. Up to the time he issued his first study of the case, the only previously published material had been written immediately after the trial when tempers and feelings were still high. These included a legal discussion in a law journal of some of the court rulings, a slim pamphlet spoofing the trial, published in Providence, and a book, *The Fall River Tragedy*, by Edwin H. Porter, a Fall River police reporter, who stoutly defended Fall River police for arresting Lizzie Borden. This book, published in Fall River, had a limited sale and circulation.

All the other books, the novels, the dramas, the innumerable magazine articles that are part of the literature available today, appeared after Pearson, and most of the writers relied heavily on the material in Pearson's books as the springboard for their own writings. I have been unable to find any evidence that any writers since Pearson actually read the two-volume official trial minutes. It is true that just one copy of the minutes is in existence and it is neither easy to locate nor readily obtainable. Also the only known copy of the official stenographic minutes of the four-volume preliminary court hearing, which contain the testimony of several witnesses who were not permitted to testify during the trial, is in private hands along with most of the exhibits introduced during the trial.

Even though Pearson indicates very strongly that Lizzie Borden was guilty, the same question can still be asked:

Did she or didn't she?

I studied the 1,930 typewritten pages of trial testimony, the many hundreds of additional pages of the preliminary court hearing, the portions of the inquest made public, newspapers and other documents of the time. I also interviewed many people, including some who knew Lizzie—and I found the answer. The legend was only a legend.

Lizzie Borden was innocent.

Legends, as a rule, are composed of few facts, much exaggeration and many freewheeling flights of fancy and fiction. The legend of Lizzie Borden is no exception.

Why does the legend say she was guilty? Why has an innocent person achieved fame as a murderess? At the time of the trial many people agreed with the jury's verdict of Not Guilty; why, today, is it difficult to find anyone, even among students of the case, who is not convinced that Lizzie Borden committed two particularly brutal murders and got away with it?

Here are the reasons. This is how the legend was born and how it grew.

Fall River is a strangely divided and volatile city. The Quequecham River, which flows from the high hills in back of it, runs underground beneath the very center of town with tremendous force. It was this source of inexpensive power and the presence of a natural harbor which led Fall River, during Lizzie Borden's lifetime, to become the largest cotton-mill center in the United States.

But there is still another hidden stream in Fall River, one that runs beneath the veneer of ordinary people and bubbles to view unexpectedly during ordinary conversations. It, too, has great force, not to spin machines but to color reasonings and judgments. The bitterness against Lizzie Borden one encounters today in many quarters of that city is not due to the murder of an elderly couple. Most of these people never knew the older Bordens, nor did they know Lizzie Borden. Lizzie, rather, is a symbol to them of a caste, of a small group against the many, of long-festering resentment and frustration. This hidden stream of dislike exists today, it existed at the time of the murders, and its beginning goes back to a time before Lizzie Borden was born. Oddly, Lizzie harbored few, if any, of the prejudices that aroused this deep-rooted caste antagonism.

The Borden murders were a windfall to Fall River reporters who served as correspondents for many large out-of-town newspapers. One of them struggled hard to come up with a simile which would immediately convey to a more sophisticated big-city audience a sense of the furor the murders were causing in Fall River. "Never since the Granite Mill fire of twenty years ago has such a sensation been created in this city," he telegraphed to the New York *World*. While it is to be doubted that many New Yorkers were able to equate a fire in a mill with the tremendous excitement and tensions that were causing mass hysteria, his choice of a mill incident was apt because the mills of Fall River played an important part in shaping the life and legend of Lizzie Borden.

When the mills first opened, the owners imported shiploads of experienced workmen from England to operate the machines. But after a while the owners realized that inexperienced and cheap labor could handle many of the routine tasks. The first great mass migration from Ireland to this country was on at that time. In Boston, only some fifty miles away, many business firms were posting signs that no Irish need apply for jobs, but the welcome mat was out for them in Fall River and many settled there. With the need for a continuing supply of cheap labor, emissaries were sent to the north and soon many French Canadians also came to Fall River. In addition there were large

Slavic groups, a sprinkling of Portuguese from the Azores and, oddly, a small enclave of Chinese.

From a small town where most of the residents were descendants of early Colonial settlers, Fall River quickly burgeoned into a city where the Yankees became a minority of the population. But this small group of families controlled the mills, the stores, the banks, the commercial life of the city. While the newcomers were welcome to work at low wages in the mills, there was no admission for them into the city's social life; Fall River was divided between the old families and the others.

Most of the newcomers were Catholic, and while there may or may not have been religious prejudice at that time, echoes of old resentments are still discernible among second- and third-generation descendants of the mill hands. Evidence of it pops out suddenly during conversations where no questions have been asked that could connect, even remotely, with some of the remarks made.

"Did you know that for many years no Catholic was allowed to teach in the city high school?" one speaker remarked to this writer in the middle of telling what he had heard of Lizzie Borden. Another offered in an equally abrupt aside: "What I've got against the old families is that they never have done anything for this town, no museums, no parks." Still a third interrupted himself to relate what he termed a "funny" story. He began with a sweeping generalization. "During the Revolutionary War naturally all the old families were Tories." He said the men equipped themselves with fancy red uniforms and set out to join the British, sailing across the Taunton River. Hidden behind shrubs and tall grasses on the opposite shore were loyal American farmers who waited until the Tories were close to landing and then opened with a withering fire, killing most of them. History records the active role played by many of the old families of Fall River in the fight for Independence; the story has little, if any, basis in fact, but it does show that there was fertile ground in Fall River in which a legend could grow about Lizzie Borden, a descendant of one of the very early settlers in the region.

A catalytic agent is usually needed to generate a legend. Fall River already had two established daily newspapers when the *Globe* was founded several years before the murders. Where its rivals were sedate, conservative and politically Republican in leaning, the newcomer was brash, breezy and an outspoken voice for the Democratic party. Its appeal was to the mass public and it soon swept into second place in circulation, but a perusal of its pages shows that many of the large old Fall River firms either refused to advertise in it or used a minimum of space.

When the murders occurred, a behind-the-scenes newspaper war was on in Fall River, and from the start of the case the *Globe* became one of the earliest practitioners of yellow journalism in this country; anything went as long as it could build up circulation. The paper drove its competitors dizzy trying to run down the wild rumors it printed and it blithely ignored making corrections when the stories were exposed as untrue. From the very first day, the *Globe* decided that Lizzie was the culprit and it whipsawed public emotion as it carried on a clamorous campaign against her. Some friendly officers leaked information to it and, in return, eagerly followed the paper's suggestions. It is interesting to note that one of its chief reporters was Edwin Porter, who wrote the book defending the police after the trial. It is also interesting to observe that Pearson quotes liberally from Porter and the Fall River *Globe*. Porter modestly took no credit in his book for one of the great scoops of the case. His reason will be shown later.

Badgered by the *Globe,* the harried police administration gave ground and they also began to fit facts into a preconceived theory. The police happily surrendered their functions when an ambitious politician, who recognized an opportunity when he saw it, arrived on the scene.

At the same time Lizzie Borden did not help her own cause. She was a complex woman, very much the daughter of her strange father, but with unexpected, soft feminine traits. She possessed a stubborn, even arrogant, pride, and at times was too forthright for her own good. Even so, she won out, but it was a Pyrrhic victory: she was totally defeated after death with the appearance of Pearson's trial book.

Pearson did more than simply collect and present legend material. He actively added to the accepted Lizzie Borden legend.

Pearson's famous trial book, the source of so much of our literature and the wellspring of so much of our limited knowledge about Lizzie Borden, has misled successive generations of readers. By the use of innuendo, by accepting unfounded rumors as positive fact, by deleting words and phrases from his presented parts of the trial minutes, by suppressing many details and even long sections of relevant testimony, and by offering incomplete and innocuous summaries of what had been telling testimony by still other witnesses, Pearson presented a distorted and inaccurate version of the case; so much so that it is one of the strangest episodes in American letters.

It matters little whether Pearson sincerely believed Lizzie Borden was guilty; he has prevented his readers from reaching their own conclusions based upon *all* of the material facts. Further, by indicating that many of the big city newspapers published stories of the trial prejudiced in Lizzie's favor, he forestalled readers from turning to these papers as a means of checking on the accuracy of his statements. Yet a comparison of the official trial minutes with the reports published in many leading newspapers in Boston, New York and elsewhere shows that their accounts were fair representations of the trial testimony.

It is true that Pearson, in his subtitle, indicated that he had edited the trial minutes, but by accepted custom and usage such editing does not ordinarily include the elimination of vital evidence or the altering of the sense of what a witness said. No reader of Pearson learned that Lizzie Borden might have been crying immediately after the murders, that directly contradictory statements, including blatant and proven perjury, were made by state witnesses, that several key witnesses were recalled to the stand with startling testimony. Perhaps Pearson was being kindhearted when he deleted an episode embarrassing to the police concerning the handle of the so-called murder weapon. He certainly was merciful when he blacked out the antics of a high police official who was so anxious to avoid answering several simple questions that he willingly stigmatized himself as incredibly incompetent. But Pearson also extended the same blackout to this man's answers when the latter was finally backed into a corner where evasions would no longer serve. Porter, the Fall River reporter, was not wasting his time when he found it necessary to defend local police in the book he wrote immediately after the trial. Pearson improved on the old saw that the pen is mightier than the sword by proving that a blot of the pen can be mightier than any ax or hatchet. His strange role will be described and documented in its proper place.

As the untold story of Lizzie Borden unfolds, I believe that the reader will be able to detect the identity of the long-unsuspected killer who used an ax on Mr. and Mrs. Borden on that scorching hot August day in Fall River.

II

The Family

Lizzie Borden was born on Thursday, July 19, 1860, at 12 Ferry Street. Curiously, heat and excitement in Fall River accompanied many of the major events in her life. The weather was hot that day. Fall River is situated at the mouth of the Taunton River and along the eastern shore of Mt. Hope Bay, in a valley where heat tends to collect during much of the summer.

The excitement that day was caused by a story in the Fall River *News,* a weekly then published on Thursdays. The editor ignored the opportunity to record the arrival of a child destined to make Fall River known in many quarters of the globe. He had more important news. The entire front page was devoted to reprinting a lengthy speech made eight days earlier in New York City before the Young Men's Republican Union. It was not politics that induced the editor to devote so much space to a, by then, stale talk, but rather a prediction by the speaker of what the South might do if Abraham Lincoln won the election. Even then the newly organized cotton mills had become the dominant economic factor in Fall River and the mills depended upon the South for raw cotton. The town was torn between its sympathies and its pocketbook. Not far from the cramped wooden house on Ferry Street was a large imposing mansion built of granite blocks, which served as an important station on the underground railway for escaping slaves.

On the back page of that same issue there was an ad, long familiar to readers, that ran week in and week out, year after year, in which the firm of Borden & Almy, undertakers, extolled the remarkable virtues of Crane's Patent Casket Burial Cases, for which they were exclusive agents. The local firm guaranteed that these superior coffins would preserve and keep intact the remains of a beloved far longer than any other casket. How anyone could possibly verify such a claim was not explained, but this play on morbid fears and the desire of many people to delay the natural return to dust was most successful. The only change that appeared in the advertising copy over the years was the expansion of the business address. Originally started at 5 Anawan Street, the ad now included two adjacent store numbers as well, indicating the steady growth of the firm. As senior partner, A. J. Borden listed his Ferry Street home address, a discreet reminder to the bereaved that they could seek him out at any hour of the day or night when his establishment was closed.

There is no notation that he was called away to attend to death while waiting for the first wail of life, but there was less excitement in the house on Ferry Street than in the town that day. For Andrew Jackson and Sarah Morse Borden this was their third child. Their first, Emma Lenora, was almost nine and a half years old. Their second, Alice Esther, had died two years earlier at the age of two.

Andrew Borden was disappointed that the new baby was a girl. He was approaching his thirty-eighth birthday, wanted no more children, and had hoped for a son to carry on his name. Under the circumstances, he did the next best thing. To keep alive his first name he gave it to this girl child as her middle one. Since it was planned to call her Lizzie, it was typical of the uncompromising father that he did not use the more formal and suitable Elizabeth at the christening ceremony. Instead, she was officially christened Lizzie Andrew Borden.

Many years later, at the inquest into the murders, District Attorney Hosea M. Knowlton had to be reassured again and again that Lizzie really was her given name when he asked these questions:

Q: Give me your full name.

A: Lizzie Andrew Borden.

Q: Is it Lizzie or Elizabeth?

A: Lizzie.

Q: You were so christened?

A: I was so christened.

Lizzie was in many ways the product of her father. He often treated her like the son he had wanted by taking the trouble to explain his business philosophies to her, and it is necessary to understand the father in order to know the daughter.

The Borden family traces its American roots to Richard and Joan Borden, colonists from England, who settled in 1638 around Portsmouth, Rhode Island, not far from Fall River. By the time Andrew was born there were more than fifty different branches of Borden families living in Fall River alone, many no longer directly related. Some of these Bordens were by now wealthy and influential, but Andrew was born into a poor Borden family.

His father, Abraham, was a fish peddler, who managed, after many years of hard work, to save enough money to buy the small, inexpensive frame house on Ferry Street. The son seems to have set out deliberately to be as unlike his father as he could. Abraham was a friendly, gregarious man who enjoyed exchanging news and gossip with his women customers as he made his rounds, crying his wares. He is remembered in later life as a portly person who enjoyed sitting in the sun, ready to yarn with anybody who passed by.

Andrew was a tall, slender man, whose weight never varied more than a few pounds throughout his adult life. He was dour, taciturn, icily reserved, and very much like his Puritan forebears; he shunned such popular vices as tobacco and liquor and lived with a single-mindedness of purpose. When he did talk, he was blunt and outspoken, and not concerned with the sensitivities of others. The poverty of his youth had bitten deeply into him, and thrift, particularly in small matters, became an obsession with him. He was determined that he would not remain a poor Borden and he subordinated everything else in his life to this one ambition. Money, to him, was not a means to a more complete or enjoyable life, but something to be amassed for the sake of acquisition.

He gave sparingly, if at all, to charity, and his attendance at church was more lip service than devotion. When the tax assessor, who was an official of his church, raised the valuation on some of his properties, he simply stopped going to church in retaliation.

Andrew Borden had a dread of debt. For a man who later controlled all the banks in Fall River and knew the value of putting other people's money to work, he had one curious boast which he repeated endlessly: in his entire business life he had never signed a promissory note or borrowed a single penny. He drove a hard bargain and was quick to take advantage of every opportunity. When the heirs to some valuable parcels of real estate squabbled among themselves over the individual distribution of the properties, Borden stepped in with an all-cash offer that was far below the recognized market value. He knew the heirs were jealous of each other and that they were afraid that one would somehow get an advantage over the others. He reasoned that they would accept an offer of immediate cash despite the sizable loss it entailed. His judgment was sound. All but one of the heirs agreed to his low offer. This one threatened court action to prevent acceptance but was forced to go along. For many years after that this heir went about Fall River denouncing Borden so bitterly that when the murders occurred he had to present an alibi before police would clear him as a suspect.

Andrew Borden had saved enough money while still a young man to think of entering a business, and he had a chance to invest in the original cotton mills then being organized. Some of the wealthier Bordens, the Durfees, and members of other old families saw the opportunities for large and rapid profits and suggested that he join them. They pointed out that Americans were grumbling openly about the shoddy quality of inexpensive cotton goods being shipped here by English firms from their mills in India. England then had a monopoly on the manufacture of cotton cloth. New York merchants had been approached and were waiting eagerly for the products of the new mills, thus assuring a steady market and reducing the risk inherent in any new capital venture.

But risk, no matter how slight, was enough to deter the prudent Andrew Borden. He wanted a safe and certain business and since nothing in life is more certain than death, he became an undertaker. It was an excellent choice for him. Naturally solemn and dignified, not given to allowing his emotions to control his judgment, he could gauge with uncanny precision the number of extras that a grieving widow could be profitably talked into buying.

He never regretted this decision. As the mills grew, so did Fall River and so did his business. He sensed the opportunities of an expanding town and as soon as he had spare cash he began to invest it in downtown real estate, particularly on Main Street. He also purchased farms in surrounding areas when foreclosures presented bargains which could be sold later at a handsome profit. But he held on to his downtown property. As he accumulated more money, he studied the mills to determine which were the best managed and making the most profit, and he bought large blocks of shares in these. He was the tortoise in the fable of the race with the hare, determinedly plodding on his course, letting nothing sway him from it. At the time of his murder the assessed valuation of his Fall River realty holdings alone, a figure which was well under the actual market value, totaled almost a quarter million dollars. This did not include his large stock holdings, other real estate outside of Fall River, and a large amount of cash he always kept in the bank for those exquisite moments when somebody needed cash in a hurry and had to accept whatever offer he made.

This was the man who was to tutor Lizzie Borden, to instruct her in thrift, to teach her how to hold her emotions in check, to point out to her the values of downtown property and to prepare her to take his place when death inevitably came. Lizzie later told friends how her normally reticent father often discussed these matters at length. As a teacher he was often successful in influencing Lizzie; sometimes he failed.

When Lizzie was two years old, two important events occurred. At that time the Rhode Island state line bisected downtown Fall River and prevented it from expanding as a unity. In an unusual swap, Massachusetts and Rhode Island exchanged land so that the city no longer was hemmed in and could grow. There was a gala celebration in Fall River. The celebration was marred for Mr. Borden and Emma when Lizzie's mother died. Lizzie was too young to understand.

The marriage of Andrew Borden and Sarah A. Morse appears to have been a genuine love match; he was twenty-three years old, she was one year younger and she did not bring him any handsome dowry. He did not have much money at the time and there was a gap of five years before their first child was born. Little is known about Sarah Morse in Fall River today. At least two of her brothers moved to the territories where new states were being created and where they homesteaded farms.

The legend of Lizzie Borden really got its start when she was not quite five years old. It was then that Andrew Borden remarried and Lizzie acquired a stepmother.

If his first marriage had been a love affair, the facts indicate that the second may have been more a marriage of convenience, at least for Andrew Borden. He had remained a widower for somewhat over two years and during that time it was Emma who had to mother little Lizzie and try to run the household as best she could, a formidable task for a girl of twelve. Some help was given by Borden's only sister, Mrs. Hiram C. Harrington, but the undertaker disliked his blacksmith brother-in-law. Some years later their quarrels resulted in a complete break and Harrington was forbidden to enter the Borden home. When the final rupture came, Lizzie sided with her father. Harrington got his revenge after the murders.

The courtship between Borden and Abby Durfee Gray was brief. It is reported that he approached Miss Gray one Sunday as she and her stepmother were emerging from church, tipped his hat, and offered to escort her home, thus publicly signifying his intentions. The elated stepmother walked home with others. The couple were married several months later on June 6, 1865.

Miss Gray probably had no illusions about her marriage. She was a spinster of thirty-seven, short, a little over five feet tall, and she had a weight problem. By the time of her murder she had ballooned up to more than 200 pounds. She was marrying a man of forty-three, a widower with two daughters, one fourteen, the other soon to be five.

Lizzie, who had no memory of her own mother, readily accepted the change in the household and followed instructions to call the new Mrs. Borden Mother. Her sister Emma, who is usually portrayed as a weak and self-effacing personality, obviously was also very much a daughter of Andrew Jackson Borden, with a will of her own. She could remember her mother and would not accord this courtesy title to the new bride, nor would she address her as Mrs. Borden. She insisted upon calling her Abby, most unusual considering the wide difference in their ages, the formality of the era, and the respect children were expected to show their elders, so firm a custom in the New England of that period. Emma won out and she remained on a first-name basis with the new wife.

The role of stepmother is difficult. Not only may there be a

latent resentment on the part of the children, but there are
relatives, friends and neighbors watching and waiting to gossip. We have been conditioned by the fairy-tale literature of
our childhood to think of the phrase "wicked stepmother" almost as one word. But there is no evidence, not even a hint of
gossip, to indicate that short and fat Abby Borden was anything
but kind to the two girls she accepted as part of her marriage.
It is probably true that in times of girlhood crisis Lizzie turned
more often to Emma for comfort. As she explained at the inquest, "I always went to my sister because she was older and had
the care of me after my mother died."

One difficulty was avoided. Andrew Borden had no thought
of starting a second family; his passion was the acquisition of
wealth, all other desires had atrophied in this cold, austere
man. Abby Borden raised no objections; she was content simply
to be married.

Lizzie's childhood was largely uneventful but it is ironic to
note that one of her early playmates was Isabel Wright, whose
father was the town marshal, the title used in Fall River for chief
of police. The little girls played at each other's homes for several years until Marshal Wright became interested in politics,
resigned his office and moved to Taunton, the county seat. Years
later when Lizzie was ordered held for trial, she was sent to the
county jail, which is under the jurisdiction of the sheriff. He
asked his wife to search the new prisoner. As Lizzie was brought
into the sheriff's office, the other woman gasped. "Aren't you the
Lizzie who used to play with my Isabel?" She was Mrs. Wright;
her husband was the sheriff.

Borden had bought two farms in Swansea for his own use,
and for many years the larger place was a favorite summer retreat for Mrs. Borden and the two girls. It was here that Lizzie
first learned how to fish, and she became an expert angler.

When Lizzie was about twelve years old the Borden family
moved to 92 Second Street. It is likely that Mrs. Borden per-

suaded her husband to move by pointing out that Emma was twenty-one and that the small, shabby house on Ferry Street was no place for an eligible young lady to entertain prospective callers. It is more than likely that Borden purchased the house without consulting the distaff side of his family; a woman could have pointed out so many disadvantages.

While Second Street had once been a fashionable address, the seeds of its decay as a residential street were apparent even then. It was a short block in back of Main Street and some business

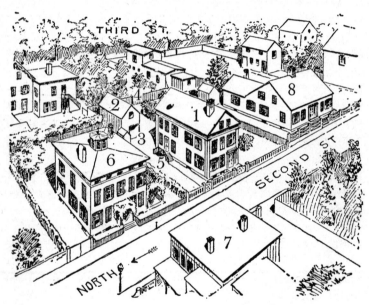

The Bettman Archive

NEIGHBORHOOD OF BORDEN HOME

1. Borden house
2. Borden barn
3. The well
4. Fence with barbed wire on top
5. Side entrance
6. Churchill residence
7. Dr. Bowen's house
8. Kelley house

firms had spread into it with stores built into the ground floors of a few homes near the corner. There were also two public stables farther up the street which added to the traffic and detracted from the general appearance. It is possible that Borden had hoped that stores would continue to spread along the block, thus increasing the value of his property as a business site. This would, to him, have outweighed any disadvantages the house might have as a home. If so, he miscalculated. Even today, the street presents the same mixed appearance, although some of the houses have been torn down for parking lots.

Since the house was the scene of the murders and its peculiar room arrangements played an important part in the legend, a careful description is necessary. Many of the homes on that block were large and spacious. Number 92 looked completely out of place among its more elegant neighbors. It was a severely plain and narrow two-and-one-half-story wooden building, not over twenty feet wide. Narrow, unadorned clapboards gave it a sharp angular look, which was accentuated by the steeply sloping roof. The house was only a few feet from the sidewalk. Although the building was on a good-sized plot, it had been erected fairly close to its neighbor on the north. The barn also was on this side, adding to the crowded effect.

The structure had been built as a two-family house with a separate railroad flat on each floor. Except for the entryways at the front and side doors, there were no inside halls. The narrow interior was cut in half by a wall running most of the length of the house and the rooms were a series of small boxes on both sides of the wall. To go from front to back, it was necessary to walk through succeeding rooms. The only running water was in a sinkroom off the first-floor kitchen, and there were no bathrooms. Before moving in, Borden installed a lavatory which, because of the lack of inside plumbing, had to be placed in the cellar. As a result, slop pails were kept in each bedroom. Although illuminating gas was then in use, no utility lines had

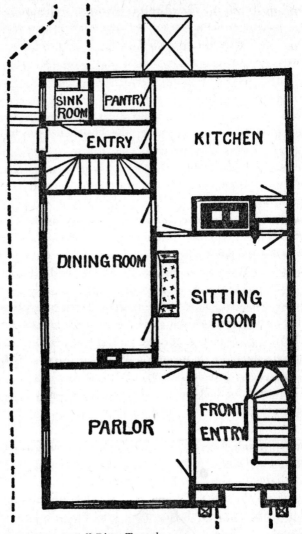

From Porter's *Fall River Tragedy*

GROUND FLOOR, BORDEN HOUSE

Mr. Borden was killed on the couch in the sitting room

been piped into the house and kerosene lamps were necessary. They were still being used at the time of the murders twenty years later when electric lights were beginning to come into use. The house did have one convenience, central heating. There was a coal furnace in the cellar and the old fireplaces had been boarded up.

Besides installing the water closet, Borden made a few minor interior changes. A wall was knocked out between two small rooms on the first floor in order to form a dining room, and the stove was removed from the second-floor kitchen, which was made into a bedroom. The interior of the house, for one-family use, was an architectural nightmare. The front door led into a small entry which contained a hall closet and a curving stairway to the second floor. On the first floor, as used by the Bordens, there was a parlor, a sitting room, a dining room and a kitchen. Off the kitchen was a pantry and a sinkroom and a narrow hall leading to the side door. In the side-door entry was a steep, dark, narrow-walled staircase going up to the rear half of the second floor and then up to the attic with its sloping roof. Because each room led not only into the room directly behind it but into the adjacent one as well, the first floor was a maze of doors. The sitting room, for example, contained five doors which led into the front entry, the parlor, the dining room, and the kitchen. All through traffic on the first floor had to pass through the sitting room.

The layout on the second floor, which was reserved for bedrooms, was similar. This meant that if the members of the family all used the front stairway, three of them would have had to pass through the bedroom at the head of the stairs in order to reach their own bedrooms. To avoid this awkward situation, the house was divided into two zones. The front stairs served a guest bedroom and separate chambers for Lizzie and Emma. The guest bedroom corresponded to the parlor, Emma's room to the sitting room and Lizzie's to the front half of the converted

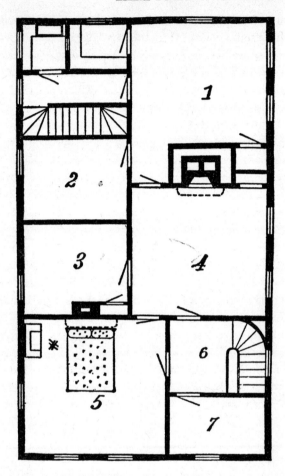

From Porter's *Fall River Tragedy*

SECOND FLOOR, BORDEN HOUSE

1. Mr. and Mrs. Borden's room
2. Mrs. Borden's dressing room
3. Miss Emma's room
4. Miss Lizzie's room
5. Guest room, in which Mrs. Borden was killed
6. Landing at head of stairs
7. Dress closet

dining room. Even so, to enter her bedroom, Lizzie had to go through Emma's room. Mr. and Mrs. Borden's bedroom and a connecting small chamber which they used as a dressing room were in the back half of the house and were reached by the steep staircase off the kitchen.

To insure further privacy, the interior door between Emma's room and the older Bordens' was kept locked. This meant that when Mrs. Borden wanted to reach the front guest bedroom from her own room, she had to go down the back stairs, walk through the first-floor rooms to the front entry and then climb the front stairs. A narrow interior hall on the second floor, just one room-length long, could have made all the bedrooms accessible to the front staircase, but Borden either did not think of it or did not want to spend the money.

If the new house on Second Street was not as appealing or as spacious as its neighbors, it still was an improvement over the old home on Ferry Street. And Borden did splurge in furnishing it. Flowered carpets were placed in all the main rooms. An upright piano was purchased for the front parlor. And, as the daughters of one of the now wealthy Bordens, Lizzie and Emma started rather late in life to take music lessons.

An undertaker is seldom a very popular person, and Borden's aloof manner and his tightfisted dealings in other business matters did not enhance his reputation. But he prospered even more after moving to Second Street and was engaged in a variety of profitable enterprises. There were four banks in Fall River and with fine impartiality he was president of one and a large stockholder and the dominant director of each of the other three. This gave him an inside track on all worthwhile foreclosures. When he was fifty-five years old he decided to sell his interest in Borden & Almy, and an auditor was brought in to make a fair appraisal. While examining the records, the accountant discovered that the firm's bookkeeper, Joseph W. Carpenter, had embezzled some $6,000 over a period of years.

The man was arrested but later, when Borden refused to prosecute, the charge was dropped. A report was soon current in Fall River that Borden let him get away with it because Carpenter threatened to reveal that Borden had substituted cheap coffins although he was paid for more costly ones. The former bookkeeper transferred $3,000 worth of property to Borden and raised an additional sum of money among friends, so the story about substituting coffins appears to be false. It was more in character for Andrew Borden to work out a private deal to get his money back rather than take a stand on any such abstract matter as justice.

His retirement as an undertaker did not slow him down. He participated actively in the loans and investments of all the banks. He helped organize a local traction company and was a director in the Merchant, Globe and Troy mills, three of the largest in Fall River, in which he held substantial interests. Because he was a shrewd judge of realty values, his services were in constant demand by the courts and others as an official appraiser. He showed only a few years before his murder that he had lost none of his business acumen. A New York corporation wanted outright ownership of the streetcar lines and offered a generous bonus above the market value for the outstanding stock. Everybody happily sold except Borden. He simply waited and finally forced the corporation to pay him double the value of the stock to remove him as a thorn in their side. At the time of his murder, when he was seventy years old, he was completing his most ambitious program. He had put together a block of property on Main Street in the heart of the downtown shopping area, torn down the old buildings, and erected a three-story office and store building which he named after himself. The A. J. Borden Building is still one of the largest of its kind in Fall River. Unable to perpetuate his name through a son, he did it with brick and mortar, not knowing that it would live on because of the way in which he met death.

The Bordens were not an affectionate family; tenderness, love, devotion, were words to them rather than feelings. Because Borden disliked Harrington, his brother-in-law, he almost never saw his only sister; she rarely came on a visit because her husband was not welcome and Borden would not enter her home. After the murders, her name was absent from the newspaper lists of mourners attending the double funeral, although this could have been an oversight by reporters.

Although Emma had been little Lizzie's protecting big sister, there was no close attachment between them when Lizzie entered her twenties and their age gap was no longer important. They were on friendly terms, always assisted each other, and, if one was away, dutifully wrote. But the love and devotion among brothers and sisters present in so many families was absent. They had few friends in common, shared almost no mutual interests, did not often go out together, and when they stopped spending summers at the farm in Swansea, quite frequently took separate vacations. Years later when they quarreled, neither made any serious attempt to patch it up; they separated and never saw each other again.

The move to Second Street had brought no rush of suitors to Emma's side. She was shy, not as outgoing as Lizzie, had far fewer friends, and left the house much less often than her sister. Young ladies in that era did not work unless it was an economic necessity, and Emma seems to have done almost nothing with her time except attend an occasional concert or lecture. She was an indifferent churchgoer and when her father walked out of the Central Congregational Church, she also stopped attending, although Lizzie continued. Later when there was a split in the Central Church and some members formed the First Congregational Church, Andrew Borden subscribed to a pew in the new church as a means of hitting back at his old enemy, the tax assessor. But his visits to the new church were infrequent. Emma went there sporadically. Mrs. Borden sometimes accompanied

Emma to the First Congregational Church and more frequently went with Lizzie to the Central Church.

Emma, who had been strong-willed enough to insist upon calling Mrs. Borden by her first name, also did not allow her father's dislike of Harrington to disrupt her relationship with her aunt. She was fond of her and visited the Harringtons regularly.

There was one unusual display of sisterly affection by Emma. When the family first moved into the house on Second Street, Lizzie was still a child and Emma was given a much larger bedroom. About the time Lizzie became thirty years old, Emma suddenly gave up her room and changed with Lizzie. Whether the switch was a form of a birthday gift or was Emma's way of announcing that she was now an old maid and that the still eligible Lizzie should have the choice room, is not known.

During the trial Prosecutor Knowlton hinted that one of the reasons for dissension in the Borden household was the desire of both daughters, particularly Lizzie, to move from Second Street to the more fashionable north hill section where many of the wealthier families now lived. While cross-examining Emma, the prosecutor went on a fishing expedition about this change in rooms, hoping it had been made to appease Lizzie. Emma testified that Lizzie had not requested the change nor had it been made because of anything Lizzie said or did. "I offered it to her," Emma said with such obvious sincerity that Knowlton immediately dropped the subject and never referred to it again.

What affection did exist in the Borden household was mainly between Lizzie and her father. His long talks were held only with Lizzie; Emma made it clear early that she was not interested. In a rare burst of emotion after her high-school graduation, Lizzie removed a ring from her finger and asked her father to wear it as a bond between them. It was an inexpensive ring and not at all suitable for a man; it would fit only his smallest finger. He wore no jewelry, carrying only a pocket watch. But during the rest of his life the dignified undertaker and banker never removed that ring; he was murdered while wearing it and it was buried with him. Whenever anybody asked about the ring he always said that it had been given to him by Lizzie. When he had the outside of the house redecorated, he told the painter to take his orders from Lizzie. "Any color she selects will be fine with me," he said.

For her thirtieth birthday Borden gave Lizzie a three-month tour of Europe, and she visited England, Scotland, France and Italy. A group of young women from Fall River made the summer tour together. Since Borden always treated his daughters alike in financial matters, he probably offered Emma the same opportunity, but she did not go. Emma never traveled outside New England in her life. During the trip Lizzie wrote to both her father and sister. The letters are filled with details of the many museums she visited. Lizzie stopped off in New York on her way home. The European souvenirs she brought back were mostly copies of museum paintings which had caught her fancy, and she gave them to friends as gifts.

There was a revealing episode during the inquest which pointed up the lack of display of normal tenderness even in the privacy of the Borden home. Lizzie readily stated that there had been no friction of any kind between her father and stepmother. Yet when she was asked whether Mr. and Mrs. Borden had been happily united, the question seemed to be one that she had not thought about. She paused so noticeably to consider it that her delay was recorded by the court stenographer. "Why, I don't know but that they were," she said finally. Asked whether her father had seemed to be affectionate to Mrs. Borden, the only answer she could give was, "I think so." The puzzled questioner, still seeking for some sign that would indicate such affection existed, inquired whether they were affectionate as a man and woman who are married ought to be. Lizzie's reply would have delighted her blunt father. She answered frankly: "So far as I have ever had a chance of judging."

The only known serious dispute in the Borden household took place about five years before the murders and apparently stemmed from a display of fondness on the part of Mrs. Borden for her half-sister, Mrs. George Whitehead. When their father died he left a small house jointly to his widow, who was Mrs. Borden's stepmother, and to Mrs. Whitehead, his daughter from his second marriage. Mrs. Borden had not objected to not sharing in the inheritance.

After some years the widow wanted to sell her share to obtain some cash. The Whiteheads, who were living in the house, could not afford to buy the other half and this meant that the house would be put up for sale. Mrs. Borden feared that a new buyer might want it all for himself and her sister would have to move out. She appealed to her husband. Borden bought out the widow's half for $1,500 and presented the title to his wife as a gift. No mention of this transaction was made by either of them to Emma or Lizzie.

Some busybodies did hear about it, however, and, as the inquest testimony shows, told the sisters. Whether the informants embroidered upon the facts can only be conjectured. Since the bearers of these tidings were meddling in a family matter, they may have been needling the sisters as well, and Emma and Lizzie did become angry. Emma's little-understood and long-hidden resentment against her stepmother, which she indicated clearly as a child when she refused to call her by anything but her first name, flared up. She testified at the trial that she had been far less cordial to Mrs. Borden after this incident than had Lizzie, and we have no reason to doubt her statement. Lizzie reacted in her direct way and showed how she felt by no longer calling Mrs. Borden Mother, but she always denied that she ever had any angry words with her stepmother over the incident.

The sisters presented a united front to their father and Lizzie acted as spokesman. "I said," she later testified at the inquest, "what he did for her people, he ought to do for his own children."

This blunt statement by Lizzie, so characteristic of both the father and the daughter, evidently seemed a fair one to Borden. He was not easily influenced concerning money matters, and yet a short time later he turned over joint title to the old house on Ferry Street to Emma and Lizzie. Since the house was then valued at $3,000 he was being scrupulously fair, giving each exactly the same amount he had given his wife. Several months before the murders he bought back the house, paying his daughters $5,000 cash which they shared; the land had become more valuable.

This incident, particularly the fact that Lizzie ceased referring to Mrs. Borden as Mother, was to play an important role in her arrest. Lizzie's testimony at the inquest on this point is interesting.

Q: Now tell me once more, if you please, the particulars of the trouble you had with your mother four or five years ago?

A: Her father's house on Fourth Street was for sale—

Q: Whose father's house?

A: Mrs. Borden's father's house. She had a stepmother and a half-sister, Mrs. Borden did, and this house was left to the stepmother and a half-sister, if I understood it right, and the house was for sale. The stepmother, Mrs. Oliver Gray, wanted to sell it, and my father bought out the Widow Gray's share. She did not tell me and he did not tell me, but some outsiders said that he gave it to her. Put it in her name. I said if he gave that to her, he ought to give us something. Told Mrs. Borden so. She did not care anything about the house herself. She wanted it so this half-sister could have a home, because she had married a man that was not doing the best he could, and she thought her sister was having a very hard time, and wanted her to have a home. And we always thought she persuaded Father to buy it. At any rate, he did buy it, and I am quite certain she did persuade him. I said what he did for her people, he ought to do for his own children. So he gave us Grandfather's house. That was all the trouble we ever had.

Q: You have not stated any trouble yet between you and her?

A: I said there was a feeling four or five years ago when I stopped calling her Mother. I told you that yesterday.

Q: That is all there is to it then?

A: Yes sir.

Q: You had no words with your stepmother then?

A: I talked with her about it and said what he did for her he ought to do for us; that is all the words we had.

While Borden supplied his daughters with a home and clothes, including fur coats, he was not generous with them in the matter of pocket money. At the time of the murders both were mature women; each received an allowance of only $200 a year. A gift of $1,500 to his wife would seem very large to them.

How well Borden had trained Lizzie in thrift can be seen in her bank records: They show that she managed to save money even from this small allowance.

Yet there was another side to Lizzie Borden in which she differed sharply from her father and family.

III

The Unknown Lizzie

The cloud of myth that has settled over the Borden murders has done more than obscure the facts of the crime. It has also obscured the flesh-and-blood Lizzie Borden. Even the descriptions of her physical appearance are inaccurate and misleading.

According to the legend, she is described, at the time of the murders, as being an embittered, homely old maid, her face lined and her disposition permanently soured by the lack of any romance in her life. She is pictured as a semi-recluse, whose insatiable greed for money was the storm center of constant dissension in the household. As an example of the futile and empty life of indolence she led, humorous mention is made of her membership in the quaint-sounding Fruit and Flower Mission, described as a small church club. The most frequently published photograph of her shows a round-faced, tight-lipped, unsmiling middle-aged woman, with a strong chin, deep lines about her mouth and wearing pince-nez glasses. In most instances the photograph is captioned as having been taken either shortly before or shortly after the trial. Her head appears to be massive and the picture suggests that she was large and powerful. Pearson accentuated this part of the legend when he wrote: "She had a strong pair of arms, could row a boat well, and drive a spirited pair of horses." Skill, not strength, is needed to row an ordinary boat, and if Lizzie ever drove a pair of spirited horses, it must have been in her youth, because the only vehicle she ever drove regularly was a pony cart.

Lizzie Borden, the old maid, was just thirty-two years old at the time of the murders; her birthday had been celebrated nineteen days before. Contrary to the legend, she was neither large nor muscular. Although Lizzie confided to friends that during the ten months she had been in jail awaiting trial she had put on so much weight that some of her dresses had to be altered for her courtroom appearance, reporters who saw her for the first time when the trial began were surprised to find themselves staring at a slight, thin-boned woman, with small hands, ears and feet, not much over five feet four inches tall, and who, despite her added weight, still appeared quite slender. She was so much smaller than most reporters had been led to believe by the already growing legend that almost all of them commented on it in their first-day stories. Most of them described her figure as petite.

She was certainly not beautiful, nor even pretty, but neither was she homely. In an era when women of her class in New England used no cosmetics except for a faint brushing of face powder, she was described in the language of the day as pleasant or plain looking. She possessed the high cheekbones, the strong chin, the full lips, and deep mouth creases characteristic of so many New England descendants of early Colonial settlers. Frequent intermarriages within a small group of families had produced a recognizable facial type, and her counterparts can still be seen today in many New England towns. Her best features were her large expressive eyes and her hair, which was invariably described as "beautiful, fine, soft and glossy." The color was described as nut-brown or auburn tinged, indicating that it had a reddish cast. She wore her hair in a large roll in back of her head.

The original of her most familiar photograph bears the stamp of a Pach Bros. studio then located on Broadway near the Flat-iron Building in New York City. An official of that firm, which is still in existence, said recently that that studio had not been opened until some years after the turn of the century, in the early 1900's. The earliest date on which this photograph could have been taken was at least ten years after the trial, when Lizzie Borden was middle-aged, had started to put on weight and begun to wear glasses. Newspapers at the time of the trial used artists who made quick drawings at the scene—drawings which were often very sketchy. Although Pearson described them as "dreadful sketches" and singled out for praise one that appeared in *Leslie's Weekly,* this is not the one he used in his trial book. Instead, he reproduced one of the unflattering drawings, one in which the artist depicted Lizzie as a thin-faced woman with a prominent nose instead of the short and somewhat tilted one that probably was her own despair.

Since Pearson praised the coverage of the trial by the New York *Sun's* Julian Ralph, whom he called this country's most distinguished newspaper correspondent at that time, let us see how Ralph described Lizzie Borden after he saw her for the first time. In his first-day trial dispatch he wrote:

"It has been said again and again that this maiden prisoner is a great strong woman, capable of extraordinary physical exertion. It is not so. She is very little, if anything, above average stature of women. She is not of large build; she does not look to weigh more than 135 pounds at the outside, and if her arms, which cannot be seen in her puffed sleeves, are large and muscular, they assuredly terminate in very small and ladylike hands." After giving a detailed description of each facial feature he added, "She is no Medusa or Gorgon."

Ralph seemed intrigued by the creases about her mouth, describing them as "deep lines of either care or habitual low spirits," and in this same dispatch he suggested they might indicate an irritable disposition. Several days later, after having observed other New England women, Ralph wired his paper: "By the way, the strangers who are here begin to notice that Lizzie Borden's face is of a type quite common here in New

Bedford. They meet Lizzie Borden every day and everywhere about town. Some here even come in the courtroom. Some are fairer, some are younger, some are coarser, but all have the same general cast of features—heavy in the lower face, high in the cheekbones, wide at the eyes, and with heavy lips and a deep line on each side of the mouth."

A listing of physical characteristics does little more than create a cardboard character. It is in our meetings and dealings with other people that we expose ourselves as we are, particularly over a long period of time. There are still some people alive in Fall River who knew Lizzie Borden before the murders and whom I interviewed.

"She was friendly and had a wonderful sense of humor," said James J. Kirby. "I was attending St. Mary's School on the same block and the Bordens had a small pear orchard alongside the house and around the back. You know how young boys are; they haven't got stomachs, they've got bottomless pits. Fresh fruit was a treat for us. Our folks didn't have much money, and we looked at those trees and got desperate for pears. Five or six of us hung around together and I was the ringleader. Mr. Borden had a reputation of being a mean skinflint and the place was all fenced in. One day I got up my courage, opened the gate and knocked on the side door, while my scared friends waited safely out on the street.

"Lizzie answered and I managed to get out my request. She told me that my friends could come in and that we could pick the fruit that had fallen to the ground, but said we must not climb the trees. We were small kids then and I suppose she was afraid we might fall and hurt ourselves. We soon found a way to beat that. We would sneak into the yard, shake a big pile of pears off the trees and then I would knock and ask for permission. I'll never forget the first time we did it. Lizzie gave a start when she saw that big mound of pears on the ground; it would have taken a full-sized hurricane to blow off that many. She caught on immediately. Her eyes danced, her lips quirked up, and you could see she wanted to laugh out loud. After that it became a game. I know she watched us through the window shaking the trees first, but she always went through the same act, telling us not to climb the trees but to pick only what was on the ground. At the same time she gave me a merry look that let me know we weren't fooling her, but she never spoiled the game for us by telling us outright that she knew. It made the pears taste even better to us and she must have realized it.

"This went on for several years, almost up to the day of the murders. I was twelve then. We went there at least twice a week, sometimes more, but she never acted as if we were pests or said a cross or angry word to us. The only times she turned us down were when we came around too early in the season and then she always explained why. 'No, they're not ripe,' she would say and you could tell from the tone of her voice that she really was sorry. Mostly it was Lizzie who came to the door. Emma came once or twice but Mrs. Borden never did. If the maid answered she always grumbled and would ask somebody inside. If Lizzie was home we got permission, otherwise not too often.

"A few times when we made too much noise in the yard Mr. Borden came out yelling and we got out of there fast. The next time we showed up, Lizzie would suggest that we be quiet, but she never scolded us. You can tell when a person comes to the door whether they are friendly or stiff. Lizzie didn't say much to us but her attitude always made us feel welcome. I saw her out on the street quite often before the murders. She seemed to know plenty of people. Some would stop and talk to her on the street and others would call out greetings. Mrs. Borden went out occasionally but Emma didn't circulate much.

"To kids, all grownups are old, but somehow I never thought of Lizzie that way. She seemed like somebody's big sister to us. Homely? I don't suppose she was pretty but she was nicer looking than many other girls I saw around at that time. I can tell you one thing about Lizzie Borden. She wasn't prejudiced."

This was the first hint of an underground feeling that I encountered so often.

"At St. Mary's we wore blue suits and white shirts; it was sort of a uniform, and since we sometimes ran over to the Borden house during recess, she certainly knew who we were, but it made no difference to her. Oh, sure, we went to other houses where they had fruit trees, but we got chased before we could even ask for permission."

Presiding Justice Benjamin Cook of the Second District Court is, unlike Kirby, a descendant of one of the early Fall River families and so moved in the same social circles as the Bordens. He is the oldest active jurist in the United States with fifty-nine years of continuous service on the bench. When I interviewed him on the eve of his ninetieth birthday, he invited me into his chambers during a brief courtroom recess.

"My earliest memory of Lizzie Borden was hearing her play the piano in our house," he recalled. "She and Emma took lessons from my mother. Lizzie must have been a young teenager then. She was about ten years my senior so her friends were in a different generation than mine, but I went around with some of the younger brothers and sisters of her friends. I would see her at the larger functions the old families attended, particularly when I would come home from Harvard during holidays and vacations. I never paid any attention to who her escorts were, but young ladies in those days did not attend unless they were accompanied by a gentleman friend. I don't know if they were suitors but she went out with young men before the murders and you can draw your own conclusions."

There must have been occasions when Andrew Jackson Borden was pleased with the visible demonstrations Lizzie gave of his careful tutoring. Her thrift, for example. With his finger in every banking pie in Fall River he probably knew that she managed to save from her meager pin-money allowance of less than four dollars a week. Her forthright manner in stating what she had on her mind probably also met with his approval since he was that way himself. If there is a hereafter, it is likely that he beamed at Lizzie's steadfast refusal during her lifetime to sell the A. J. Borden Building, because of his oft-repeated lecture on the value of holding on to downtown property. But there must have been many occasions during his life when he was puzzled, if not outright alarmed, at some of her actions and at what she did with the money she so painstakingly saved.

At the time of the murders the Fall River newspapers vied with each other in describing the life of one of their wealthiest citizens. They spoke of Borden's humble origins and of his slow but steady rise in station. They listed his impressive array of business affiliations, his directorship in so many important corporations, his banking connections. They wrote of his industry, his thrift, his economy; they praised him for living a simple and unostentatious life. They avoided any mention of the enemies he had made, merely stating that he had offended few people. They quoted his fellow bankers and directors who said in a variety of ways that he had been a solid citizen. Conspicuously absent from these stories was any mention of his work for the community, for the welfare of the people, for civic improvement, for social reforms. The papers did not report any helping hand he might have extended to others, or any charities that might have engaged his attention. There were no quotes from the civic leaders, the welfare organizations, the community associations. The omissions were not deliberate; nothing was written, nothing was said, because there was nothing to write or say. If Borden dropped more than an occasional silver coin in an alms box he managed to keep it secret even from the groups that were looking for aid to help others. If he served on an occasional jury, he had discharged his civic obligations. Although Borden's industry and wealth were held up to Fall River as an example to follow, he contributed little to his community. He was a taker, not a giver.

With such a father, it is not difficult to understand why the legend says that Lizzie Borden's greed made her fear that her stepmother would siphon away his fortune, and that she murdered them both to prevent it. It is ironic that after twenty-seven years of married life the major portion of Mrs. Borden's estate consisted of her half-share in the small house, for which her husband paid $1,500, and her request for that had not been made on her own behalf but for her half-sister. His second marriage had been a typical Borden bargain: it was cheaper than hiring a housekeeper.

Even before the murders Lizzie had an aversion to publicity; she never sought it and her known activities indicate that she tried hard to avoid it. Her name seldom appeared in the local papers. Yet she had a record of community service before the murders which, for her time, is as impressive as her father's is bleak.

She was eighteen years old when she graduated from high school. Few women in that era attended college; in Fall River it was almost unheard of. To Andrew Borden it would have been unthinkable: when a young woman finished school, she stayed home and waited for marriage, performing household chores to train herself for her future life. Since the Bordens had a servant girl these chores were lightened. Most young ladies then did very little traveling; they lived a closely circumscribed life. Although the population of Fall River grew until that city became the fourth largest in the state, the number of old families with whom a proper alliance could be made was small. It was further reduced because the young men in the best families went off to college and many of them met and married eligible young ladies elsewhere. This was the tragedy of many young women in New England in that period, the reason why many in the smaller cities and towns never married.

Emma was an example. When her school days were over, she remained at home, saw only her very small circle of friends. With almost no outside activities, her days must have been dreary and endless repetitions.

Lizzie retained many of her school friends and acquired many new ones through her outside activities. She appears to have been the one member of her family who was sincerely religious. Church meant more to her than merely attending Sunday services. She actively participated in many of the women's groups in her own church, and was one of the leaders of the Christian Endeavor Society. She also volunteered her services to the Mission Church on Pleasant Street and for several years taught a Sunday school class of Chinese men; later she taught a class for girls employed in the mills. Since liquor never entered the Borden home, it is not surprising that she was a member of the Women's Christian Temperance Union.

She seemed to have inherited much of her father's drive. Long before it became fashionable for young women of leisure to devote themselves to public service and charitable organizations, Lizzie Borden engaged in a full round of such activities. The Fall River Fruit and Flower Mission was actually a worthwhile city-wide group like the volunteer groups who work in hospitals today. The members visited the poor and friendless who were ill in institutions, brought toys for children, gifts of food for adults, read books and papers to the afflicted, and performed disagreeable and thankless tasks that relieved nurses from time-consuming chores. They also visited the aged and bedridden at home. Hospitals understand the psychological values to patients of these services and seek such volunteer workers.

While still in her twenties Lizzie was elected a member of the board of the Fall River Hospital, one of the few women to serve in that capacity, and the youngest. The appointment was not made because of her father's position, and most certainly not because of any contributions he made; it resulted from her own devoted efforts on behalf of the hospital.

Her interest in children included more than allowing a group of neighborhood boys to pick unwanted pears from the ground. With a group of friends she organized annual Christmas and Thanksgiving dinners for poor children and newsboys and she was an active worker in the kitchen, cooking and loading their plates.

Unlike her father, she did not save money simply to accumulate it, but gave it away freely, which must have shocked him. She donated regularly to the organizations in which she was interested and eventually became treasurer of almost every group she joined because her co-workers knew that she paid many expenses out of her own pocket and personally made up any deficit when the funds gathered were insufficient.

Her high-school years must have been very happy ones because she maintained cordial relations with her former teachers long afterward. When she learned from them of bright and deserving students without much money, she would give the teachers tickets to lectures and concerts to pass on to the students, requesting that her name not be mentioned.

On one occasion one of her former teachers who had retired and was living on a small pension learned that her aged mother needed a major operation and was without funds to finance it. Lizzie quietly arranged for medical specialists, the hospital room, and paid all the bills from her savings. Later when the teacher's mother died, Lizzie paid the funeral expenses. She never discussed or mentioned any of her charitable acts or her work, and this one came to light only after Lizzie's arrest when the schoolteacher first told it to friends. A bemused researcher, unable to believe such information about a daughter of Andrew Borden, mentioned it to the director of the Fall River Historical Society. "I can vouch for the story," she said. "I heard the schoolteacher tell it before she died." And she added, "Whatever may be said about Lizzie Borden, there is no doubt that she was a very kind person throughout her life."

Lizzie was intensely loyal and devoted to her friends. During the early days of the investigation reporters noticed that whenever she left the house she was always accompanied by Mrs. Mary Brigham, wife of a young clerk in town. In its typical fashion the Fall River *Globe* soon gave its own explanation. The paper reported that police had placed an undercover agent in the household to watch Lizzie and report back everything she said and did.

Mrs. Brigham was neither an undercover agent nor a policewoman and she testified as a defense witness for Lizzie during the trial. She and Lizzie had been friends from childhood. The year before Mrs. Brigham had lost a young son and her grief was so deep that many feared her health would be affected. Her husband appealed to Lizzie for help and she stayed with Mrs. Brigham, talking to her, cajoling her into going outside, awakening her interest in other matters, and gradually restoring her to the extent that she could accept her loss. The friend later realized what Lizzie had done for her, and when Lizzie became a suspect Mrs. Brigham promptly came to her aid. Even decades later these facts were not too difficult to obtain and verify.

In some ways Lizzie and Emma were alike. Both were exceptionally fond of animals. On one occasion when the hired man at the Swansea farm was using a scythe, he failed to notice a cat in the tall grass and inflicted a severe gash. Lizzie, who was at the farm that day, treated the injury and then made daily trips from Fall River to change the dressings until the cut was healed. At their deaths both sisters left substantial legacies to animal shelters.

Love of animals as a lone virtue is meaningless—many coldblooded killers have loved their pets; but it must be considered here as part of the factual and more complete portrait of Lizzie

Borden, because stories were printed after the murders that she butchered dogs and cats.

Lizzie and Emma also shared an unusual household habit. Although the name of the servant girl at the time of the murders was Bridget Sullivan, both of them called her Maggie, the name of a former maid. The elder Bordens used her correct name. This is cited as proof that Lizzie was indolent, that she was too lazy to bother learning the girl's name, a view contradicted by her many and varied activities. It could indicate, instead, that there had been a rapid turnover in the household servants and the sisters had given up trying to remember the names of the quickly departing maids; it could not have been too easy to work for outspoken Andrew Borden with his acute preoccupation with trifling economies. It may be significant that when Bridget Sullivan was asked immediately after the murders how long she had been working for the Bordens, she replied without hesitation that it was two years and nine months, an answer that might mean she had been ticking off the days.

Bridget's main duties, as she described them, were to "cook, wash, iron and sweep." Except for keeping the kitchen in order, her inside cleaning tasks appear to have been light. She testified that she never entered the front parlor and that Lizzie took care of that room. Mrs. Borden and Emma shared the daily dusting of the other first-floor rooms. Lizzie and Emma also ironed their own dresses and personal things. As far as the daily making of the beds and the cleaning of the bedrooms was concerned, "Themselves took care of their own rooms," was the way Bridget phrased it. In fact, when the various members were not in their bedrooms, the doors were kept locked. Bridget could not enter them if their occupants were not present. Her own bedroom was a low-ceilinged chamber in the attic, at the top of the back staircase. Part of her room space was taken up by a water tank that had previously supplied running water to the former second-floor kitchen, now used by the Bordens as their bedroom. The tank had not been removed when Mr. Borden converted the house to one-family use.

A strange rite Andrew Borden performed each morning was to lock his bedroom door, come down the stairs and put the key on a shelf in the sitting room before going out. How locking the door and leaving the key behind could prevent anybody from entering the room remains a mystery.

The front and side entrances to the house were kept locked at all times. During the summer months when a screen door was used at the side entry, this was locked with a latch. This practice may have arisen because two burglaries, one in the house and the other in the barn, had occurred a year or so before the murders. Actually, the flimsy locks on the bedroom doors could not have served as any real barrier to a thief skillful enough to enter the house.

The legend gives Lizzie a sour disposition, but it is quite likely that she had a sense of humor; others besides Kirby have commented upon it. In fact, a humorous note she had written caused a one-day sensation right after the murders when it was misinterpreted as meaning that she had bought a sharp ax. Several days before the murders Lizzie wrote to some friends that before coming up to visit them she would get a sharp ax to make certain she did not freeze. She was referring to an episode that had occurred the previous summer when they were to- gether at the same cottage. On the first chilly evening they found that the logs on hand were too large for the fireplace and the ax so dull they could not chop the wood to fit. They had to search constantly for small branches and twigs in order to keep warm. A reporter who went to Marion to interview Lizzie's friends after the murders either misunderstood her reference in the letter or let his imagination run wild. He wrote that Lizzie had bought a sharp ax just prior to the murders. Before police learned the real meaning of the letter, officers questioned every hardware merchant in Fall River and for miles around. They found no one to testify that Lizzie had purchased an ax.

She had her father's same intensity and took her varied duties seriously. Her original summer plans had been to go to this cottage at Marion in late July with a group of friends. She was, as usual, treasurer of the Endeavor Society and in late spring had also accepted the additional post of secretary. When she learned that this group was to hold a roll call meeting on the first Sunday in August, she canceled her vacation plans. She said that, as secretary, it would not be proper for her to miss the meeting, and she also had reports to prepare for the session. Her friends urged her to join them after the meeting and stay with them for the brief remaining time. She agreed to do so in the letter she wrote just before the murders.

Lizzie missed the roll call meeting after all; the murders intervened.

Whether Lizzie Borden had any serious suitors before the murders we do not know. We know that she did attend social functions with escorts, and she did have what are today called dates. Her looks were no particular handicap as far as marriage was concerned, and the fact that she was a potential heiress to a comfortable fortune certainly would not keep men away. She demonstrated that she liked children, she did perform many kind acts, and she had a variety of interests, all of which could be counted as marriage assets. Her hobby of fishing could be appealing to some men.

It is true that her family was distinguished by its lack of warmth and she was not an effusive person. And, as her father's daughter, she would have discouraged any man who she thought was attracted by the Borden wealth.

Courting in those days was largely done in the girl's home. A hopeful swain would first have to pay his respects to the assembled family, which, in this case, was a formidable one. There was the grim Andrew Borden, whose interests were confined

Lizzie Borden prior to the murders

The Borden house at the time of the murders in 1892

Little-known snapshot of Lizzie, probably taken shortly after the trial

The handleless hatchet which the prosecution claimed was the murder weapon

Andrew J. Borden

Mrs. Abbie D. Borden

District Attorney Hosea M. Knowlton

Defense Attorney George Robinson

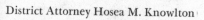

Mr. Borden's body

Mrs. Borden's body

Brown Brothers

In her teens   In her twenties

About the time of the murders   In the early 1900s

Courtesy of Fall River Historical Society

Actress Anne Meacham, who played the part of Lizzie Borden in *The Legend of Lizzie* on Broadway, looks into the guest bedroom from the stairs where Bridget saw Mrs. Borden's body.

Mrs. Adelaide B. Churchill

Miss Alice M. Russell

The guest room as seen from the position on the stairs where Miss Meacham is standing. Notice how little space there is between the bed and the floor.

Fall River *Herald News*

Druggist Eli Bence

Assistant Marshal Fleet

Sketch of Lizzie Borden
made by a Boston newspaper artist
at the trial.
Compare with full-page photo.

Bridget Sullivan,
the Borden maid

Maplecroft, imposing home Lizzie and Emma bought after the trial

largely to the wonders of Crane's Patent Burial Casket Cases and the fine print in intricate mortgages; there was the grotesquely fat Mrs. Borden, a sight to blunt romantic thoughts; and the dull Miss Emma with virtually no interests at all.

The narrow cramped house, with its peculiar first-floor layout of rooms, was another hurdle. Romance does require a modicum of privacy in order to develop and flourish. But with doors opening into the rooms from all sides, the probability that household traffic might have to pass through at any moment must have been a restraining factor, if not an outright deterrent, to anything beyond formal conversation. More privacy and spontaneity could have been achieved in a crowded railroad station.

If, as the poets sing, "Love will find out the way," we have no evidence that love had found its way through the locked doors of 92 Second Street prior to the morning of August 4, 1892.

IV

The Prelude

The first week of August 1892 opened with deceptive quiet at 92 Second Street. Only three members of the Borden family were home. Emma was visiting friends at Fairhaven, on the other side of New Bedford harbor, and her return was not expected for several weeks. Lizzie had also been away for three or four days, having left with Emma, to visit some of her own friends in New Bedford. She then returned home. During her brief stay in the former whaling town, Lizzie must have occasionally passed New Bedford's old courthouse on the square where, not long afterward, she was to stand trial for her life, the focus of world attention.

A joint of mutton, also soon to receive international fame, probably made its first appearance that week as a roast for the Borden Sunday dinner. It must have been a very large roast. The Bordens ate their formal dinner at noon each day and a lighter meal at suppertime. After dinner on Sunday Lizzie saw various acquaintances and discussed a problem with them: Her friends at Marion were still urging her to come up to the cottage even if she couldn't get away until after the roll call the following Sunday. Since she had already missed most of the vacation with them she wondered if she should bother going. One of those she consulted was Alice M. Russell, a former next-door neighbor who was Emma's age. Miss Russell was on friendly terms with both sisters and a frequent visitor at the Borden home. She advised Lizzie to go, because even a short time away from Fall

River during the hot weather was worth the effort, and the papers were predicting another long heat wave. Lizzie said she would think it over.

The heat wave did arrive on Monday. It was a languid sort of day for most of the household. Borden, nearing seventy, was not as active as he had once been. He still left the house every morning by nine o'clock and discussed the problems that required his attention at the various banks, but he stayed no longer than necessary. His A. J. Borden Building was almost completed and many of the stores and offices had been rented, but some of the tenants needed changes to meet their specific needs and he made a daily inspection of the work being done. He was usually back home by mid-morning. A short narrow band of gray whiskers, extending from ear to ear, gave his face a white-fringed halo effect. Fat Mrs. Borden was content to move about as little as possible in the heat. Lizzie spent most of the day upstairs in her room pondering her Marion problem and working on her reports for the coming roll call. The only really busy person in the house was Bridget Sullivan. Monday was wash day and she spent a good portion of her time at the cellar tubs scrubbing sheets, pillowcases, tablecloths and assorted household linens.

For dinner there was mutton again.

Tuesday continued hot and much of the early part of the day was a replica of the preceding one. Bridget was no longer scrubbing the laundry, she was ironing it. Mutton made another appearance at the breakfast table, but there was a change in diet for the remaining meals. Swordfish was prepared for dinner that noon, and what remained was warmed over for supper that evening. Bridget, perhaps tired from her day's ironing and unable to face the prospect of again stoking up the wood-and-coal-burning stove in the already hot kitchen, did not bake any bread for supper but went to a bakery and purchased a loaf. On her return she told her mistress this, and Mrs. Borden paid

Bridget the money she had spent, a nostalgic five cents. All three Bordens ate the bakery bread for supper. Bridget testified later that she did not eat any.

During the night, Mr. and Mrs. Borden both had attacks of violent cramps and nausea. Lizzie, in her adjacent room, heard them retching. She knocked on the doubly-locked connecting door and asked if she could do anything to help them. She was thanked and told to go back to bed, that they would be all right. Lizzie said later that she also suffered an attack but that it was milder and she did not vomit. The only one who escaped unscathed was Bridget, who had not eaten the bread.

Wednesday morning, still weak and shaken by her experiences during the night, Mrs. Borden told Lizzie she suspected that the family might have been poisoned. When she insisted upon seeing Dr. Seabury W. Bowen, a friend and neighbor who lived diagonally across the street, Borden tartly commented, "Well, my money shan't pay for it." Mrs. Borden visited him anyway and said afterward that Dr. Bowen had laughed at her talk of poison and said that some of the food might have become spoiled. Concerned about the elderly banker, the doctor came over to examine him. Borden refused any medical attention and berated Dr. Bowen for making a call without being asked. After the physician left, Borden was persuaded by his wife and Lizzie to take a home remedy consisting of a dose of castor oil followed later by medicinal tea. Whether Lizzie left the house at any time that busy morning is a point in dispute.

Although all three Bordens were not feeling well and a light meal seemed indicated, some of the mutton roast still remained and the main course for dinner that noon was mutton. Something new, though, had been added. Enough meat had been carved from the bone to put that to use and so hot mutton soup, in the midst of a heat wave, was also on the menu. Lizzie could not recall later whether she had eaten this dinner or had remained in her room; one mutton meal seemed to have tasted very much like another.

About 1:30 that afternoon the Bordens had an unexpected visitor with the arrival of John Vinnicum Morse, a brother of Borden's first wife and an uncle to Lizzie and Emma. Morse was one of the brothers who had gone to Iowa to homestead a farm near Hastings. Selling out at a good price a year or so earlier he had returned to Massachusetts, settled in South Dartmouth and made occasional visits to the Bordens. Although retired, he sometimes dabbled in horse trading, selling mustangs from the West; and as an experienced farmer, he would inspect Borden's two farms and offer helpful advice and suggestions. Even though he brought no luggage, he planned to stay at least overnight.

When Mrs. Borden learned that he had not eaten dinner, she hurried into the kitchen to warm up the specialty of the house —mutton and mutton soup.

Morse heard from Mrs. Borden the story of their sudden illness during the night, and she told him that Lizzie had also been ill and was still not feeling well, an indication that Lizzie may not have come down for dinner. During most of the afternoon Morse and Borden sat talking in the sitting room. At one point, annoyed by their loud voices while trying to take a nap, Lizzie closed the door to her bedroom, shutting off any cross ventilation in the hot upstairs. If she recognized her uncle's voice, she did not go down to greet him. Morse left late in the afternoon, rented a rig from one of the stables up the street and drove to the Swansea farms to inspect his brother-in-law's cattle. Due to his advancing years, Borden no longer kept a horse or carriage.

Lizzie also did not eat any supper that evening. Mercifully for those still suffering from the aftereffects of the previous night, the mutton did not appear; the meal consisted mainly of bread and butter, cake and coffee. Morse had not returned by seven o'clock when Lizzie came down and walked to Miss Russell's home on nearby Borden Street. She had reached a decision and her first words to her friend were that she had taken her advice; she had written to Marion saying that she was coming up the following Monday, the day after the Endeavor Society roll call.

Lizzie's visit lasted for two hours and it was during her conversation with Miss Russell that she made her famous prediction, "I am afraid that somebody will do something."

Lizzie said that she felt depressed, mentioned the episode of the illness the previous night, and raised the possibility that the milk or bread had been poisoned. Miss Russell replied that it was most unlikely. Lizzie told her about the burglaries of the house and barn, spoke of the discourteous way her father treated people, and expressed a fear that his enemies might some day burn down the house. "I am so ashamed, the way Father treated Dr. Bowen. I was so mortified," Miss Russell later quoted her as saying.

Lizzie returned home not long after nine o'clock. Following the nightly custom of the house, she triple-locked the front door by closing the patent lock, turning the key in the regular lock and finally shooting a bolt home into the door jamb. Her uncle was then in the sitting room with her father; Mrs. Borden had retired for the night. There was no light on in the sitting room. If the men were silent when Lizzie entered the house she would not have known her uncle was there. No one knows. She still had not seen or spoken to her uncle. She went directly up the stairs to her room. Morse was seated where he could not see into the hall. He did not call out to greet her.

The last member of the household to arrive that night was Bridget Sullivan. She had spent part of the evening at a friend's home and they later took a walk on Main Street. Bridget said she returned shortly after ten o'clock. By this time everybody else had gone to bed. Morse was using the front guest bedroom.

The Bordens always left a kerosene lamp lit in the kitchen for Bridget when she was out late and she had her own key to the side door. This door was also triple-locked each night. After making certain that she had set each lock, Bridget drank some milk and used the lamp to light her way up the back stairs to her attic bedroom.

Five people went to bed that night in the Borden home; two of them were murdered the following morning. It is almost certain that one of the people mentioned so far in this account was the killer.

The murder morning, Thursday, August 4, 1892, dawned hot and clear. The heat and humidity had been rising steadily all week and were still going up. The movements within the house of all five people have been accounted for until about nine o'clock that morning; then there is a gap of two hours.

Accustomed to early rising from his farming days, Morse was the first one up. Lizzie's door was closed as he passed it on the small second-floor landing. Bridget awakened about 6:15 and it was her turn to be ill; she said she had a sick headache and felt queasy. She came downstairs, went to the cellar to get wood for the kitchen stove and then made another trip for coal. By the time she got the fire going, Mrs. Borden reached the kitchen, told her what to prepare for breakfast, and joined Morse in the sitting room. Five minutes later Borden came down.

One of the unforgettable little details of daily life in this household is the picture of Borden following his normal morning custom. The dignified banker came down the back stairs, fully clothed except for his suit jacket, solemnly carrying a slop pitcher in one hand and the key to his locked bedroom in the other. He went first to the sitting room where he placed the key on the shelf. He paused next in the kitchen to don what Bridget described as a "dressing gown," but what was actually a cardigan jacket or sweater. Carrying the slop pitcher he went out into the back yard, emptied its contents upon the ground, and then unlocked and opened the barn door. Borden paused to pick a basket of fallen pears which he brought back into a house already containing many pears; perhaps he feared a visit that day by young Tom Kirby and his hungry cohorts. These chores done, Borden washed his face and hands at the kitchen sink, still the only source of running water in the house above the cellar. He then joined his wife and guest for breakfast.

In explaining her absence from the table that morning, Lizzie said she seldom ate a real breakfast at home. It is easy enough to understand why: the meal served that morning, with the temperature already in the upper eighties at seven o'clock, would have given pause to even an ardent trencherman. The menu included johnnycakes, bread, coffee, cookies, the ubiquitous and by now very tired mutton, and hot mutton soup; it must have originally been a *tremendous* joint of meat. For those with any hollows left to fill there was a bowl of fresh fruit, including bananas. Morse may have found room for a banana since he mentioned this fruit several times in discussing the breakfast. Later, during the trial, he agreed that it had been an ample meal.

Bridget served the others in the dining room. During the half-hour breakfast Morse said he heard Mrs. Borden tell the maid, "Bridget, I want you to wash these windows today." The servant ate in the kitchen after Borden and Morse went to the sitting room. Mrs. Borden, equipped with a feather duster, started cleaning the first floor. Between 8:40 and 8:45 Morse left the house. He wanted to go to the post office and then walk to Weybosset Street, about a mile and a half away, where a niece and nephew from Excelsior, Minnesota, were staying on a visit. Oddly, he had learned of their presence in Fall River from Borden only the previous night. Mrs. Borden called to him to be sure to be back by noon for dinner. He agreed. Borden accompanied him to the side door, unhooked the latch, let him out, and relocked the screen door. Bridget saw Morse leave. Border then entered the kitchen where Bridget was working at her stove, brushed his teeth, got his bedroom key from the sitting room and went up the back stairs.

A few minutes later—it was then about nine o'clock—Lizzie came out of her room for the first time that morning, walked down the front stairs and stopped in the dining room, where Bridget said she heard her talking to Mrs. Borden. Lizzie had missed her uncle again. She then came into the kitchen and spoke to Bridget. A short time later Bridget's headache, combined with the breakfast she had eaten, caught up with her. She fled to the back yard where she was sick for ten to fifteen minutes. Bridget also said that upon returning to the house she went to the dining room, was told by Mrs. Borden to wash the windows and prepared to do so.

Borden, still somewhat weak from his illness and the purge he had taken, seems to have left the house later than usual that morning. Lizzie gave him a letter she had written to Emma and asked him to mail it. His departure set the stage for murder.

V

The Discovery

On the last morning of his life Andrew Borden had a busy hour in town; neither heat nor illness had kept him from his appointed rounds. He appeared at the first bank at 9:30, and a half hour later he had completed his tour of all four. At one of them a hopeful borrower was anxiously awaiting his arrival. John Burrill, the cashier, later testified that he had talked with Borden "and a colored man regarding a loan." The conference was over in ten minutes. It is unfortunate that Burrill made no mention of Borden's verdict, the final banking decision of his life.

Not long afterward Borden performed an act that was characteristic of him. He had stopped off at the A. J. Borden Building where a carpenter, Joseph Shortsleeves, and his assistant, James Mather, were lowering the front window of one of the stores to meet the specifications of Jonathan Clegg, the hatter. Clegg, who was moving his shop to Borden's new building, must have been a nervous type of tenant. Twice that week he had gone to Borden's home to discuss the store and earlier that morning had called to the banker as he was walking on the opposite side of the street and had talked to him again. Borden inspected the work the carpenters were doing and noticed a lock they had discarded. He picked it up and examined it. Shortsleeves explained that he had removed it from an old door. Borden put it down and went upstairs to check on the work being done there. When he came back down to the street level, he re-entered the store, picked up the lock and put it in his pocket. "It was all broken to pieces," was Shortsleeves' puzzled description. Borden probably was pleased with this last act of thrift.

Borden returned to his home on Second Street shortly after 10:45. He now had less than a half hour to live. Mrs. Caroline Kelly, wife of a physician, who lived next door on the south, was on her way to keep a dentist's appointment when she saw Borden come around from the side of the house, where he had tried the screen door and found it latched. She saw him go to the front door carrying a small paper-wrapped parcel, which was later found to contain the broken lock.

A few minutes earlier Bridget had completed washing the outside of the ground-floor windows. She had just started on the top half of her first inside window in the sitting room when she heard Borden having difficulty at the front door. She hurried to the entry, opened the patent lock, then turned the knob to admit the head of the household. The door did not budge. The assorted fates seemed to be having a tug of war deciding whether Borden should die then; had he been a superstitious man he might have taken heed from this double warning to stay away, but he waited patiently outside. When Bridget realized that the other two locks on the front door were still in place, she exclaimed out loud.

It was immediately after she made her explosive remark that she heard Lizzie laugh.

The maid finally got the other two locks open and Borden came in. He entered the sitting room and sat down to read, but when Bridget resumed her washing of the windows there, he stepped into the adjacent dining room where Bridget heard him talking to Lizzie. In reply to her query he told his daughter, "I feel no better, no worse." He said there was no mail for her, all the letters he had picked up at the post office were for him. He had mailed her letter to Emma. Bridget then heard Lizzie tell her father that Mrs. Borden had received a note and had gone out. Borden made no reply to this. He went up to his room briefly, getting the key from the sitting-room shelf, then came back down.

By this time Bridget had completed the sitting-room windows and shifted to the dining room. Borden returned to the sitting room and lay down on the horsehair sofa. According to Bridget, Lizzie was preparing to do some ironing on a board placed on the dining-room table and the following conversation took place between them:

"Maggie, are you going out this afternoon?"

"I don't know; I might and I might not. I don't feel very well," Bridget replied.

"If you go out be sure and lock the door, for Mrs. Borden has gone out on a sick call, and I might go out, too."

"Miss Lizzie, who is sick?"

"I don't know, she had a note this morning. It must be in town."

Bridget soon completed cleaning the dining-room windows and then entered the kitchen. While she was washing the rags she had been using, Lizzie said to her, "There is a cheap sale of dress goods at Sargent's this afternoon, at eight cents a yard." There was an interesting change in testimony on this point during the trial. Bridget said she replied, "I am going to have one," and a short time later went upstairs to her attic room to rest.

Bridget was able to fix this time as exactly 11 A.M.; she heard the City Hall tower bells ringing the hour and she glanced at the alarm clock at her bedside, verifying the time. Bridget said she stretched out on top of her bed without removing her shoes or any of her clothes. She did not believe she had napped; there were no sounds within the house.

It was about ten minutes later when Bridget heard Lizzie shout up the stairwell, "Maggie, come down!"

"What is the matter?" Bridget called back.

"Come down quick. Father's dead. Somebody came in and killed him."

Bridget hurried down the back stairs and started for the sitting room. Lizzie, who was standing near the side door, stopped her and told her she needed a doctor in a hurry. She repeated twice, "I have got to have a doctor."

The servant rushed across the street to Dr. Bowen's home. The physician was out on his morning rounds but his wife expected him back momentarily. After returning with this information, Bridget asked Lizzie where she had been. "Didn't I leave the screen door locked?" she asked.

"I was out in the back yard and heard a groan, and came in and the screen door was wide open," Lizzie replied. She then directed the girl to get Miss Russell, who lived around the corner at Borden and Third Streets, because she did not want to be alone.

Meanwhile, Mrs. Adelaide B. Churchill, the Bordens' next-door neighbor on the north, returned from a brief marketing trip and saw Bridget walking very fast from Dr. Bowen's house and looking "very white." She entered her kitchen and glanced out of the window. The two houses were separated by little more space than is required for a double-width driveway. When she saw Lizzie standing just inside the screen door looking very "excited and agitated," she opened the window and called out to her. Lizzie hurriedly replied, "Oh, Mrs. Churchill, do come over. Someone has killed Father."

Since a four-foot-high board fence separated the two properties, Mrs. Churchill had to go out into the street to reach the nearby side entry. Bridget had just left to get Miss Russell and Lizzie was sitting on a lower step of the back stairway. Mrs. Churchill also asked the inevitable question, "Where were you when it happened?" Lizzie replied, "I went to the barn to get a piece of iron." She added, "Father must have an enemy for we have all been sick, and we think the milk has been poisoned."

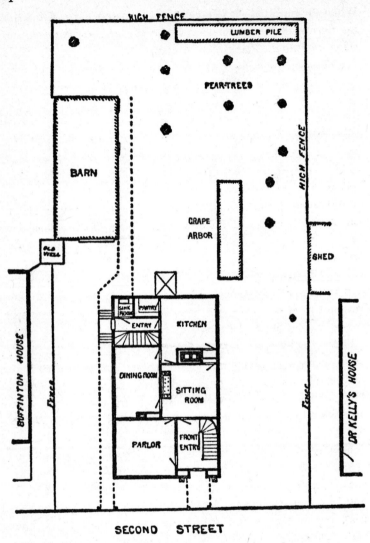

From Porter's *Fall River Tragedy*

PLAN OF BORDEN HOUSE AND YARD

When she repeated that she must have a doctor, Mrs. Churchill ran over to Hall's stable where her yardman had taken the carriage and told him to find a physician.

Memories sometimes can be faulty. Both Bridget and Mrs. Churchill testified that Lizzie told them her father had been "killed." At the inquest Lizzie insisted that she had told Bridget that her father had been hurt. She said that upon returning from the barn she had stepped into the doorway of the sitting room and saw her father's battered skull with fresh blood dripping from it and her first thought was to send Bridget for a doctor. It is impossible, of course, to state with absolute finality whose memory was at fault, but there is a possible signpost in the actions of John Cunningham, a news dealer, who was lounging at the stable and heard Mrs. Churchill speaking to her yardman.

Cunningham was the first one to think of police. He went across the street to a store with a telephone and rang up the central station house. The call was received at 11:15 by Marshal Rufus B. Hilliard. Cunningham did not report a murder. "There's a row at the Borden house," Marshal Hilliard said after hanging up. Cunningham also notified the newspapers. In fact, he played favorites. He telephoned the *Globe* even before he called the police but did not notify the other papers until after he spoke to Marshal Hilliard. In none of the calls did he use the word "murder" or even mention that Borden was dead.

Shortly after Mrs. Churchill hurried back, Dr. Bowen arrived, closely followed by Bridget and Miss Russell. The physician stepped into the sitting room while Bridget, Miss Russell and Mrs. Churchill took Lizzie into the kitchen and began fanning her, rubbing her hands and applying cold cloths and toilet water to her face. When Miss Russell wanted to loosen Lizzie's dress, the other said, "I don't feel faint."

Dr. Bowen found Borden stretched out on the sofa, his head on a pillow, his long legs resting on the floor. The couch was too short for him to stretch out full length and so he usually napped that way. He was wearing Congress shoes. His suit jacket was neatly folded on a sloping arm of the sofa and he was wearing a cardigan jacket, the one described by Bridget as a dressing gown. Fresh blood was still oozing from the massive skull wounds and the severed eye was hanging down out of its socket. Dr. Bowen had to clean the face before he was able to recognize Borden. He estimated that the banker had been dead no longer than twenty minutes, placing the time of the murder as shortly after eleven o'clock. It was apparent that Borden had been killed in his sleep.

The Fall River *Globe* quoted Dr. Bowen as saying, "Physician that I am, and accustomed to all kinds of horrible sights, it sickened me to look upon the dead man's face." At a court appearance later, the doctor denied having made any such statement. His denial was probably correct since he thought the sight of his chopped-up neighbor so interesting that he stepped out of the sitting room and called to Mrs. Churchill, "Addie, come in and see Mr. Borden." Mrs. Churchill emphatically declined.

Marshal Hilliard had sent Patrolman George W. Allen, who was on duty inside the station house as committing officer, to find out what had happened at the Borden house and report back. He ran part way and made the trip in four minutes. The legend becomes highly melodramatic at this point. It says that Allen was so frightened at the sight of the body that he ran screaming out of the house and returned to the station house gibbering, "He's dead," without stating who was dead. It makes a good story but it does not square with the facts. Officer Allen had enough presence of mind after viewing the body to notice that the sitting room showed no signs of a struggle, that a stand containing two books was within three feet of the sofa, and that the front door was locked and bolted. He even made certain to safeguard the house before he left. John S. Sawyer, a painter, had been attracted to the front of the house when he saw Allen running up, and the patrolman deputized him to stand before the side door with instructions to admit nobody but police or a doctor until officers returned to start the investigation. It wasn't until 6 P.M., when Sawyer complained that he was getting hungry, that police realized he had been doing guard duty all day and replaced him with a uniformed officer.

As part of the same myth, much fun has been poked at the police force because the murder occurred on the day of its annual picnic, the story being that the investigation had to be delayed for hours. Actually it was a patrolmen's picnic and limited to those who were off duty. Marshal Hilliard was in his office and Assistant Marshal John Fleet, who headed investigations for Fall River police, was testifying in court only a few blocks away from the Borden home. The special officers, a designation then used for detectives, were also on duty along with an almost complete complement of the regular day force. In fact, even before Officer Allen returned to the station house, one of the detectives was on his way to the Borden home. He had returned from a routine call, learned of the message from Cunningham, and decided to go to the Borden house to see if a detective's services were needed.

When Dr. Bowen completed his brief examination, he requested a sheet to cover the body. Bridget said she was too frightened to go up to Borden's bedroom and Mrs. Churchill volunteered to go with her. Dr. Bowen got the key from the sitting-room shelf and Bridget took Mrs. Churchill to the bedroom door and told her in what drawer the sheets were kept. Mrs. Churchill unlocked the door, entered the room alone, and got a sheet while Bridget waited outside. At Lizzie's request, Dr. Bowen went to the telegraph office to send a wire to Emma at Fairhaven. Lizzie told him, "Put it as gently as you can because there is an old person there and the shock might be too much for her."

Mrs. Churchill appears to have been the first person to think about Mrs. Borden. She asked Lizzie where her stepmother was and Lizzie told her about the note. Then she added, "I don't know but she is killed, too, for I thought I heard her come in." She suggested that Bridget look for her stepmother, but again the maid refused to go alone and for the second time Mrs. Churchill agreed to accompany her. With Bridget leading the way, they went through the dining room, hastily cut through a corner of the sitting room where the sheet-covered body of Borden lay on the sofa, and started up the front stairs.

Bridget was part way up the steps when she suddenly stopped, made an exclamation, and then ran up the rest of the flight and darted into the guest room off the landing. When Mrs. Churchill reached the same step where Bridget had paused, her eyes were just level with the floor of the landing, and by peering through the open door of the guest room she saw part of a woman's body on the floor on the far side of the bed. The neighbor did not go up any farther. She saw Bridget open an inner shutter on one of the two windows. The two women quickly came down the stairs and went into the kitchen where Lizzie and Miss Russell still sat. Whether Mrs. Churchill sighed when she sat down or whether the expression on her face told the story, neither could recall, but Miss Russell asked:

"Is there another?"

"Yes, she is up there," Mrs. Churchill replied.

Dr. Bowen returned shortly after from the telegraph office, learned of the second murder and went upstairs. Mrs. Borden was lying face down on the carpet. The physician noticed that the blood had started to coagulate, indicating that she had died some time before her husband. Again there were no signs of a struggle. The bed was completely made, even the fringed spread was smooth and in place. Despite the greater number of skull injuries, less blood had been splattered about the room; there were several stains on the pillow shams.

It was about 11:40 that morning when Morse, the temporary member of the household, returned from his morning outing. A small cluster of excited onlookers already had started to gather in front of the house, but Morse said later that he did not see either them or Sawyer on guard at the side door. He slowly sauntered along the side of the house, went to a tree in the back where he selected three pears and quietly ate one of them. With the other two still in his hand, he ambled over to the side door. Stopped by Sawyer, he said he was Borden's brother-in-law and walked inside. It wasn't until he saw Lizzie for the first time since his visit began that he learned of the murder of his host and hostess. It has been suggested that Morse, fearing a third serving of mutton soup and mutton within twenty-four hours, had taken the pears as a means of dulling his appetite before going inside for dinner.

Dr. William A. Dolan, the medical examiner, was driving by the Borden house when he saw the crowd beginning to form. Learning of the murders he went in and, with Dr. Bowen, examined Mrs. Borden, counting the wounds. When they turned the body over they saw a cut in the forehead with a flap of flesh hanging loose. Later, during a preliminary autopsy, the Medical Examiner found another wound in the back slightly below the neck.

He searched Borden's pockets and found his watch and $80.65 in bills and silver. He also observed a ring on the little finger of the banker's left hand. After learning from Lizzie of the sudden illness on Tuesday night, he took samples of the milk in the house and sealed them in containers. He also arranged for photographs to be taken of the bodies before they were removed in the afternoon for the autopsies.

One of the earliest spectators outside was Dwight Waring, a young boy then, today a retired cotton broker. "Not long after I got there," he recalled recently, "I saw a woman come out with a shawl over her head. I always thought it was Bridget Sullivan, although it could have been Mrs. Bowen. She hurried across the street. I noticed that she was sort of limping." In her testimony, Bridget mentioned wearing a shawl each time she left the house. She had made four trips that morning: first to Dr. Bowen's home, then for Miss Russell, again to the Bowen home, this one to summon the doctor's wife, and later to a Mrs. Miller, who also lived across the street.

By coincidence, Waring later married the daughter of Andrew J. Jennings, who had been Borden's lawyer and was one of the defense attorneys for Lizzie Borden. Waring never discussed the case with his father-in-law. Jennings died in 1923, the year before Pearson revived interest in the case with his first book. It was some years after her father's death when Mrs. Waring sold the family home and moved out. An old tub, covered with tarpaulin, was on a side porch of the house. Mrs. Waring had thought it was filled with the kind of useless effects that are put aside because they might come in handy one day. She was about to instruct that it be thrown out when she decided to examine its contents. Concealed under the other things was part of her father's original files on the Lizzie Borden case. Included were many of the actual exhibits introduced into evidence during the trial, an account book filled with notations about witnesses, cryptic references to other files (unfortunately not in the tub), plus a large batch of newspaper clippings and four volumes of a stenographic report, which some people have thought to be a copy of the inquest minutes. An examination by this writer established that these are the minutes of the preliminary court hearing held in Fall River—the only known copy.

VI

The Furor

Fall River in 1892 was a city of some 83,000 people. Its harbor was crowded with vessels from many far-off places, long lines of freight cars were constantly being shunted in and out. As the steamship terminus of the Fall River Line, it was an important gateway to New England, played host daily to thousands of transients, and boasted a large, many-storied hotel—the newly opened Mellen House. It was less than twenty miles from Providence and about fifty miles from Boston. This was not an isolated, ingrown community; it was somewhat more cosmopolitan than many other cities of its size. Yet, seldom has any city reacted to a crime as Fall River did that day.

As news of the murders spread quickly through the town, many workmen abandoned their machines and dashed out of the factories. Others never returned from their noontime meal. By early afternoon most of the mills shut down for the day, not out of respect for Andrew Borden, but simply because there were so few workers still on the job. Thousands of them gathered in Second Street in a tightly packed, hot and sweating mass, filling the street and roadway from side to side, blocking all traffic. Hundreds of others gathered in clusters, some on Main Street, others in front of the newspaper offices, the station house, City Hall—wherever they thought they might glean more information. Saloons enjoyed an unexpected bonanza.

But this was not a crowd in a holiday mood. There was excitement, but under it there was tension and fear that was almost panic. The mysterious murder of a man and his wife in bright daylight in their own home on a busy street made each person in the crowd realize how vulnerable he and his family were. The fragmentary details of the brutal, almost inhuman and savage slaughter suggested the possibility of a demented ax-wielder, a maniac who might strike again at any moment without reason.

Newspapers were then enjoying their golden days; there was no radio, no television, to broadcast bulletins and news flashes. The newspapers were the sole source of information. With its very first story, the Fall River *Globe* left no doubt that it intended to increase its circulation and advertising by any means. It boasted, in its initial headline, that one of its reporters had been the first on the scene. As a flat declaratory statement, it was true; as an implication that it had scored a beat over its rivals, it was false.

The *Globe* had been tipped off first, but its reporter did not reach the scene until after Officer Allen had returned to the station house and Sawyer was already guarding the side door. Sawyer still did not know that Mr. Borden had been murdered. The *Globe* newsman sat on the outside step to await the return of the police and was still waiting there when he was joined by his colleagues from the other papers. They all got the news of the murders at the same time. This did not deter the *Globe* from making its boast or from quoting Dr. Bowen in such a gory fashion that he later protested.

Five days later the *Globe* showed what it had on its mind when it published a front-page box stating that its circulation had jumped 10,000 copies, an impressive figure which implied that its rivals were losing readers in droves. A different story emerges from a careful reading of the fine print. Actually, the *Globe's* average daily circulation had jumped about 2,000 copies and the paper had multiplied this increase by the number of days, a unique system for calculating circulation! Even so, a daily increase of 2,000 would be substantial, but all the other Fall River papers also increased their circulation. The papers began publishing all day with new editions or extras almost hourly, and many of the same readers bought several editions. Some of the extras issued consisted of a single sheet, printed on one side.

The first newspaper stories gave their readers little hope that there would be any quick solution of the murders. Bridget said she had been up in her room, Morse stated he was away from the house visiting a niece, and Lizzie said that after her father lay down on the sofa she had gone to the loft of the barn. The reporters had been admitted into the house and although the papers said that Lizzie spoke freely to them, unfortunately none used any direct quotes. The stories were so written that it cannot be determined exactly what information they obtained from her.

Unable to explain several puzzling aspects of the Borden murders, the legend makers have hinted that police were so slow to arrive that vital evidence against Lizzie Borden may have been destroyed or smuggled out by her friends. The documented facts show that the investigation began with Special Officer Patrick Doherty who arrived even as Officer Allen was reporting to Marshal Hilliard. From that moment on there was a steady procession of officers and officials to the house including State Detective George F. Seaver, who came from Taunton early that afternoon. By noon there were well over a dozen men actively at work on the murders and at least seven of them held separate interviews with Lizzie. The only outsiders who had entered the Borden home before the arrival of police were Mrs. Churchill, Miss Russell and Dr. Bowen. He was the only one who left the house, when he hurried to the telegraph office, and this was before Mrs. Borden's body had been found. His only conversation with Lizzie had been in the presence of all the others. When friends and neighbors began to stream in to offer their sympathies or comfort to Lizzie, police were there observing them. Miss Russell remained fairly close to Lizzie and went with her to her room when she went upstairs shortly after noon. In view of later developments, it is extremely unlikely that Miss Russell missed any suspicious action. Emma did not arrive home until late that afternoon.

As the news began to spread that Mrs. Borden had been hacked to death an hour or more before her husband, most people realized that it was highly unlikely that a maniac could have been in the house all that time without being discovered either by Lizzie or Bridget. Suspicion began to center on those connected with the household.

Uncle John Vinnicum Morse quickly became the favorite suspect of the man on the street and of many of the officers working on the case. He was cast in that role because he was a stranger to most people in Fall River, the murders had occurred less than twenty-four hours after his unexpected arrival, his alibi was so perfect that this was suspicious in itself, and to top it all off, he was a horse trader. In the popular mind horse traders then had the reputation that some used-car dealers have today.

News of the double homicide was flashed by telegraph to newspapers throughout the country, and many wired requests to Fall River asking local reporters to serve as correspondents. Some of the reporters began working for three to five out-of-town newspapers as well as for their own. A few of the papers in Boston, New York and other Eastern cities rushed reporters of their own to Fall River.

In many of the stories filed at the end of the first day, Morse was publicly named as the prime suspect and his early arrest was even predicted. By Friday evening, the day after the murders, public feeling against him was already so strong that when he left the Borden home to walk to the post office a menacing crowd, estimated at more than two thousand, began following him down the street. Several officers who had been assigned to watch him hurriedly brought him back to the safety of the house.

Porter, in his book written immediately after the trial, described the first day's activities of the police in detail, stating that they had searched the house, cellar, yard and barn, and that Mayor John W. Coughlin, a physician, took an active part in the search along with Medical Examiner Dolan. "From cellar to attic," he reported, "the police and physicians delved into every nook and corner; every particle of hay in the barn loft and every blade of grass in the yard was turned over, and when the day was done the harvest had been nothing." It is true that police had searched the house, barn and grounds, but it is unlikely that the first day's search was quite as intensive or thorough as Porter described it.

Lizzie's most fateful interview that day was probably the one with Special Officer Philip Harrington. According to Porter, it was Harrington who first suspected her. This statement was probably true, since it was Porter's paper, the Fall River *Globe,* which obtained exclusive reports of Harrington's activities, and the *Globe* stopped pointing its finger at Morse and switched to Lizzie Borden not long after Harrington's session with her. Unless this officer was the victim of an unusual number of coincidences, it is logical to suppose that he was on very friendly terms with one or more members of the *Globe* staff and did not mind the paper featuring reports of his activities above those of everybody else.

Oddly, it was not so much what Lizzie said that aroused Harrington's suspicions, it was what he described later as her "cool and steady" behavior. There is no doubt that her conduct was in sharp contrast with that of Bridget Sullivan. When police and reporters questioned the servant girl they found her so agitated that she was confused and incoherent. The first newspaper reports, based on what Bridget told reporters, said she was washing windows on the *third* floor. Lizzie, on the other hand, had her emotions well in check. She was not observed by police to be crying, and during the first hour readily and clearly answered all questions. Later, when she wearied of hearing the same question repeated by each officer who sought her out, she bluntly stated that she was getting tired and asked that they be brief—an arrogant attitude not calculated to make friends of the investigators. Shortly afterward she became nauseated and Dr. Bowen gave her the first of several sedatives.

One incident stood out in Harrington's mind. The officer, who appears to have spoken in language lifted straight out of a Victorian novel, testified that he had remarked to her, "Owing to the atrociousness of this crime perhaps you are not in a mental condition to give as clear a statement of the facts as you will be on tomorrow." Lizzie, he said, made a "stiff courtesy" and answered, "No, I can tell you all I know now just as well as at any other time." Her calm reply somehow convinced Harrington that Lizzie knew more about the crime than she was telling.

Two events occurred during the first day that later played an important part in the case and legend. During Assistant Marshal Fleet's questioning of Lizzie, she mentioned the sudden illness in the house on Tuesday night and the possibility that the bread or milk might have been poisoned. Following this lead, Fleet directed Harrington and Doherty to check all drugstores for recent purchases of poison and they started this investigation assignment late the same day.

Meanwhile, searching officers had found an ax resting on a chopping block in the cellar. Dr. Dolan later examined the head with a magnifying glass and said there were several stains that could be blood or rust. He also saw hairs clinging to the ax head which he placed carefully in an envelope. Later examination showed the stains were rust spots and the hairs were from a cow. When Lizzie was asked if there were other axes in the house, she said she knew of only the one and called Bridget to assist the police. The servant led several men, including Patrolman Michael Mullaly, to a small room in the cellar. She reached up into a box on a shelf and lifted out two hatchets which she handed to Mullaly. Mullaly later showed them to Fleet. The Assistant Marshal asked to see the box. Fleet took it down from the shelf, lowering it so that both men could look inside. A handleless hatchet, its head covered with ashes or ashy dust, was among other items in the box. The handle had been broken off near the head and the wood around the break was not dark with age. Fleet replaced the broken hatchet in the box. This episode was to have unexpected repercussions at the trial.

On Friday morning, the day after the murder, the *Globe* had a real scoop with Special Officer Harrington cast as the hero. The headline read: WHAT DID LIZZIE WANT OF POISON? Harrington, the story stated, had visited the D. R. Smith Pharmacy at the corner of South Main and Columbia Streets and questioned Eli Bence, a clerk who told him that on Wednesday morning, the day before the murders, a young woman had come into the store and asked for ten cents' worth of prussic acid. She said she needed it to kill moths in a fur garment. When Bence told her that the dangerous poison was sold only on a doctor's prescription, the woman left. He identified her as Lizzie Borden. Frederick E. Hart, another clerk in the store, and Frank H. Kilroy, a student, corroborated his story, and they both added that Lizzie had carried a fur cape over her arm.

In its earlier editions the previous day, while Morse was still being mentioned as the chief suspect, the *Globe* had explained Lizzie's calm demeanor by stating, "In temperament she is extremely phlegmatic and is never easily excited or disturbed. She is extremely matter-of-fact and not given to betraying her emotions."

But Lizzie was no longer phlegmatic in the paper's account

of the poison incident: "The demeanor of Miss Lizzie Borden through the trying ordeal of being confronted with the man who says that she asked about the poison was that of contempt and scorn; in fact, her conduct as seen by the police has been strange."

As will be shown later, no such confrontation scene took place, but the *Globe* seldom let facts get in the way of a good story. It soon had additional information about and against Lizzie. It quoted unidentified former schoolmates as describing her to be "rather eccentric," and added, "Lizzie's friends are now talking of her peculiarities." The schoolmates and friends were not named, and what the eccentric acts were or in what way she was peculiar was not stated. The paper also quoted another authority on Lizzie, Hiram C. Harrington, the blacksmith husband of Borden's sister, to whom neither Lizzie nor her father had spoken in years. He was quoted as saying: "Mr. Borden was an exceedingly hard man concerning money matters, determined and stubborn, and when he once gets an idea, nothing can stop him. As for the motive for this crime, it was money, unquestionably money. If Mr. Borden died he would have left something over $500,000, and in my opinion that estate furnished the only motive and a sufficient one for the double murder.

"Last evening I had a long interview with Miss Lizzie who has refused to see anyone. She was very composed, showed no signs of any emotion, nor were there any traces of grief upon her countenance. This did not surprise me as she is not naturally emotional."

He said Lizzie told him her father had returned home at 10:30 the morning of the murder, that she had been very solicitous, assisting him to remove his coat and put on his dressing gown, asked about his health, and volunteered to adjust the windows so he could take a nap. She estimated she left the house for the barn about 10:45 but could not state exactly how long she had remained in the barn "as she was cutting lead into sinkers." He also said Lizzie told him that the previous spring, while her father and stepmother were at Swansea, a large amount of money, "together with diamonds," was stolen from the house.

"Yes," he continued, "there were family dissensions though it was kept very quiet. For nearly ten years there have been constant disputes between the daughters and their father and stepmother. It arose, of course, with regard to the stepmother. Mr. Borden gave her some bank stock, and the girls thought they ought to be treated as evenly as the mother. So he deeded them the homestead on Ferry Street, an estate of 120 rods of land with a house and barn, all valued at $3,000. This was in 1887. The trouble about money matters did not diminish, nor the acerbity of the family ruptures lessen, and Mr. Borden gave each girl ten shares in the Crystal Spring Bleachery Company, which he paid $100 a share for. They sold them soon after for less than $40 a share. He also gave them some bank stock at various times, allowing them, of course, the entire income from them. In addition to this he gave them a weekly stipend, amounting to $200 a year. In spite of all this the dispute about their not being allowed enough went on with equal bitterness. Lizzie did most of the demonstrative contention, as Emma is very quiet and unassuming, and would feel deeply any disparaging or angry word from her father. Lizzie, on the contrary, was haughty and domineering with the stubborn will of her father and bound to contest for her rights. There were many animated interviews between father and daughter on this point.

"Lizzie is of a repellent disposition, and after an unsuccessful passage with her father, would become sulky and refuse to speak to him for days at a time. She moved in the best society in Fall River, was a member of the Congregational Church, and is a brilliant conversationalist. She thought she ought to entertain as others did, and felt that with her father's wealth she was expected to hold her end up with others of her set. Her father's constant refusal to allow her to entertain lavishly angered her. I have heard many bitter things she has said of her father, and know that she was deeply resentful of her father's maintained stand in this matter. This house on Ferry Street was an old one, and was in constant need of repairs. There were two tenants paying $16.50 and $14 a month, but with taxes and repairs there was very little income from the property. It was a great deal of trouble for the girls to keep the house in repair, and a month or two ago they got disgusted and deeded the house back to their father. I am positive that Emma knows nothing of the murder."

The feud between Harrington and the Borden family, with the exception of Emma who still visited the Harringtons, was no secret in Fall River. All the papers, except the *Globe,* mentioned this fact so that their readers could judge for themselves the value of Harrington's statements.

One reporter, who had seen the blacksmith go in, timed the length of Harrington's stay. With tongue in cheek, he wrote that Harrington had managed to get a surprising amount of information from Lizzie considering that he had been inside the house exactly three minutes.

While the *Globe* was freely predicting Lizzie Borden's immediate arrest, the police, under Marshal Hilliard, continued their investigation. They were flooded by reports about mysterious and sometimes blood-soaked strangers wandering around everywhere. All of these reports were checked.

A determined search was made for the person who wrote the note and for the messenger who delivered it to Mrs. Borden. A New York publication, *Once a Week,* offered a $500 reward to the writer of the note if he or she would come forward. Morse's alibi was investigated. A report was received that Carpenter, the man who had embezzled funds from Borden and who had left town in disgrace after repaying the money, had been seen in Fall River. Men were assigned to find him.

For the second day in a row, the Borden house, grounds and barn were searched. Porter devoted an entire chapter of his book to this search to show how thorough it was. Five top officials supervised the search: Marshal Hilliard, Assistant Marshal Fleet, State Detective Seaver, Medical Examiner Dolan and Captain Dennis Desmond. When the search party entered the house, a squad of patrolmen, whose instructions were not to let anyone enter or leave while the search was in progress, surrounded the building and guarded all doors and windows. "The five officers," Porter wrote, "spent over three hours ransacking rooms, bureaus, beds, boxes, trunks and everything else where it was thought that anything they would like to find might be hidden. Then the yard and barn were again searched, but with the same result. Nothing was found . . ."

The inclusion of Dr. Dolan in the searching party is significant. He was brought along not for any ability to find secret hiding places but because he could recognize bloodstains on a garment. At the end of the search Dr. Dolan remarked, "We examined everything down to the slightest bump in the wallpaper." Reports of this thorough search appeared in all the papers. A partly filled old well near the barn was cleaned out, and several piles of lumber against the back fence were moved board by board. Even the *Globe* admitted that Lizzie had cooperated completely with the officials, opening all locked trunks and compartments for them. This Friday search disappeared into limbo during the trial; no officer mentioned it.

On Saturday Fall River was in turmoil. The *Globe,* which had expected the immediate arrest of Lizzie Borden, was highly displeased; its lead news sentence on the Borden case that day read: "It may seem strange that no arrest had been made up to 10 o'clock this morning." The pot boiled more furiously when the Fall River *News,* the oldest and largest paper in the city, printed the following announcement:

$5,000

REWARD!

The above Reward will be paid to any
one who may secure the

Arrest and Conviction

of the person or persons, who occasioned
the death of

Mr. Andrew J. Borden and Wife.

**EMMA J. BORDEN,
LIZZIE A. BORDEN.**

It was apparent that there was a difference of opinion within the police department. Some of the officers, notably Harrington and Fleet, wanted to arrest Lizzie. Marshal Hilliard was reluctant to act without some physical evidence such as a bloodstained garment or the murder weapon. For the third time in three days a searching party again went through the house, the grounds, and the barn of the Borden home. The arrival of out-of-town newspapers in which the local force was criticized for not yet solving the murders added urgency to the new search.

This was the day of the Borden funeral and some 4,000 people pushed, shoved and jostled their way into a monumental jam on Second Street to watch it. About twenty patrolmen were needed to clear a way through the crowd for the funeral coaches. The services had raised a delicate problem in protocol: Lizzie was a staunch member of the Central Congregational Church but her father had left that church and had been a non-attending pew holder at the rival First Congregational Church. Which minister should conduct the services? A satisfactory compromise was reached. Since Lizzie was also active in the Mission Church, the Reverend Edwin A. Buck of that organization and the Reverend Dr. Adams of the First Congregational Church were asked to share the ministerial duties. Private services were held in the home. Hiram C. Harrington was not listed among those present. Lizzie was the first of the mourners to emerge from the house, leaning on the arm of undertaker Winward. She was followed by Emma. The sisters seemed to have flouted convention; the papers reported, "Both ladies were without veils."

No graveside rites were held. Both bodies were placed in the receiving vault at Oak Grove Cemetery and the funeral cortege left at once. The actual burial was delayed at the request of Dr. Edward S. Wood, professor of chemistry at the Harvard University Medical School and one of the country's foremost experts in forensic medicine. He had received the various axes and hatchets found in the cellar, as well as the stomachs of both murder victims. After the mourners departed from the cemetery, Dr. Dolan, acting upon the request of Dr. Wood, entered the vault with several physicians. The heads of both victims were severed and the grisly relics were sent to the Harvard professor. The news was withheld from the family.

The search was suspended during the funeral until the Borden family lawyer, Andrew Jennings, came to the house. Marshal Hilliard was taking no chances that anyone might accuse the police of planting evidence while no witnesses were present. The police head was overcautious. Again nothing was found.

Fall River police had reached an impasse. There was a rising clamor everywhere for action. The stories in the *Globe* had not gone unnoticed and its voice was loud. Marshal Hilliard, who had the authority to ask for a warrant for Lizzie Borden's arrest, was reluctant to act on the information he had. He telephoned District Attorney Knowlton of the Southern District and asked him to come from New Bedford to Fall River.

He may have become uneasy over the sudden appearance of O. M. Hanscom, superintendent of the Boston office of the Pinkerton Detective Agency, who had been hired by Lizzie and Emma on the advice of Jennings. Hanscom remained in Fall River only two days, after which it was generally believed that he had dropped out of the case. However, in the memorandum book found years later by Jennings' daughter, the lawyer had listed Hanscom's name with references to file numbers, indicating that he had received a good many reports from the detective agency.

Knowlton arrived that afternoon and went directly to the Mellen House for a conference with Marshal Hilliard, State Detective Seaver, Mayor Coughlin and Medical Examiner Dolan. According to Porter, this unpublicized Saturday session lasted almost five hours. While no statement was made after the conference, indications are that the District Attorney had decided to prosecute Lizzie Borden. Not long after the conference, Mayor Coughlin and Marshal Hilliard appeared at the Borden home and the Mayor suggested that all members of the family remain in the house for several days. "I believe it would be better if you do so," he said.

Lizzie realized what the Mayor's words implied and asked, "Is there anybody in this house suspected?"

Mayor Coughlin tried to avoid a direct answer by pointing out Morse's experience when he was almost mobbed on the street, but Lizzie would not be put off and said she wanted to know the truth.

To this the embarrassed official replied, "Well, Miss Borden, I regret to answer, but I must answer yes; you are suspected."

Lizzie replied promptly, "I am ready to go now."

Emma spoke up for the first time and remarked, "We have tried to keep it from her as long as we could."

The murders had one unexpected result: they healed the breach between the rival churches. The Reverend W. Walker Jubb, recently installed as pastor of the Central Congregational Church, announced that joint memorial services for the murdered couple would be held Sunday at the First Congregational Church. No member of the family attended, however, because of Mayor Coughlin's instructions.

On Monday, reporters who had previously published statements by police officials saying that they would arrest on sight any member of the household who left the Borden home, discovered that Bridget Sullivan had spent only one night in the Borden house since the murders. She left Thursday night, returning Friday morning. She left again that night and was gone until Monday morning. She was accompanied by a cousin who lived in Fall River and at whose home she had been staying.

While the reporters were questioning Bridget, Hilliard secretly visited Judge Josiah C. Blaisdell in his chambers at the Second District Court and obtained a warrant for Lizzie's arrest. It was a poorly kept secret. Newspapers soon had the news, but the warrant still had not been served at 5 P.M. when Knowlton came back from New Bedford. Reporters quoted him as saying at the station, "There will be action at once." If they thought this meant that the warrant would now be served, they erred. Later they were told that the District Attorney wanted to hold a hearing.

Under Massachusetts law, an inquest does not have to be held before a coroner and a jury in public. A prosecutor can elect to hold a secret inquiry before a judge with no one else present except an official court stenographer. Witnesses are sworn and both the judge and the prosecutor have the right to question a witness. A suspect does not have the right to be represented by counsel.

Although such an inquest began on Tuesday and Jennings was denied permission to be present while Lizzie Borden was questioned, officials insisted to newsmen that no inquest was being held.

"Authorities seemed to want it understood that there was no inquest," Porter wrote. "Some of them intimated that the Government was simply conducting an informal examination with a view to drawing from the witnesses their last stories and making a comparison of them. . . . It was reported that no oath was administered."

On the first day of the secret inquest only two witnesses were examined: Bridget Sullivan and Lizzie in that order. When Officer Doherty arrived at the Borden home to get Bridget and take her to the inquest at the central police station, the servant burst into tears because she thought she was being placed under arrest.

The pretense that it was not an official secret inquest was dropped the following afternoon when Attorney General Albert E. Pillsbury, the chief prosecuting official of the state, attended part of the session. At its end late in the day, District Attorney Knowlton issued this bulletin: "Inquest continued at 10 o'clock. Witnesses examined [today] were Lizzie Borden, Dr. S. W. Bowen, Mrs. Adelaide B. Churchill, Hiram C. Harrington, John V. Morse and Emma Borden. Nothing was developed for publication."

With no news coming from the inquest, reporters followed the police about and reported that Marshal Hilliard and Officer Harrington went to the Borden house with a carpenter who removed bloodstained woodwork. An expert who was brought from Boston opened a safe in Borden's bedroom and found nothing but papers connected with his work as a bank official.

The *Globe* ran what it claimed was a summary of Bridget's inquest testimony, but since it had her saying that she was washing windows on the third floor at the time of Borden's murder, repeating the mistake of the garbled first-day murder story, it is fairly safe to assume that the paper was substituting imagination for information. No police officers were allowed inside the inquest room.

On Thursday, as on the other two days, Lizzie was on the stand most of the time. The other witnesses questioned were the three men who had been in the drugstore when the attempt to purchase the poison had been made. Then the inquest ended. Lizzie was asked to wait in a small room and Knowlton and Hilliard went to Jennings' home and informed the lawyer they had decided to arrest her. The Marshal produced a new warrant, not the one he had obtained on Monday. In this one Lizzie Borden was accused of the murder of her father.

When the formal arrest was made Lizzie broke down in public for the first time. She sobbed, had a violent attack of nausea, and Dr. Bowen was summoned to the station house to treat her. On Thursday, August 11, one week after the murders, the news of her arrest flashed around the world. Fall River papers printed extras.

The *Globe* could not resist making its usual editorial comment even in its news headline, shown below:

LOCKED UP.

Lizzie Borden At Last In Custody,

VII

The Antics

If the Fall River police thought they had been under fire before the arrest, they soon learned to look back upon that period as one of comparative calm. The week-long investigation had created national, even international, interest, and the arrest increased the excitement. I recently examined the 1892 issues of a now-departed Long Island paper known for its boast that its news columns carried local news only. A catastrophe could occur twenty feet beyond the limits of its territory and the paper would ignore it. True to tradition, the paper had not carried a single line of news about the Borden murders, but the editor could not resist commenting on it and, within a few weeks, wrote three editorials about the case.

Lizzie Borden was kept in the matron's room of the station house over night. The next morning she was arraigned before Judge Blaisdell. Jennings objected to his sitting on the case because he also had presided at the inquest. The reporters were more interested in the prisoner than in the legal argument. They noted that she was wearing a dark-blue suit and a black straw hat trimmed in front with red flowers. Except for a slight trembling of her lower lip she had completely regained her composure and showed no other signs of emotion. The court ordered her held without bail for a hearing on August 22 and she was taken to the county jail in Taunton where she had the unexpected reunion with Mrs. Wright, the sheriff's wife and the mother of a former childhood playmate. The Reverend Mr.

Jubb was allowed to accompany her on the train. A large crowd of curiosity seekers had gathered at both the Fall River and the Taunton stations.

A barrage of letters descended on the Fall River police after the arrest; some praised them, some denounced them. The officials could ignore the letters, but not the rising emotional tension in the town, nor the rising incidence of brawls which began as arguments over Lizzie's innocence or guilt. The men who were working on the case quickly learned that it was best not to mention it in the presence of pugnacious strangers.

If Lizzie was a symbol to some people in Fall River of an old family being cut down to size, she also became a symbol to women's organizations throughout the country who were fighting for equal rights—the suffragettes, the Lucy Stoners and other feminists. Somehow, the leaders of these organizations equated Lizzie's position of being under arrest for murder with the question of women's rights. Petitions began to shower on police and the courts demanding that Lizzie Borden be released from jail until her trial. Among the most demanding were some of the national members of the Temperance Union, whose Carry Nation, soon after, made another hatchet famous in another fashion.

The Reverend Mr. Jubb and City Missionary Buck were firm in their support of Lizzie. They had been present at the Borden home throughout the week of the investigation and at the police station daily while the inquest was held. The Reverend Mr. Jubb, who had arrived from England the previous year to accept the call from the Central Congregational Church, bitterly protested American court procedure that allowed one of his active church members to be placed in a cell.

But while the behavior of some of Lizzie's supporters led later commentators to ridicule them, there was also substantial and meaningful support from Lizzie's friends and associates. A reporter went to Marion to interview the friends whom Lizzie had been planning to join. These included the Misses Anna C.

Holmes, Elizabeth M. Johnson, Isabel J. Frazer, Louise Remington and Mary L. Holmes. Which one of them acted as spokesman, the reporter neglected to mention, but he left no doubt that the speaker expressed the opinion of them all.

"I and several others here have known Lizzie since she was a little girl," the speaker said. "She has never changed except to grow older in years from what she always was, self-contained, self-reliant, and very composed. Her conduct since her arrest is exactly what I should have expected. The very idea of her killing Mr. and Mrs. Borden is preposterous.

"Her stepmother and she were not fond of each other, a state of affairs that, as everybody knows, is not uncommon between second wives and grown-up daughters. As for Lizzie and her father, they were, without being demonstrative, very fond of each other.

"She is a monument of straightforwardness. I never shall believe, even were she convicted of the deed, that she committed it, unless she were to confess herself, and then the marvel would be greater to me that she had concealed her act than that she did it."

While Lizzie had missed that Sunday roll call of the Endeavor Society, its members did not forget her; they sent the following communication to her in Taunton: "We, the members of the Young People's Society of Christian Endeavor, desire to extend to our fellow member, Miss Lizzie A. Borden, our sincere sympathy with her in her present hour of trial, and our confident belief that she will soon be restored to her place of usefulness among us."

The Fall River *Globe* did not approve of any of this and five days after Lizzie's arrest headlined a story: SENTIMENTAL NONSENSE FAR TOO PREVALENT.

Even after arrest the police continued to work on the case; their efforts naturally were directed toward finding additional evidence for the prosecution. The only trip Lizzie had made away from home in a year had been her visit to New Bedford the week before the murders. Inspectors Hathaway and Parker of the Fall River police went to that city and called upon every drugstore in it. They reported on their return that there had been no sales of any poison, nor any attempt to make such a purchase during the time Lizzie had been in New Bedford.

One of the early clues that had excited Fall River had been furnished by Dr. Benjamin Handy. He informed police that while driving by the Borden home on the morning of the murders he had observed a medium-sized young man, extremely pale, dressed in a light suit of clothes, acting strangely in front of the house. He said the man kept his eyes fixed on the sidewalk and was moving very slowly with a peculiar rigid walk. He emphasized that the man was not drunk but appeared to be under severe mental strain. The doctor said his actions were so unusual that he turned in his carriage to watch him. The physician had more than an average interest in the Borden home since his daughter was one of Lizzie's friends and it was his summer home in Marion to which she had been invited. Dr. Handy reported this incident to police shortly after the murders. At that time the *Globe* was already calling for the arrest of Lizzie Borden. The paper poked fun at the clue and, although Dr. Handy said the man had kept his head down and he never saw his eyes, it dubbed the stranger: Dr. Handy's "Wild-Eyed Man."

In some fashion, a private detective named Edwin D. McHenry of Providence became associated with the Fall River police, and he claimed that they had engaged him. Later, no police official would admit either hiring McHenry or even knowing how and why he was allowed to take an active part in much of the investigation. McHenry located a drunken millhand, known as "Mike the Soldier," who had passed the Borden home that morning. Mike had been suffering from a hangover when he arrived late at the mill and had been sent home. He was still

wearing the same trousers he had worn the morning of the murders, a distinctive and vivid shade of blue. Dr. Handy, called
to the station house to look at Mike, said he did not resemble
the man he had seen.

After Lizzie's arrest, several reporters asked State Detective
Seaver if any further effort was being made to locate the man
described by Dr. Handy. "It's being worked for all it's worth,"
he replied, "and in my opinion it's not worth much."

Lizzie was brought back to Fall River for the scheduled
August 22 hearing but it was postponed for three days. During
this time she was held at the local station house under the guard
of Matron Mrs. Hannah Reagan, and she was visited daily by
Emma, the ever loyal ministers and many of her friends, including Mrs. Brigham and Mrs. Charles J. Holmes.

On the eve of the court hearing, Edwin Porter came up with a
tremendous news beat that created headlines throughout the
country. His story said that Lizzie had quarreled with Emma
and had accused her older sister of giving her away. Although
Porter was a staff member of the Fall River *Globe*, he also was
serving as local correspondent for a Boston newspaper among
others. Curiously, he gave the scoop to the Boston paper, not to
his own.

His story said that Emma had arrived at Lizzie's room in the
police station shortly after 8:30 that morning for her customary
daily visit. Matron Reagan left the sisters alone while she cleaned
an adjacent room. Attracted by loud voices in the room she had
just left, she hurried back and stood in the doorway. She saw
Emma bending over Lizzie, who was lying on a couch. Lizzie
was talking:

"Emma, you have given me away, haven't you?"

"No, Lizzie, I have not," the older sister replied.

"You have, and I will let you see I won't give in one inch,"
the prisoner retorted, sitting upright and holding up a finger.

There the conversation ended. Lizzie flounced angrily back

onto the couch, turned on her side toward the window and closed her eyes. Emma sat beside her and the two sisters remained mute, not talking to each other, for almost two and a half hours, until Jennings arrived to see his client. Emma then left.

This conversation obviously implied that Emma had some secret knowledge about Lizzie's guilt, and the report was treated in a sensational manner in the Boston newspaper. When copies arrived in Fall River this scoop must have really jolted the twenty-six out-of-town reporters waiting there for the hearing to open. Most of them dashed to the police station to confirm the event with Mrs. Reagan. Lizzie's friends also hurried there and the Reverend Mr. Jubb soon drew up a statement which he requested Mrs. Reagan to sign.

Porter mentioned the quarrel in his book but failed to give himself credit as the reporter responsible for breaking the story. The fact that this report later was thoroughly discredited at the trial may have accounted for his modesty.

In preparation for the District Court hearing, Jennings engaged Melvin O. Adams, a Boston lawyer, as associate counsel. Most of the witnesses who testified during the six-day hearing also appeared at the trial; their testimony will be given later in the trial chapter and will be compared to their testimony at the hearing. The poison testimony by Eli Bence and his associates, who were not permitted to testify at the trial, will be given in the chapter concerning Pearson.

Bridget Sullivan, who left the Borden home after the murders, attended the District Court hearing accompanied by her lawyer, James T. Cummings. While she was still on the stand testifying, the hearing was halted for the day and she was seen entering an office with Prosecutor Knowlton, who showed her the testimony she had previously given at the inquest. When she was cross-examined about this the next morning, she replied she could not remember what she and Knowlton had talked about.

The District Attorney read to the court portions of Lizzie Borden's testimony at the secret inquest. Knowlton emphasized that Lizzie had testified that when Bridget was fumbling with the locks on the front door to admit her father, she was on her way down the steps. Lizzie said she had brought up some clean clothes from the cellar laundry and had stopped to baste a loop on a dress, estimating that she had been up in her room about five minutes. This placed her upstairs next to the guest bedroom where the body of her stepmother lay on the floor, and the door to this room was open. During the second and third days of her questioning she changed her story and insisted she had been downstairs in the kitchen when her father entered the house. Although she still said she was upstairs at one point during the morning, she was vague as to the time. Knowlton thought her change of story was of extreme importance, indicating a guilty knowledge. The inquest testimony showed she had told the story of going up into the hayloft looking for lead and had searched through a small box. She admitted she had not been in the barn for many months prior to that morning.

Q: Where was that box you say was upstairs, containing lead?

A: There was a kind of a workbench.

Q: Is it there now?

A: I don't know, sir.

Q: How long since you have seen it there?

A: I have not been out there since that day.

These questions seemed to indicate that no such box had been found in the barn. Knowlton asked Lizzie to describe the contents of the box and particularly what kind of lead, if any, she found in it. She told him that there were nails, some old locks, a doorknob and some pieces of a form of sheet lead that were doubled over and not usable for sinkers. When he asked her if she owned a fishline, she replied, "Not here; we had some at the farm." He also asked her if she had sinkers at the farm. Lizzie replied she thought there were some at the farm but she didn't know if there were any on her own lines since she had not used that equipment in five years. Knowlton then demanded to know why she had been searching for lead up in the loft of the barn on a hot day when she had sinkers on the farm. Lizzie explained that she wanted the sinkers for her trip to Marion, that she had no way of getting the equipment at the farm. She had planned to buy new line and hooks and wanted to see if she could find lead to use as sinkers before purchasing the new equipment; if she found the lead, she would not have to buy the sinkers.

The inquest also brought out the information that several days after the murder Lizzie had turned over to police the clothes she had been wearing the fatal morning. Her dress consisted of a blouse and skirt. Asked to describe the material she replied, "Some call it bengaline silk."

The fact that Lizzie admitted being upstairs and had not reported seeing the body of her stepmother weighed heavily with Judge Blaisdell. "Suppose for a single moment a man was standing there," he remarked. "He was found close by that guest chamber, which, to Mrs. Borden, was a chamber of death. Suppose a man had been found in the vicinity of Mr. Borden; was the first to find the body, and the only account he could give of himself was the unreasonable one that he was out in the barn looking for sinkers; then he was out in the yard; then he was out for something else; would there be any question in the minds of men what should be done with such a man?"

Judge Blaisdell then ordered her held for action by the grand jury.

This same hearing established that Lizzie Borden had been seen by many people, including police and officials, shortly after the murder of her father, and nobody saw the slightest trace of blood on her clothes or person. At the end of the hearing the Fall River *Globe* ran the following surprising editorial:

"We sincerely hope that Lizzie Borden will be able to establish her innocence and we know that the courts of Massachusetts will accord her every opportunity to do this. . . . As we have already remarked, the State will have to present a stronger case than it already has, to establish the guilt of the accused beyond a reasonable doubt or to satisfy public opinion."

This unusual behavior on the part of the *Globe* did not last long. Although newspaper reporters had been besieging the Taunton jail hoping to get in to interview Lizzie Borden, she had declined all requests. A Mrs. McGuirk, the wife of a former Fall River reporter, who had moved away several years before the murders, had been associated with Lizzie on the Fruit and Flower Mission and several other charitable organizations. She wrote a letter to Lizzie reminding her of their former friendship and asked for an interview for the New York *Recorder*. It was the right approach by Mrs. McGuirk. Lizzie was known for her loyalty to friends and she agreed to be interviewed.

Mrs. McGuirk came to the Taunton jail on a Saturday and her story appeared in the New York paper the following Monday. In it she quoted Lizzie as saying, "I know I am innocent, and I have made up my mind that no matter what happens, I will try to bear up bravely and make the best of it. There is one thing that hurts me very much. They say I don't show any grief. Certainly I don't in public. I never did reveal my feelings and I cannot change my nature now."

The story stated that Lizzie spent most of her time in jail sewing or reading but was not allowed any light in her cell at night. The woman reporter mentioned for the first time in print some of the charitable work she knew Lizzie had been doing while she was associated with her. Mrs. McGuirk gave considerable space to a description of the dress Lizzie had been wearing: "plum-colored gown, a pattern dress with embossed velvet bands of trimming, a narrow white ruche and a pretty brooch, with a child's head on it, at the throat, and a white apron over the skirt front."

Mrs. McGuirk had achieved the dream of all reporters at that time, an exclusive interview with Lizzie Borden, and the other papers had to pick up her story from the *Recorder*.

The very next day the Fall River *Globe* had something to say about it:

"The flap-doodle, gush, idiotic drivel, misrepresentations and in some instances, anarchic nonsense, which is being promulgated by women newspaper correspondents, W.C.T.U. conventions and other female agencies in connection with the Borden murder just now, may originate in good intentions but do not strengthen Lizzie Borden's case much in the opinion of the public. The Commonwealth of Massachusetts will, for the present, adhere to the forms of law in conducting its criminal cases, regardless of the clamor or criticism of any petticoat propaganda."

In the very same edition, the paper dropped a blockbuster of its own. Under the headline, ANOTHER LINK IN THE DAMAGING CHAIN OF EVIDENCE THAT IS BEING FORGED ABOUT LIZZIE BORDEN, it published a story saying that she had consulted with a well-known Providence lawyer six months before the murders and had discussed with him the disposition of certain property in the event of death. The story indicated that she had described her father's large realty holdings. The paper added:

"His name, which is now in possession of the *Globe*, together with his exact address, is not mentioned because the *Globe* has no desire to go further than the legitimate search for news."

The Fall River *Globe* now had the satisfaction of seeing other newspapers pick up its exclusive story and reprint it. It boasted of this fact the following day. Reporters from other papers set

out to learn the identity of the lawyer. They questioned police
and other officials only to learn that the information in the
story was also news to them. After inquiring at the office of every
lawyer in Providence, the other papers reported that the story
was false.

The *Globe* promptly retorted, "There is no occasion for extended comment upon such proceedings. If the story is 'utterly
false' as our contemporary [the Fall River *News*] asserts, its action in publishing it as news on Wednesday is also utterly inde-
fensible." The paper refrained from pointing out that its rivals,
in reprinting the information, had carefully credited it to the
Globe, steering clear of guaranteeing its authenticity. Several
days later the *Globe* dropped all mention of this story, tacitly
admitting it had been untrue.

Although no one can pinpoint with any accuracy the exact
date, it was while these wild stories and rumors were making
their rounds that the four-line verse concerning Lizzie Borden
and the ax made its first appearance. The author has never
been identified. Kirby said that there were at least a dozen
other stanzas that the children of Fall River used at that time in
playing games, but since he was a firm believer in her innocence, he had not learned them and they seem to have been lost
to posterity. Although the original verse was not published in
American newspapers of the day, it spread rapidly by word of
mouth throughout the country and soon was being published
abroad.

It was now the turn of the Boston *Globe* to heat up the case
against Lizzie Borden. The Boston paper had the curious distinction of receiving Porter's scoop on the supposed quarrel between Lizzie and Emma. Evidently this experience was not
enough to make it cautious, or it may have been trying to
emulate its Fall River namesake in convicting Lizzie Borden
before trial and even before indictment.

Private Detective McHenry played a prominent role in this one. He had teamed up with a Boston reporter aptly named Henry G. Trickey and on October 10, 1892, in a story that ran for more than a solid page of type, almost thirteen full columns, the Boston *Globe* printed what it called LIZZIE BORDEN'S SECRET.

LIZZIE BORDEN'S SECRET.

Mr. Borden Discovered It and Hot Words Followed.

Startling Testimony from Twenty-five New Witnesses.

Emma Was Kicked During That Quarrel— Family Discord and Murder.

Trickey, through McHenry, revealed that the prosecution now had some twenty-five new witnesses, whose stories all dovetailed in building up an ironclad case against Lizzie. The witnesses had seen almost everything except the actual blows delivered.

Whether it was Trickey's flashy imagination or McHenry's that supplied the names of the witnesses could never be determined, but the story gave both their names and addresses. They came from far and wide. One was listed as living on East 126 Street in New York City, another in "the second Queen Anne cottage on the street below Rhodes' pavilion on the right-hand side of Broad St., Pawtuxet, Rhode Island." If the purpose in giving such an address was to convince a city editor of the story's authenticity, it seemed to succeed.

The story told, witness by witness, how one person had been passing the Borden house at 9:40 on the morning of the murder and heard a horrible cry that nobody in the Churchill home, less than twenty feet away, ever heard. Attracted by the fearsome wail, this newly discovered witness glanced up at the house and there, nicely framed in the guest-room window, was a woman whose head was covered with a rubber cap or hood, possibly from a waterproof, which neatly explained how Lizzie Borden avoided the bloodstains. This man's story was confirmed by the Pawtuxet woman who, in some peculiar fashion, was transported so far from home and was pushing a baby carriage along Second Street. There were still other witnesses who happened to be on Second Street when Borden came home. They saw him about to enter the house and at the same time espied Lizzie peering through the blinds of the guest bedroom where the butchered body of her stepmother lay in its own gore.

The collaborators on this fantasy either recognized a weakness in the motive that seemed to satisfy police and prosecutor, or they felt that the Lizzie Borden story needed some additional beefing up, and so they produced a love interest, including a great big scarlet A for Lizzie. A couple identified as Mr. and Mrs. Frederick Chace were reported to have visited the Borden home on the night before the murder, overheard Lizzie quarreling with her father, and heard him say, "I will know the name of the man who got you into trouble!"

With these immortal words ringing in their ears, the Chaces apparently beat a hasty retreat.

To lend authentic coloring to the story, the names of Bridget Sullivan, John Vinnicum Morse and Mrs. Hannah Reagan were used. Matron Reagan was quoted as saying that Morse had visited Lizzie in the police station and she had heard the prisoner tell her uncle, "Get those things out of the way in my room, and then they can do their worst." Bridget was quoted as saying that she heard Lizzie and her father quarreling.

Although Fall River police would have been happy to have such witnesses as the ones generously supplied by McHenry and Trickey, they had to say that virtually every line in the thirteen columns of newsprint was untrue.

The Boston *Globe* tried to slide out of it the next day. It stated that the story had been proven wrong in "some particulars." McHenry, in an outburst of virtuous indignation, said that naturally the names of the actual witnesses had been changed, since he would not want to give away their identities. But the paper dropped all attempts to salvage its pride when it was threatened with a libel suit. It profusely apologized, in a prominent box on page one, to Lizzie Borden and to Uncle Morse. Authorities and reporters who questioned McHenry got such a medley of confused accounts from him that they in turn became confused, withdrew, and left him alone. Officials did learn that Trickey had attempted to bribe Bridget Sullivan. He was indicted and fled to Canada. Later he slipped in a railroad yard and was killed by a train.

During the week of November 7, District Attorney Knowlton began presenting his evidence to a grand jury. In a highly unusual move, the prosecutor notified Jennings that he would be allowed to offer witnesses and evidence for the defense before the grand jury. It was not accepted. I gave this, as a hypothetical case, to some lawyers, judges and district attorneys, all skilled in criminal law. All were appalled at the thought of a defense attorney, in advance of an indictment, gratuitously presenting to a district attorney the names and information possessed by his witnesses, while the prosecution reserved to itself the information it had gathered. They also were disturbed at the attempt to have a case tried before a grand jury. They said the purpose of a grand jury is to listen to the witnesses for the prosecution and to determine whether there is sufficient information to warrant the lodging of a charge. They emphasized that an indictment is not proof of guilt, nor does a grand jury rule on the question of innocence or guilt. Whatever Knowlton's motives were, the fact remains that when the grand jury reconvened on November 21, the day it normally handed down its indictments, it postponed any action on the Lizzie Borden case until December 1. Newspapers reported that the grand jury had refused to issue an indictment against Lizzie on the basis of the information it had received.

It was after this story was published that Miss Russell went to the prosecutor and informed him that she had seen Lizzie burn a dress in the kitchen stove on the Sunday after the murders. Miss Russell later repeated her information to the grand jury, and an indictment charging Lizzie Borden with murder was presented to the court the very next day. Actually, there were three indictments against Lizzie by the grand jury, one for the murder of her father, another for the murder of her stepmother, and the third charging both murders. The vote by the grand jurors was twenty for and one against.

There are indications that Attorney General Pillsbury was skeptical of the case the prosecution had against Lizzie Borden. It was after he appeared in Fall River that officials dropped the subterfuge that the three-day secret inquest, during which Lizzie Borden had been on the stand most of the time, was some sort of an informal hearing. As the chief prosecuting official of Massachusetts, the attorney general in those days usually headed the staff in many prominent trials. This did not mean that he personally asked the questions and delivered the various addresses to the jury. The county prosecutor was relied upon to carry the bulk of the trial, with the attorney general occasionally taking part, perhaps summing up. It was his presence, not his active participation, which gave an aura of importance to the case, and the fact that the attorney general was there in person impressed the jury; in effect, it threw the full weight of his office against a prisoner.

Attorney General Pillsbury reviewed the case with Prosecutor Knowlton. After this conference in April 1893, two months before the trial of Lizzie Borden, Pillsbury announced that for reasons of "ill health" he would not be present for the trial.

As a prelude to the trial, a Taunton reporter sent out a flash announcing that Lizzie Borden was ill and might be dying. Sheriff Wright's office was immediately flooded with calls from newspaper offices all over the country as well as from many hundreds of individuals. The harried official assured all callers that Lizzie was not even sick. The reporter had seen a doctor drive up to the prison and had promptly made a running broad jump to the conclusion that he was visiting Lizzie. The newsman did not even bother to inquire at the jail. The doctor's call had actually been made to treat one of the male inmates.

VIII

The Ordeal

She is either the most injured of innocents or the blackest of monsters. She either hacked her father and stepmother to pieces with the furious brutality of the ogre in Poe's story of the Rue Morgue or some other person did it and she suffers the double torture of losing her parents and being wrongfully accused of their murders.

—JULIAN RALPH, New York *Sun*
opening day story on trial

It is no exaggeration to say that on Monday morning, June 5, 1893, the attention of a great many people throughout the world was centered on a small, square brick building, with four make-believe stone columns in front, resting in an oasis of closely cropped grass and early-blooming flowering shrubs. In this building, and on that day, ten months after the murders, the trial of Lizzie Borden began in the Massachusetts Superior Court in New Bedford.

If a trial is a drama, then a trial for murder with a defendant's life in balance is high drama. And when that defendant is a woman, and the double crime involves the rarest murder of all, patricide, and is only a brief step away from the equally rare crime of matricide, then the drama touches everyone emotionally.

Under the rules of the Superior Court at that time, murder trials were held with three judges sitting on the bench. Because of the importance of this one, Chief Justice Albert Mason assigned himself and two senior members of the state-wide court, Associate Justices Caleb Blodgett and Justin Dewey, to preside with him. The Chief Justice, in preparation for the expected crowds, had the seating arrangements in the second-floor courtroom altered, increasing its capacity from 182 to 219 seats. In keeping with the town's whaling tradition, a barricade of heavy nautical rope was strung about the building's walks. Even so, the court underestimated the overwhelming public interest the case had aroused; only twenty-five seats were set aside for the press, fifteen for the Bristol County newspapers, four for the press associations and the remaining six for Boston newspapers. But requests for press seats came from all the papers in New York City, many national publications such as *Leslie's Weekly*, and from papers in St. Louis, Chicago, Cincinnati and Canada, to name just a few. An additional press section had to be prepared in a hurry.

With Attorney General Pillsbury resting in Florida, far away from the scene, Knowlton asked William H. Moody, the district attorney for the Eastern District, to assist him with the prosecution. The two men were in sharp contrast. The New York *Sun's* Julian Ralph described Knowlton as a "veritable Cromwell, a round-headed, powerful and bustling big man, built like a bull, with a thick neck, bristling hair, a red beard, heavy jaws and plump cheeks." Moody, forty years old, was six years younger than Knowlton, more slender and of medium height, with a striking facial resemblance to Theodore Roosevelt, in whose cabinet he later served. Knowlton would roar at a witness he wanted to rattle, but Moody always kept his voice at a low even pitch. His hands provided a clue to the emotions that were gripping him. "He busies them with his coattails, violently and incessantly," one observer wrote. "He does his coattails up in a bundle, he rolls them up like a scroll, he ties them in a knot, he jiggles them with his fingers, and he pulls them apart.

This reflects his every emotion, failure and success. Rolling them up indicates plain sailing, doing them in a bundle means triumphant success, and sundering them indicates a failure to make a witness understand him."

Jennings had asked George D. Robinson, who had served three terms as governor of Massachusetts, to join the defense along with him and Adams. Robinson interviewed Lizzie Borden in her cell at the Taunton jail, and then, in early February, he accepted. Robinson could have served as a model for the familiar cartoon figure of a Yankee farmer—he had a long and narrow face, a prominent nose and a dab of chin whiskers. Reporters, who had expected the mellifluous bursts of oratory usually associated with political figures, were surprised to find that he used a more homespun approach. They soon learned that he had considerable ability in cross-examining a witness.

Most out-of-town newspapers had relied upon local correspondents or had sent regular staff members to cover the investigation and the preliminary hearings. But for the trial they assigned their most brilliant reporters, men whose by-lines were long familiar to readers, to handle the running account of the trial. A few of journalism's early sob sisters were also present to cover human-interest sidelights. Few of the top reporters covering the trial had seen Lizzie Borden, and their only information had come from news clippings and the rumors that had been spreading for the ten months since the murders. All of them eagerly awaited their first look at Lizzie and were in their seats long before the three judges entered to take their places on the bench. No spectators were admitted the first day; all seats, except those for the press, were reserved for the panel of prospective jurors. Out of 148 veniremen summoned from all over the county, only three did not appear, a further indication of the interest in the trial. The entire first day was devoted to selecting a jury and 108 of the panel were examined before the twelfth juror was seated. None of the jurors lived in Fall River.

The assembled newsmen were content with the time it took to pick a jury, since it gave them an opportunity to concentrate on staring at, appraising, and all but dissecting Lizzie Borden. Their surprise at her small, slender figure has already been noted. She entered the courtroom accompanied by the faithful Reverend Mr. Jubb, who sat by her side behind the defense attorneys. Emma, Mrs. Brigham and Mrs. Holmes, three others of Lizzie's constant attendants, were not in the courtroom; all witnesses were excluded up to the time of their testimony. Lizzie had been transferred from the county jail to the New Bedford House of Correction, two short blocks away from the courthouse. A closed carriage was used to transport her to and from the court.

Reporters' descriptions of her dress differed: some thought the material was brocade while others wrote that it was sable cloth. Whatever the material, it was a black dress, ornamented with narrow velvet ribbon; the skirt stopped just short of sweeping the floor. Lizzie wore a poke-shaped black straw hat trimmed with blue feathers and velvet rosettes. Her only jewelry was a large pin with an enameled engraving of a pansy, worn at her throat. Ralph stated at least six times in his dispatch that she looked like a lady or was ladylike, and he was not alone. "She was," he wrote, "modest, calm and quiet, and it was plain to see that she had complete mastery of herself, and could make her sensations and emotions invisible to an impertinent public." Lizzie did display one sign of emotion during the first day when one of the prospective jurors stated that he was related to her. She stared with obvious astonishment at the man. It developed later that he had married a relative. He was excused.

Knowlton had elected to try Lizzie Borden on the indictment charging both murders. With the words, "Upon the fourth day of August of last year, an old man and woman, husband and

wife . . . were . . . severally killed by unlawful human agency,"
Moody began the opening address to the jury for the prosecution. An opening statement by a district attorney is not evidence but rather an announcement of intent. In it, the speaker
reviews the crime, describes the scene, gives the prosecution's
version of what might have occurred, and most important, out-
lines the state's case against the prisoner. He tells what the state
hopes to prove. As a rule, district attorneys avoid making exag-
gerated claims or charges in their opening statements because
they have learned from experience that their words can return
to haunt them if they fail to back up their statements with con-
vincing proof. Sometimes, however, a prosecutor will overload
his statement when he has a weak case; he gambles on fooling
some of the jurors.

During the ninety minutes Moody spoke he made these points
against Lizzie Borden: He emphasized the ill feeling that had
developed between her and her stepmother as a result of the
house incident and promised to produce witnesses to show that
this ill will had continued. He reviewed the attempt to buy
poison the day before the murders and said, "I think, gentlemen,
you will be satisfied that there can be no question that the person who made this application for this deadly poison was the
prisoner." He mentioned the difficulty Bridget had in opening
the front door locks to admit Mr. Borden, and stated, "The
prisoner from the hall above made some laugh or exclamation.
At that time, gentlemen, Mrs. Borden's body lay within plain
view of that hall, dead probably more than an hour." In discussing Lizzie's statement to her father that Mrs. Borden had gone
out in response to a note, he told the jurors, "That, gentlemen,
we put to you as a lie, intended for no purpose except to stifle
inquiry as to the whereabouts of Mrs. Borden." He implied that
Lizzie had tried to lure the maid out of the house when she mentioned the sale of cheap cotton goods to Bridget, thus leaving
her free to murder her father. He reviewed the varying state-

ments of her trip to the barn and inferred that she had not been
up in the loft when he said he would offer testimony that there
were no footprints in the dust on the loft floor. He claimed that
Lizzie had turned over a silk dress to police and it was not the
one she had been wearing the morning of the murders, that the
actual dress had been burned in the kitchen stove. Moody produced the various axes and hatchets found in the house and
stated that the handleless one probably was the murder weapon.
He indicated he would be able to offer proof that the handle had
been destroyed.

"The time for idle rumor, for partial, insufficient information, for hasty and inexact reasoning, is past," he informed the
jurors in his closing remarks. When he sat down, the Reverend
Mr. Jubb leaned toward Lizzie Borden with a bottle of smelling
salts in his hands. Some of the reporters sent out a flash saying
that she had fainted; others reported that she had pushed aside
the bottle and had taken a drink of water.

The moment the testimony got under way, the prosecution
was placed on the defensive by its own witnesses. The first one
called was Thomas Kieran, a civil engineer, who had been hired
by the state to make various measurements and scale drawings.
Reporters, who knew that their readers were not interested in
the fact that it was exactly 900 feet from City Hall to the Borden home, or that the ceilings on the first floor were six inches
higher than the ceilings on the second floor, paid scant attention as the witness gave these routine measurements. Jennings
arose to cross-examine and Kieran agreed that the closet in the
front entry of the Borden home was large enough to conceal a
person. Jennings had made that experiment in Kieran's presence. Many spectators in the courtroom smiled at this; the possibility of a killer lurking in the hall closet for some ninety
minutes between the murders was a remote, catching-at-straws
theory. Jennings did not spend much time on this point. He suddenly shifted and asked Kieran if he had conducted any experi-

ments in connection with the guest bedroom where Mrs. Borden had been murdered. The witness said he had.

Reporters leaned forward with interest. Kieran was a witness for the prosecution, hired by Knowlton's office, and his experiments had been conducted on behalf of the prosecutor, yet the District Attorney had neither mentioned any experiments nor questioned the witness about them. Jennings had been present, watching.

The engineer testified that he had his assistant lie down on the floor in the guest bedroom, between the bed and the bureau, in the same position and place Mrs. Borden's body had been found. While he did not know the height of his assistant, he was a much taller person than Mrs. Borden; the assistant's feet had projected beyond the bed while Mrs. Borden's feet had not.

"Then I went downstairs," Kieran testified, "and came up the stairs in the middle of the stairs, as I would if I had not been trying to see this man." Knowlton immediately rose to his feet and objected to the latter portion of the answer. It was the first of several objections he made as the testimony continued, but Kieran's story did emerge. He was allowed to state that in going up the steps in the usual or normal way a person ascends a flight of stairs, he had not seen the body of his assistant stretched out on the floor, even though he knew it was there. It was only after pausing carefully on each step and staring through the open door of the guest bedroom that he found just one point on the staircase where he could see his assistant. This was when his eyes were just a little above the level of the floor. Even then, he testified, it was only because he knew his assistant was there and deliberately looked for him that he managed to glimpse him. At all other points on the stairs, he said, it was impossible to see the body. The courtroom buzzed at this unexpected testimony. The prosecution was contending that since Lizzie admitted she had gone up the stairs to her room that morning she should have seen her stepmother's body. Chief Justice Mason had to rap his gavel for order.

Jennings was not finished with the witness. Lizzie's bedroom was at the head of the stairs, the guest bedroom was further forward on the small second-floor hall. She had been standing either at the top of the stairs at her door or was coming down the steps when Bridget heard her laugh.

Q: How was it when you stood upon the floor of the hall upstairs, in front of the door which we will call Miss Lizzie's room?

A: I couldn't see him.

Q: As you stood in the hall did you stand in the hall in front of Miss Lizzie's room and look for him?

A: I did.

Q: Could you see any portion of his body from that position?

A: No, sir.

Spectators in the courtroom glanced curiously at the prosecutors. In the opening address, only a few minutes earlier, the prosecution in mentioning Lizzie's laugh had stated, "Mrs. Borden's body lay within plain view of that hall." This statement was being contradicted flatly and positively by the state's own expert witness. Jennings rammed home one further fact. The assistant's feet had projected beyond the bed, making it even easier to see him while walking up and down the stairs.

Q: Could you see his feet from any position on the stairs?

A: I could not.

By prior arrangement both sides had agreed that as soon as Kieran completed his testimony the jury would be taken to Fall River to inspect the Borden house and grounds. Kieran was still on the stand the second day when the court was recessed to enable the jurors to make this trip. How many of them conducted experiments similar to those described by the engineer is unknown; no one except court attendants was allowed inside the house with the jury.

When court reconvened for the third day, Kieran completed his testimony. The prosecution did not re-examine him on the experiments he had conducted. After a photographer identified the official pictures he had taken of the house and the bodies, John Vinnicum Morse was called to the stand. His direct testimony told the familiar story of his unexpected arrival and his activities on the morning of the murders. He said that on a visit three or four weeks earlier he had not seen Lizzie, but he had seen her on still another visit three or four months before that. He told about being in the sitting room with Borden the night before the murders and sleeping that night in the guest room, the two rooms in which the murders occurred.

Morse testified that during the now famous breakfast he heard Mrs. Borden say to the servant girl, "Bridget, I want you to wash these windows today." Morse said that after leaving the house he walked to the post office and then on to visit his nephew and niece whom he had not seen in fifteen years. He missed his nephew but remained with his niece until it was time to catch the 11:20 horsecar. He got off at Pleasant and Second Streets, not far from the Borden home. "Nothing attracted my attention at first," he testified. Police officers and doctors were already inside the house when he arrived and Sawyer was guarding the door.

After he went in and saw Borden's body, he went part way up the stairs to view Mrs. Borden's body. "I went up far enough so I could look under the bed where I slept the night before, and I saw Mrs. Borden lying there with blood on her face." (By this time Mrs. Borden's body had been turned over.) He said he had been told she was there, so he knew where to look.

The importance of his testimony to the prosecution was that it established his alibi and removed him as a suspect. The defense made no effort to upset his alibi.

Under cross-examination, Morse testified that Mrs. Borden told him that Lizzie was sick on Wednesday from the illness that had stricken all members of the family. The prosecutor objected to this statement on the grounds that it was hearsay evidence, and the court agreed. Spectators chuckled twice during Morse's testimony. He was unable to give Lizzie's age correctly, missing it by some years. After describing the breakfast he had eaten he was asked if it had been a good breakfast. "Plenty of it," was his hearty reply.

Morse testified that he had watched the police search the house on Thursday and Friday. Speaking of Thursday's search he said, "I see them overhauling everything. I unlocked a chest or a trunk or something of that kind in the attic that they couldn't get into." He added they also had made a thorough search of the cellar, including "a washroom, a coal room, a wood room."

The prosecution then introduced a group of bank officials and other witnesses who traced Borden's path on the morning of the murder. The earliest he had been seen was at 9:30 when he entered the Union Savings Bank. The last witnesses who saw him were Joseph Shortsleeves and James Mather, the carpenters. Mather said Borden left at 10:40; he had glanced at the City Hall clock because he customarily ate his dinner in midmorning and wanted to see if it was time for him to stop and eat. Borden apparently made one further stop, possibly at the nearby post office, to wrap up the broken lock he had thrust into his pocket. He was carrying it wrapped when he entered the house.

The defense scored another surprise. The popular story was that Lizzie had murdered her father to prevent him from changing his will. Abraham G. Hart, treasurer of the Union Savings Bank and a close associate of the murder victim, testified under cross-examination that Borden had died intestate, without any will. As an officer of the court, Jennings then stated for the trial record that he had been Borden's lawyer for many years and the banker never had asked him to draw up a will

nor had he ever discussed making a will. Knowlton accepted
Jennings' statement as uncontested fact.

There was a stir in the courtroom when Bridget Sullivan
took the stand. She was the only other person known to have
been around the house at the time of the murders and was expected to be a key witness for the prosecution. Ralph described
the servant as a "rosy, brown-haired girl with a generous figure,
eyes near together, and her mouth looked irritable." She was
wearing a brown serge dress, a black Van Dyke hat, and a circle
of white lace around the neck, and "kid gloves of generous size
concealed her hands."

Bridget said she had been born in Ireland and had come to
this country when she was nineteen years old. She was the only
domestic employed by the Bordens; a man came from the farm
to do occasional chores. She testified that on the murder morning
she came downstairs at 6:15 after awakening with a dull headache and busied herself with her normal pre-breakfast chores.

The servant said that Lizzie came down after Morse left and
shortly after she had seen Mr. Borden go up the back stairs to
his room. "She came through the kitchen and she left down
the slop pail, and I asked her what did she want for breakfast.
She said she didn't know as she wanted any breakfast but she
guessed she would have something, she would have some coffee
and cookies. She got some coffee, got her cup and saucer and got
some coffee; I went out in the back yard, and she was getting
her own breakfast."

Asked why she went out to the rear yard, Bridget replied, "I
had a sick headache and I was sick to my stomach." She said
she remained in the rear vomiting from ten to fifteen minutes
before returning inside. She said she did not see Lizzie on her
return. She resumed washing the dishes and then took them to
the dining room.

"Mrs. Borden was in the dining room as I was fixing my
dining-room table, and she asked me if I had anything to do

that morning. I said, No, not particular, if she had anything for me to do. She said she wanted the windows washed. I asked her how and she said inside and outside both, they are awful dirty." At that time Mrs. Borden was dusting the door between the dining room and the sitting room. Bridget testified that this was the last time she saw Mrs. Borden alive. She did not see Mr. Borden, Morse already had left the house, and she said Lizzie was not around.

After getting her orders to wash the windows, Bridget testified, she cleaned off the stove, went to the dining room and sitting room where she closed the windows, picked up a pail in the cellar and took it outside. While she was outside, she said Lizzie came to the side door and asked her if she was going to wash the windows. "Yes," I says, "you needn't lock the door; I will be around here; but you can lock it if you want to; I can get the water in the barn." Lizzie did not lock the door. Bridget said she went to the barn to get the handle for the brush and then washed the sitting-room windows on the south side of the house. She paused for a few minutes to talk over the

The Bettman Archive

Bridget Sullivan under cross-examination

fence with Mrs. Kelly's servant girl. She made several trips in and out of the barn to get clean water as she washed the outside of the sitting-room, parlor and dining-room windows. At no time, while washing those windows, did she see anybody in those rooms.

Bridget testified that after finishing the outside windows she came back into the house, locked the screen door, got a hand basin and a stepladder and began washing the inside of the same windows. While she was doing the top half of the first window she heard, "Like a person at the door was trying to unlock the door but could not; so I went to the front door and unlocked it. The spring lock was locked. I unbolted the door and it was locked with a key; there were three locks." She said she made an exclamation out loud at this point and heard Lizzie laugh immediately after she said it. During her testimony in the District Court, when Bridget was asked what exclamation she had made, she hesitated so long that the question had to be repeated. She finally stated she had said, "Oh, pshaw." When asked the same question during the trial, she no longer hesitated and replied promptly, "Oh, pshaw." Whatever exclamation she made to express her annoyance at finding all three locks in place, her testimony left no doubt that it was this remark that had caused Lizzie to laugh. This destroyed another piece of the legend the prosecutor had used in his opening statement.

Bridget testified that she heard Lizzie telling her father that Mrs. Borden had received a note and had gone out. He made no reply. She said that while she was washing the inside of the dining-room windows, Lizzie brought an ironing board in from the kitchen, placed it on top of the table and began to do some handkerchiefs. Lizzie then asked her if she planned to go out that afternoon and repeated the story of the note in advising her to make certain the doors were locked.

Bridget then testified that after she completed the inside windows, "I washed out the cloths that I had washing the windows, and hung them behind the stove. As I got through, Miss Lizzie came out and said, 'There is a cheap sale of dress goods at Sargent's this afternoon, at eight cents a yard.' I don't know that she said, 'this afternoon,' but 'today.' And I said, 'I am going to have one.' Then I went upstairs to my room."

Bridget's testimony on this point differed from her statement at the District Court hearing where she used the phrase "this afternoon" without qualifying it in any way. In both instances she testified to giving the same answer, "I am going to have one," and then going up to her room to rest.

The servant repeated her testimony that she heard the City Hall clock strike eleven and had confirmed the time by glancing at her own clock. She testified she heard no sound or noise in the house until Lizzie called to her to come down, saying that her father had been killed. "I run downstairs; I hadn't taken off my shoes or any of my clothing."

Q: Let me ask you in this connection if you are able to tell us what dress she had on that morning?

A: No, sir. I couldn't tell what dress the girl had on.

When the prosecutor attempted to ask what dress Lizzie usually wore in the morning, the defense objected and the question was withdrawn. Bridget was not shown the dress Lizzie had given to police.

In describing how she found Mrs. Borden's body, Bridget testified, "I went upstairs. I saw the body under the bed. I ran right into the room and stood at the foot of the bed."

Q: How far up the stairs did you go before you saw the body?

A: I don't remember how far, but I remember to see the woman's clothes.

The maid testified that she had not seen any note, or any messenger deliver it, and stated she first heard about it from Lizzie.

Bridget was examined by Robinson for the defense and his questions soon established differences in her testimony from that given previously at the inquest and at the District Court hearings, both held shortly after the murders. The maid was reluctant at some points to give detailed answers and the facts had to be brought out step by step.

The defense tackled almost immediately the problem of dissension in the household. In response to questions Bridget testified that she had not seen any conflict among members of the family, that they never quarreled, and that Lizzie and Mrs. Borden always spoke "pleasantly" to each other.

In his opening statement Moody had said that this ill feeling caused Lizzie and Emma to stay away from the dinner table while Mr. and Mrs. Borden were eating. Robinson questioned Bridget closely on this point.

Q: Now the daughters, Miss Emma and Miss Lizzie, usually came to the table, did they not, as the father and mother did?

A: No, sir, they did not.

Q: I thought you said they did?

A: No, sir, they did not.

Q: Didn't you say this morning that they ate at the table with the family?

A: Nobody asked me whether they did or not.

Q: Didn't they eat with the family?

A: Not all the time.

Q: But they did from time to time and day to day, did they not?

A: Yes, sir.

Q: What?

A: Sometimes the family—most of the time they did not eat with their father and mother.

Q: How was it at dinner?

A: Sometimes at dinner; a good many more times they were not.

Repeated questioning along these lines brought similar responses by Bridget. Robinson then asked Bridget how Lizzie acted when Mrs. Borden was not feeling well. She replied that she didn't know, that Mrs. Borden was not particularly sick while she had been there.

Q: Did not Lizzie treat her properly and help her?

A: I did not see anything; I know that she was sick one time and none of them went into the room while she was sick.

Questioned further about this illness, Bridget said Mrs. Borden had remained in her room less than a day. He then read from the inquest minutes in which Bridget had testified, "If anything was the matter with Mrs. Borden, Lizzie did all she could for her." Bridget's reply to Robinson was that she could not remember being asked that question.

Robinson again abruptly shifted his line of questioning and now his purpose became apparent to the seasoned reporters familiar with trial techniques; the lawyer was trying to show a reason for Bridget's changes in testimony. He asked her where she had been living since the murders and she replied that she was living in New Bedford.

Q: Where?

A: Mrs. Hunt's.

Q: Where does Mrs. Hunt live?

A: On Court Street.

Q: What is Mr. Hunt's occupation?

A: Keeper.

Q: Keeper of what?

A: Of the jail house.

Q: Then you have been at the jail, have you, helping work all the time?

A: Not in the jail.

Q: I don't mean at the jail, but at the keeper's house?

A: Yes, sir.

Q: And you have been there all the time?

A: Yes, sir.

Q: And are still there employed?

A: Yes, sir.

Q: You came right over from Fall River?

A: Yes, sir.

Q: And you have been there all the time?

A: Yes, sir.

Bridget testified that she had been released as a material witness to City Marshal Hilliard and State Detective Seaver who obtained the job for her. Asked if she had talked to "Miss Lizzie, Miss Emma or anybody representing her" since the arrest, Bridget said she had not. Robinson then asked her if she had seen any of the police officers who had worked on the case since she moved to New Bedford. She named about a half-dozen men who came to see her from time to time, but when she was asked if she had discussed the case in any way with these officers on their various visits, she surprised the spectators in the courtroom when she answered, "No, sir."

Having shown Bridget's reluctant behavior to the jury, Robinson again returned to the question of the eating habits of the household, this time with a copy of her inquest testimony.

Q: Now do you recall what you testified at the inquest about their eating together? I have asked you about it. Have you a clear memory of it now?

A: I don't know if they asked me anything about it.

[*All quotation marks in the following are from the minutes of the inquest in which Bridget had previously been questioned by Knowlton.*]

Q: Well, you were asked this: "Did she generally get up to breakfast?" and you said: "Very seldom, she generally came down about nine o'clock."

A: Yes, sir.

Q: "And then helped herself to breakfast?"

A: Yes, sir.

Q: "Did she always eat at the same table with Mr. and Mrs. Borden?" and your answer: "Always did eat dinner and supper when she was in the house."

A: Yes, sir, she ate the meals when she was in the house.

Q: That is so, isn't it? "They always ate together when she was in the house except when she was out on an errand." Is that so?

A: Yes, sir, they always ate in the same dining room.

Robinson was not interested in this still different answer and he repeated part of the previous question:

Q: Always ate together in the dining room?

A: Yes, sir.

It had taken Robinson well over an hour to get Bridget to admit to her previous testimony at the secret inquest during which she had been questioned by Knowlton one week after the murders.

The maid also testified that she had started to wash the windows about 9:30 that morning. She said she had left the screen door unlocked while she had been outside. She agreed that she did not have the side door under continuous observation while she had been washing the windows on the south side of the house, while she had been talking to the Kelly servant or while she was inside the barn on her various trips to get water. She said she had not seen any blood on Lizzie when she rushed downstairs from her attic room. "Not on her face or hands or anywhere. As far as I can remember, her hair was in order."

The prosecution had indicated that the bedroom doors had been kept locked because of the bitter feelings that existed in the divided household. Robinson turned his attention to this point. He asked Bridget if the second-floor bedrooms had always been locked, and the servant testified, "Once in a while I used to see the girls, Miss Lizzie and Miss Emma, coming down the back stairs." Seeking to show that the bedroom doors were kept locked as a result of burglaries in the barn and house, Robinson questioned Bridget about them. Bridget said that the house had been robbed about a year before the murders when all members of the family had been in Fall River. Knowlton objected to any further questioning about the burglaries because they were too remote to be connected with the murders. The court upheld him and Robinson had to drop this line of questions. Bridget confirmed that she had not slept in the Borden house on Thursday night and had left again over the weekend, returning Monday morning.

The New York *World* in recounting the evidence given so far by Kieran and Bridget headlined its story: BORDEN BOOMERANGS. DEFENSE PLAYS DUCK AND DRAKES WITH THE STATE'S WITNESSES.

Julian Ralph, in the New York *Sun,* was more conservative. "Unless the Government has got more than it has shown," he wrote, "the Borden case will pass into history as one of the most mysterious of the celebrated cases of the century. Most fairminded persons here are of the opinion that there has been nothing brought forward that does not tend to prove the woman innocent quite as much as to suggest her guilty."

The pace quickened on the fourth day of the trial. The examination of witnesses was briefer, enabling more to take the stand than previously.

Dr. Bowen testified that when he arrived at the house only Lizzie and Mrs. Churchill were there and both were standing near the side-door entry. He said Lizzie told him her father had been killed or stabbed, he did not know which word she had used, and he hurried into the sitting room, where he saw that Borden was dead. "His face was hardly to be recognized by one who knew him." The physician noticed that nothing had been disturbed in the room. Lizzie told him she had not seen anyone and when he asked her where she had been she replied, "In the barn looking for some iron."

The prosecution indicated that it was claiming that the dress Lizzie had burned was the one she had been wearing that morning when seen by various witnesses.

Dr. Bowen testified that he could not remember the color of the dress Lizzie had been wearing, and the prosecutor read his inquest testimony in which he said, "It is pretty hard work for me [to recall the dress]. Probably if I could see a dress something like it I could guess, but I could not describe it; it was a sort of drab, not much color to it to attract my attention—a sort of morning calico dress, I should judge."

The prosecutor insisted that the use of the word "drab" was the description of a definite color, while Dr. Bowen equally insisted that what he had said was most indefinite and he had made no attempt to describe a definite color, simply an impression. Shown the dress Lizzie had turned over to police, he was asked if that was the dress she had been wearing the morning of the murder. "I don't know, sir," was his reply. Asked to describe the dress being shown to him, he answered, "I should call it dark-blue."

The defense brought out in questioning the doctor that it was he who had directed Lizzie to go up to her room and rest. He said he noticed a group of women, including his wife, Mrs. Churchill, Miss Russell, and Bridget Sullivan, all working over Lizzie, rubbing her hands, her face, fanning her, loosening her clothes. He had not seen any bloodstains on her clothing or person. He later went to her room and gave her bromo caffeine to quiet her, and administered a second dose an hour later. The following day, because of her mental distress and nervous excitement, he prescribed an eighth of a grain of morphine to be taken at bedtime. On Saturday he doubled the dose and ordered it continued. He testified he was still prescribing the drug all through the week after the murder up to the time she was arrested. He was asked:

Q: Does not morphine given in double doses to allay mental distress and nervous excitement somewhat affect the memory and change and alter the view of things and give people hallucinations?

A: Yes, sir.

News that Lizzie Borden had been kept under constant sedation since the afternoon of the murders, information so contrary to the legend portrait of her as an unemotional iron-willed woman, created a sensation in the courtroom. Moody set out to destroy the damage of this testimony by re-examining Dr. Bowen. He asked the physician how many times he *personally* saw Lizzie take the medicine. Dr. Bowen said he saw Lizzie take the bromo caffeine twice on Thursday afternoon.

Q: Is bromo caffeine a medicine which has a tendency to create hallucinations?

A: Yes, sir.

Q: A week after taking it?

A: No, sir.

On this ingenuous note, as if doctors personally watch patients take medicine, Moody ended his redirect examination of Dr. Bowen.

At this point Robinson requested permission to recall Bridget Sullivan to the stand for further cross-examination. He asked her about her trip to the cellar with Officer Mullaly to get the hatchets. She said they were kept in a room off the furnace.

Q: And did you take them out?

A: No, sir, I did not.

Q: Are you sure about that?

A: No, sir. I didn't put my hands at all on them. I don't think I put my hands on the hatchets at all.

Q: Well, are you sure about that?

A (*emphatically*): Yes, sir, I am.

The word "emphatically" was inserted in the official trial minutes by the court stenographer. Reporters in describing her testimony said she was highly excited when she made the statement.

Bridget testified that on the morning of the murders she had been wearing a blue calico dress with a white cloverleaf design. She described the color as dark indigo blue.

The maid became upset for the second time on her recall when Robinson questioned her about Lizzie's appearance after she was called down from the attic bedroom.

Q: Was she excited?

A: She seemed excited to me more than I have ever seen her before, but not crying.

[The latter part of her answer was volunteered since Robinson had not asked her if Lizzie had been crying.]

Q: What do you say?

A: Yes, sir. She seemed excited to me more than I ever saw her before.

[This time Bridget omitted the phrase about not crying.]

Q: Was she crying?

A: No, sir.

Q: Are you right about that?

A: Yes, sir; I am.

Q: Have you ever said differently about it?

A: No, sir. I never said no different.

Q: Didn't you testify at the inquest—give your testimony over there?

A: Yes, sir.

Q: Now let me read and ask if you didn't say this. The questions were asked you by Mr. Knowlton, weren't they?

A: Yes, sir.

Q: "Was the screen door open then?" "I don't know, I couldn't say. She was leaning against the inside door that locks, the large door." Is that right?

A: Yes, sir.

Q: "Not the screen door, but the regular door?" "Yes, sir." Is that right?

A: I said the inside door was open, but I didn't say anything about the screen door only I couldn't tell whether it was locked or not.

Q: Well, the question is that she was leaning against the regular door, and not against the screen door and to that you said Yes. That is correct, isn't it?

A: Yes, sir.

Q: "How did she seem?" Answer: "She seemed to be excited more than I ever saw her." That is right, isn't it?

A: Yes, sir.

Q: "Was she crying?" "Yes, sir; she was crying."

A: Well, that must be wrong; I couldn't say that.

Q: That must be wrong?

A: Yes, sir; I didn't say that, for I couldn't.

Despite repeated questions on the same point, Bridget insisted that she had never said Lizzie was crying. For the sake of convenience, it might be added at this point that the official court stenographer who had taken the inquest minutes was called to the stand later in rebuttal. Reading directly from her stenographic notes, she said that at the inquest Bridget had testified that when she came down from the attic Lizzie was crying. District Attorney Knowlton, who had conducted the inquest and was familiar with the testimony given by Bridget, did not cross-examine the court stenographer nor did he dispute the accuracy of her minutes.

Mrs. Churchill, the next-door neighbor, followed Bridget's second appearance on the stand. She told how she had seen Bridget hurrying from Dr. Bowen's home and then had looked out of her kitchen window and seen Lizzie standing inside the screen door.

"She looked as if she was leaning up against the east casing of the door, and she seemed excited or agitated to me, as if something had happened, and I stepped to the other window and asked her what was the matter." She testified that she heard Lizzie ask Dr. Bowen to send the telegram to Emma and quoted Lizzie as asking the physician to "put it as gently as he could, because there was an old person there and it would shock her."

The prosecution scored an important point when Mrs. Churchill described the dress Lizzie had been wearing in these words: "It looked like a light-blue-and-white groundwork, it seemed like calico or cambric, and it had a light-blue-and-white groundwork with a dark, navy-blue diamond printed on it." She was then shown the dress Lizzie gave to police and testified it was not the one Lizzie had been wearing the morning of the murder. She was definite on this point.

During cross-examination Mrs. Churchill said she had seen Bridget rinsing one window, the north parlor window. It was the only one she saw her working on that morning. She stated that she had been standing directly in front of Lizzie fanning her and later rubbing her hands and saw no bloodstains on her dress, her hands, or her face. Lizzie's hair was not disarranged. She remained steadfast in her testimony that the dress Lizzie gave to police was not the dress she had been wearing.

Ever since the newspapers had reported that Lizzie Borden had been indicted as a result of Miss Russell's belated report of the dress-burning incident, there was great public interest as to what her actual testimony would be. District Attorney Knowlton had told reporters before the trial that he expected her to be the state's star witness. He said she is "no longer able to stand the gnawing pangs of conscience," and indicated that her testimony, almost single-handed, would convict Lizzie.

Miss Russell testified that she had formerly lived in the house occupied by Dr. Kelly and knew all members of the Borden family. She related the story already given of Lizzie's visit to her the night before the murders in which Lizzie, saying that she was depressed, gloomily predicted that some disaster would strike the family.

She was led to the morning of the murders when she had come to the house with Bridget. Miss Russell testified that Lizzie told her she had gone to the barn to get a piece of iron or tin to fix her screen, she could not remember which. She had fanned Lizzie, bathed her with cold water and at one point started to loosen Lizzie's dress until the other protested that she did not feel faint.

Q: Are you able to give us any description of the dress she had on that morning?

A: None whatever.

Miss Russell said she accompanied Lizzie to her room and came down to speak to Dr. Bowen. He then went up a short time later and prescribed the bromo caffeine. When Miss Russell returned to Lizzie's bedroom, she testified Lizzie was just coming out of Emma's room tying the ribbons of a pink-and-white striped wrapper. In answer to Moody's question she said she did not hear anybody tell Lizzie to change her clothes. On Sunday morning, she left the Borden house after breakfast, returning shortly before noon.

Q: Will you state what you saw after you returned?

A: I went into the kitchen, and I saw Miss Lizzie at the other end of the stove; I saw Miss Emma at the sink. Miss Lizzie was at the stove, and she had a skirt in her hand, and her sister turned and said, "What are you going to do?" and Lizzie said, "I am going to burn this old thing up; it is covered with paint."

Miss Russell said she left the room at that point. When she returned and saw Lizzie tearing part of the garment, she testified she told her friend, "I wouldn't let anybody see me do that." Lizzie did not reply but moved one step nearer the cupboard door. The witness said she noticed a part of the dress was inside the cupboard. Continuing her testimony, Miss Russell said she saw Hanscom, the Pinkerton superintendent, the following morning and had a conversation with him. She then went into the dining room where Lizzie was seated and said, "I am afraid, Lizzie, the worst thing you could have done was to burn that dress. I have been asked about your dresses." She quoted Lizzie as replying, "Oh, what made you let me do it? Why didn't you tell me?"

It was shortly after this part of her testimony that Moody turned to Robinson and said, "Your witness."

There is little doubt that up to that point Miss Russell's testimony was all that the prosecution had claimed it to be—harmful to Lizzie Borden. Robinson had just started to question Miss Russell and had asked only one question which the witness was answering, when Moody stood up and interrupted with, "Oh, excuse me; an important matter I forgot."

Q (by Mr. Moody): Miss Russell, will you tell us what kind of a dress—give us a description of the dress that she burned, that you have testified about, on Sunday morning?

A: It was a cheap cotton Bedford cord.

Q: What was its color?

A: Light-blue ground with a dark figure—small figure.

Q: Do you know when she got it?

A: I am not positive.

Q: Well, about when she got it?

A: In the early spring.

Q: Was your attention called to it at the time she got it in any way?

A: At the time I first saw it?

Q: Yes, at the time you first saw it, and by what?

A: She told me that she had got her Bedford cord and she had a dressmaker there, and I went there one evening and she had it on, in the very early part of the dressmaker's visit, and she called my attention to it, and I said, "Oh, you have got your new Bedford cord." That is the only time I saw it until this time.

Q: Until the time it was burned?

A: Yes, sir.

Q: To make it clear, between the time you saw it on Miss Lizzie Borden and had the talk about it in the spring, you did not see it again until the Sunday morning after the homicide?

A: I never remember of ever seeing it, and I am quite sure I did not—that I never had.

Q: Can you give me any further description of the dark-blue figure?

A: No, sir.

Q: Could you give any further description?

A: Nothing, only that it was small.

Q: A small dark-blue figure?

A: Yes, sir.

Moody once more turned the witness back to Robinson. Miss Russell testified that after they went upstairs Lizzie complained that her head ached and she felt ill. She said she had noticed some ironed handkerchiefs in the dining room with others sprinkled to be ironed when she arrived at the house on the morning of the murders. She said again that she could not describe the dress Lizzie had worn on the morning of the murders. And like the other witnesses who had bathed and fanned Lizzie, she said she saw no traces of blood on her clothes or person. Asked if she had seen any blood on the dress Lizzie burned, she replied she had not. "The edge of it was soiled as she held it up. The edge she held toward me like this (illustrating), and this edge was soiled." Robinson's questions brought out that the incident occurred in broad daylight, that there were police officers outside in the yard, and that you could look into the kitchen from the yard through three windows that faced on two sides of the house.

Reporters, who had expected Robinson to subject Miss Russell to severe cross-examination, were startled when he ended his brief questioning. It wasn't until they had reviewed their notes that they realized why Robinson had been satisfied with her direct testimony and had had little need to examine her. Miss Russell had testified in a most positive way that she had seen the Bedford cord dress exactly twice; once in the spring before the murders when it had just been made, and then three days after the murders when it was burned. She did not remember what dress Lizzie had been wearing the morning of the murders, but her testimony made it clear that it was *not* the Bedford cord dress. The prosecution had been trying to prove, with the questioning of Dr. Bowen and Mrs. Churchill, that Lizzie had been wearing the Bedford cord dress when they saw her after the murders and that she had burned it to destroy unnoticed bloodstains. Miss Russell's testimony in no way contradicted Lizzie's claim that she had turned over to police the dress she had been wearing. Her answer to Moody's last-minute added questions had been a severe blow to the prosecution.

The District Attorney's theory that Lizzie had burned the dress because it was bloodstained had placed Fall River police in an awkward position since newspapers had carried accounts of the three different searches in the house—on Thursday, the day of the murders, on Friday, and again on Saturday. The dress was not burned until Sunday, after three days of intensive searching by police. Many observers at the trial wondered what reasons the police would give to explain why they did not find a bloodstained dress. They received their answer when Assistant Marshal John Fleet, the second highest officer in the city and the man who headed the active investigation for Fall River police, took the stand.

Fleet testified that he arrived at the Borden house at 11:45 on the morning of the murders and spoke to the various officers already there. He did not interview Lizzie until after she had gone up to her room with Miss Russell, so he was one of the last officials to question her. He said that Lizzie told him that after her father came home, he went into the sitting room, sat down in a large chair, took out some papers and looked at them. She was ironing handkerchiefs in the dining room. "She saw that her father was feeble," he testified, "and she went to him and advised and assisted him to lay down upon the sofa." After that, she went out into the yard and up in the barn. "I then asked her what she meant by 'up in the barn.' She said, 'I mean up in the barn, upstairs, sir.' " She told him she was up there about half an hour, came into the house and found her father dead. After learning from her of Morse's visit, he asked her if she thought her uncle had anything to do with the murders. "She said no, she didn't think that he had, because Mr. Morse left the house before nine o'clock and did not return until after the murders. . . . I asked her if she thought Maggie [Bridget] had anything to do with the killing of these. She said no, that Maggie had gone upstairs previous to her father's lying down on the lounge, and when she came from the barn she called Maggie downstairs."

Q: Anything else?

A: I then asked her if she had any idea who could have killed her father and mother. Then she said, "She is not my mother, sir; she is my stepmother; my mother died when I was a child."

He testified that at another point in this same conversation Miss Russell, who was in the room, advised Lizzie to tell him everything. "And she looked at Miss Russell, and then she says, 'About two weeks ago a man came to the house, to the front door and he had some talk with Father and he talked as though he was angry.' And I asked her what he was talking about. She said, 'He was talking about a store, and Father said to him, "I cannot let you have the store for that purpose." 'The man seemed to be angry.' "

Fleet testified that after his talk with Lizzie he came downstairs, conferred with officers and then returned with two men to make a search of her room. "While the search was still going on I said to Lizzie, 'You said this morning that you was up in the barn for half an hour. Do you say that now?' She says, 'I don't say half an hour, I say twenty minutes to half an hour, sir.'"

After the search Fleet went downstairs where Officer Mullaly showed him the two hatchets Bridget had given him. He went with the patrolman to a room in the cellar where he took down a box from a shelf and saw the handleless hatchet, the one the prosecution was claiming had been the murder weapon. He described the hatchet as covered with fine ashes on both sides of the blade and testified that these ashes were also adhering to the break in the handle, which he termed a "new break." The other items in the box were small tools and pieces of iron which were covered with a light dust.

Asked if he had made any other search of the house, Assistant Marshal Fleet replied that he had searched the house on Saturday. He testified that Marshal Hilliard, State Detective Seaver, Captain Desmond and lawyer Jennings were also present. Fleet did not mention the search conducted on *Friday* when these same officials were accompanied by Medical Examiner Dolan.

Fleet testified that the Saturday search began at 1 P.M., after the funeral procession left, and continued until shortly after five o'clock. There was a stir in the courtroom during his direct examination when he mentioned that during a visit to the barn loft he saw a basket on a workbench that contained "iron and lead, something of that kind." He indicated that he had paid little attention to it.

His cross-examination by Robinson quickly developed into a duel. It must be pointed out that Robinson had entered the case many months after the murders. He missed the significance of

Fleet's omission of any mention of the Friday search. All Robinson knew was that police had searched the house.

Robinson set out to show that Fleet had made one important change from his earlier testimony. At the District Court hearing in Fall River, Fleet had not testified that Lizzie had assisted and advised her father to lie down on the sofa. Pointing to this omission in his earlier testimony, Robinson asked Fleet if his memory was sharper now, ten months after the murder, than it had been only three weeks after the crime. Fleet replied he thought he had mentioned it at the preliminary hearing, that if he didn't it was an oversight. Robinson then turned his attention to the search of the house. Fleet stated flatly that he did not search the house as thoroughly as he should have. He repeated this many times during cross-examination.

Q: But you took each dress and looked at it, is that so?

A: Yes, sir; I think it is about so.

Q: Were you looking to see if you could find any bloody garment?

A: Not very closely, it was—

Q: Did you have that in mind?

A: Yes, sir.

Q: Is that so?

A: Yes, sir.

Robinson then took Fleet on a room-by-room explanation of his search. The following is but part of the examination of Fleet by Robinson, dealing only with the search in Bridget's room, and it is typical of all of Fleet's replies as recorded in the official trial minutes:

Q: Did you see in that room any dresses?

A: I think there was some clothing in one of the rooms.

Q: Did you examine it?

A: Just looked at it, that is all.

Q: Did you take it down to look at it?

A: No, sir.

Q: You didn't examine that clothing?

A: Not to take them down, but just looked at them.

Q: Not to take them down? And you three officers were there making a search, wasn't you?

A: Yes, sir.

Q: And you did not make a search up there?

A: Didn't we?

Q: Did you?

A: Yes, sir.

Q: Did? Such as you described?

A: Yes, sir.

Q: Was there any blood on Bridget's dresses?

A: On Bridget's?

Q: That is what I asked you.

A: Not that I discovered.

Q: You didn't discover at all?

A: I did not discover anything in the line of blood.

Q: You did not really look for blood, did you, on her dresses?

A: No more than I did on the others.

Q: That is not quite correct. Did you look for blood on Bridget's dresses?

A: I looked at Bridget's dresses.

Q: Just tell the jury how you looked.

A: Just looked at the dresses as they were—some were thrown on the bed.

Q: Were they in the closet?

A: There were some in a closet.

Q: Did you take them down?

A: I threw them on the bed, that was all.

Q: Now what did you really look at those dresses for?

A: To see if we could discover anything, or any blood, or anything like that.

In each part of the search Fleet began by stating that he just looked, that was all, but then as Robinson continued to question him, demanding step by step just what he had done, it developed that each garment was picked up, taken out of closets, drawers, trunks and examined individually for any traces of blood-stains.

The cross-examination of Fleet occupied the greater part of the afternoon and he still was on the stand when court convened for the fifth day of the trial.

A similar duel occurred when Robinson questioned Fleet about the handleless hatchet. Each time he described the blade as being covered with ashes while everything else in the box was "dusty." It was the prosecution's contention that Lizzie Borden had washed the blade of the hatchet and then thrust it damp into ashes which would account for ashes being on both sides of the blade. Fleet gradually admitted that there was a pile of ashes on the cellar floor only a few feet from the shelf where he had found the box. He finally estimated that this pile of ashes might fill at least fifty bushel baskets, and that this was where Borden dumped the ashes from the furnace. He agreed that the dust he noticed on the other items in the box might have come from the ashes, but he would not use the word "ashes" in describing anything else but the handleless hatchet.

Q: Had you noticed whether either of the other two hatchets were covered with ashes?

A: The smaller one was somewhat dusty.

At one point during this exchange, Robinson appears to have lost his temper when he said suddenly:

Q: Tell me if you see any ashes on it. Tell me in your judgment as a man, not a police officer.

Knowlton promptly rose. "Is that a proper way to address a witness?" he demanded.

"I withdraw it. I don't think it is," Robinson replied.

Fleet also testified that after finding the handleless hatchet he put it back in the box; it was not removed until Monday. When he first saw it officials believed that an ax found on the cellar chopping block was the murder weapon. Medical Examiner Dolan sent the ax to Professor Wood at Harvard. After the toxicologist reported that the stains were rust and the hairs caught in the handle were cow hairs, the hatchets were sent to him.

Philip Harrington, the police officer whose many discoveries appeared exclusively in the Fall River *Globe,* followed Marshal Fleet to the stand. Harrington testified that he had jumped from the rank of patrolman to captain since the arrest of Lizzie Borden. He told of his conversation with her in her bedroom, previously given, and stated that her voice was "steady" and he did not see her crying. He had arrived at the house about an hour after the murders had been reported. In his direct testimony Harrington said he went to the barn after speaking to Lizzie. He stated that the windows in the loft were shut and emphasized that it was very hot and close up in the loft. Harrington also testified to another discovery. He said he observed Dr. Bowen standing near the kitchen stove with scraps of notepaper in his hand and noticed the word "Emma" written on one of the pieces.

Q: Now then, what did you do with that paper?

A: I asked him again what they contained, and he said, "Oh, I think it is nothing. It is something, I think, about my daughter going through somewhere." He then turned slightly to his left and took the lid from the stove and threw the papers in, or the pieces in.

Q: Now then, did you observe anything as he lifted the lid from the stove?

A: Yes, sir.

Q: Go on and state what you did and what you observed.

A: I noticed the firebox. The fire was very near extinguished. On the south end there was a small fire which I judged was a coal fire. The embers were about dying. It was about as large as the palm of my hand. There had been some paper burned in there before, which was rolled up and still held a cylindrical form.

Q: Now will you describe that roll of burned paper by measuring it with your hands, please?

A: Well, I should say it was about that long. (*Indicating*) Twelve inches, I should say.

Q: And how large in diameter?

A: Well, not over two inches.

The inference was clear to everybody in the courtroom. The prosecution had indicated in its opening address that the handle to the handleless hatchet had been burned. Harrington's description of the roll of burned paper which was the right size backed up their claim.

Robinson also conducted the cross-examination of this witness. He read from Harrington's testimony given at the District Court hearing that at least one of the windows in the loft of the barn had been open. Harrington admitted that the testimony he had just given in direct examination was in error, and agreed that a window in the barn loft had been open. The lawyer now took up the matter of the scraps of paper burned by Dr. Bowen.

Q: When you were in the kitchen you saw Dr. Bowen with the notepaper in his hand?

A: Yes, sir. I saw him put it in the stove.

Q: And you saw the name Emma in one corner?

A: Yes, sir.

Q: And there was no attempt to withhold it?

A: No, sir.

Harrington remained adamant about one point in his testimony, and that was his description of the cylindrical roll of burned paper in the stove.

The sensation caused by Harrington's testimony lasted until the appearance of Officer Michael Mullaly on the stand a few minutes later. In his direct testimony he stated that Bridget Sullivan had led him to the box and she reached up and took two hatchets from it. He then showed them to Fleet and brought the Assistant Marshal to the box. "I showed him a box where Bridget had taken them from," he testified.

Q: What did you do after you showed him the box?

A: He took a hatchet out of there. . . . It looked to me as if smaller than one of them. The handle was broken and he put it back. It was covered with ashes or something like that, it looked to me.

Mullaly produced his sensation while being cross-examined by Robinson. He confirmed again that Bridget had led them directly to the two hatchets which she removed from the box, despite her emphatic denial of this. He then told how Fleet had taken the box down and found the handleless hatchet. In describing the contents of the box he mentioned that there had been *a broken handle in the box.*

"What?" Robinson shouted in complete surprise. The lawyer hurriedly picked up the handleless hatchet. The small piece of broken wood that had been in the eye had been removed by Dr. Wood in order to make his tests. Robinson showed these to Mullaly.

Q: Well, that was in the eye, wasn't it?

A: Yes; then there was another piece.

Q: Another piece of what?

A: Handle.

Q: Where is it?

A: I don't know.

Q: Was it a piece of that same handle?

A: It was a piece that corresponded with that.

Q: The rest of the handle?

A: It was a piece with a fresh break in it.

Q: The other piece?

A: Yes, sir.

Q: Was it a handle to the hatchet?

A: It was what I call a hatchet handle.

Q: Well, did you take it out of the box?

A: I did not.

Q: Did you see it taken out?

A: I did.

Q: Who took it out?

A: Mr. Fleet took it out.

Q: You were there?

A: I was there.

Q: Anybody else?

A: Not that I know of.

Q: Did Mr. Fleet put it back, too?

A: He did.

Mr. Robinson (*to Knowlton*): You haven't it in your possession, may I ask?

It was obvious to everybody in the courtroom that the District Attorney also had been taken completely by surprise by Mullaly's testimony that the broken handle to the handleless hatchet was in the box.

"I don't know where it is. This is the first time I ever heard of it," Knowlton informed Robinson.

The lawyer hurriedly ended his examination of Mullaly and requested the court's permission to recall Fleet to the stand. The judges directed Mullaly to take a seat and sent a court attendant to find Fleet and bring him back without talking to anybody. A police officer who was in the courtroom got up and started to leave. An attendant told him to return to his seat. When Fleet came back to the witness stand, the prosecution attempted to question him first, but the court ruled against this action.

Robinson then had Fleet relate again how he had taken down the box shown him by Mullaly.

Q: Will you state again what you found at the time you looked in?

A: I found a hatchet head, the handle broken off, together with some other tools in there and the iron that was inside there. I don't know just what it was.

Q: You did not find the handle, the broken piece, not at all?

A: No, sir.

Q: You did not see it, did you?

A: No, sir.

[The same question was repeated with the same answer.]

Q: Did Mr. Mullaly take it out of the box?

A: Not that I know of.

Q: It was not there?

A: Not that I know of.

Q: You looked in so that you could have seen it if it was there?

A: Yes, sir.

Q: You have no doubt about that, have you at all?

A: What?

Q: That you did not find the other piece of the handle that fitted on there?

A: No, sir.

[Re-Direct]

Q (*by Moody*): A single question has been suggested: Did you see anything other than metallic substances, except this piece of wood driven into the eye of the hatchet in that box, or around that box?

A: I don't recollect that I did.

[Re-Cross-Examination]

Q (*by Robinson*): You saw no piece of wood with any fresh break in the box, around the box or near it?

A: No, sir, not that I am aware of; I did not see any of it.

The last important witness of the day was Mrs. Churchill, the next-door neighbor who was recalled to the stand. Mrs. Churchill was the only witness the state had produced so far who stated positively that the dress Lizzie had turned over to police was not the dress she had been wearing on the morning of the murders. Hoping to nail down that she had seen Lizzie wearing the Bedford cord dress, Moody asked the witness the direct question. Her reply jolted the prosecution when she said she didn't know the Bedford cord dress, had never seen it. She thought the dress Lizzie had been wearing was a calico or some similar material. When the witness was turned over to Robinson, he asked her what dress Bridget had been wearing that morning. She replied that it was a light-colored calico. Bridget had testified earlier that she had been wearing a dark indigo-blue dress. Robinson read this description to her. Mrs. Churchill was certain that Bridget's dress had not been indigo-blue but a much lighter color. Mrs. Churchill's recall to the stand had greatly weakened the value of her previous testimony. Bridget also had testified in the lower court, shortly after the murders, that she had been wearing the indigo dress. Since Mrs. Churchill apparently was mistaken about Bridget's dress, she could, therefore, be equally mistaken about Lizzie's dress.

The prosecution, which had been embarrassed by the conflicting testimony over the handle to the handleless hatchet, found itself in an even worse predicament as testimony continued on Saturday, the sixth day of the trial.

The first witness that day was Lieutenant Francis L. Edson who testified that on the Monday after the murders, six officers went to the Borden house to continue searching and also to pick up the handleless hatchet.

Ever since Fleet had said that he had seen a basket on the workbench in the barn loft, Robinson had been trying to find a police officer who had examined it. He struck pay dirt with Edson. The lieutenant testified that he had picked up the basket and had taken it to the police station where he examined its contents. He listed three pieces of sheet lead folded over, a door knob, and several other items, all of which matched the description given by Lizzie Borden to District Attorney Knowlton during the inquest. This helped to corroborate Lizzie's statement that she had been up in the loft of the barn.

Edson was followed by William H. Medley, the officer who had said he found no footprints in the dust in the loft, although his own were clearly visible. Medley had been rewarded by being promoted from patrolman to inspector with the permanent rank of lieutenant.

The witness testified that he reached the Borden house shortly before Fleet. About ten or fifteen minutes after Fleet arrived Medley heard about Lizzie's story of her visit to the barn loft, and, acting on his own, went there. He said the barn door was closed, with an iron pin in the hasp.

He testified that after entering the barn, he walked part way up the steps and looked around the loft and saw that an accumulation of dust and hay particles on the floor appeared to be undisturbed. He put his hands on the loft floor and noticed they left an impression. He then walked up into the loft and took four or five steps along the edge near the stairs. He stooped down and said he could see his footmarks plainly in the dust, but he could see no other foot impressions on the floor. He reported his discovery to Fleet.

During his direct examination, Medley testified that he was the officer who had picked up the handleless hatchet from the box on Monday, wrapped it up and brought it back to the station house so that it could be sent to Professor Wood.

Under questioning by Robinson, Medley said his entire visit to the loft, including his experiments, took about two or three minutes. Asked about the handleless hatchet, he described it as covered with "coarse dust such as the empty ashes nearby." After his experiences with Fleet and Mullaly, Robinson apparently was taking nothing for granted with police witnesses.

Medley had mentioned in his direct examination that he had wrapped up the handleless hatchet in paper.

Q: Where did you get your paper?

A: In the basement.

Q: A piece of newspaper?

A: I think it was a piece of brown paper. I wouldn't be sure of that. It was a piece of paper, that was all I remember surely.

Medley was given a piece of paper and he demonstrated to the jury how he had folded the paper around the hatchet head.

He was followed on the stand by Captain Dennis Desmond, who said he took part in the search of the house on Saturday, the one described by Fleet as less thorough than it should have been. Desmond also testified that he was with Medley on Monday and he picked up the handleless hatchet in the "ash cellar." "I gave it to him wrapped up in a newspaper. I suppose he carried it away in that condition."

Under cross-examination, Captain Desmond gave an entirely different picture of the search on Saturday than Fleet had given. Desmond stated on the stand that nothing was overlooked, that they even turned the mattresses on all the beds in the house in their search for bloodstained items or the murder weapon.

Robinson quickly picked up Desmond's statement about retrieving the handleless hatchet on Monday.

Q: Are you certain about your taking it up?

A: Positive. I got the paper from the water closet there to do it up with.

Q (*handing witness the handleless hatchet*): Well, won't you wrap it up in about as large a piece of paper?

A: I shall have to get a full-size newspaper to do it, much larger than that, sir. (*Referring to a piece of paper handed witness by counsel*)

Q: You got a piece out of the water closet?

A: Yes, sir.

Q: Brown paper?

A: No, sir, regular newspaper, but a larger piece than that.

Q: You wrapped it in a newspaper?

A: Yes, sir.

Q: You are sure about that?

A: Positive.

The courtroom was absolutely silent as a poker-faced Robinson handed the witness a piece of the Boston *Globe* and said, "Well, take that and give us the way you wrapped it up." Only a few minutes earlier, Medley had testified under oath that he had been the officer who had picked up the handleless hatchet from the box on Monday and demonstrated to the jury how he had wrapped it. Now Captain Desmond, testifying to the identical incident, stated he was the one who had taken the handleless hatchet from the box, wrapped it up and turned it over to Medley. When he completed his demonstration Captain Desmond handed the package to Robinson. "I wrapped it up in some such form as that, and passed it to him," he testified.

Robinson could not resist one final question when he gravely asked:

Q: You don't remember what the newspaper was?

A: No, I don't.

The police woes for the prosecution were still not over. State Detective George Seaver, the next witness, testified that he had taken part in the search of the Borden house on Saturday. He also contradicted Fleet's story about the search and said he and the Assistant Marshal had examined the dresses together. "I removed each dress off the hook and he examined them as well as myself, he more thoroughly than myself, and I took each garment then and hung it back as I found them."

Seaver gave a minute description of well over one hundred bloodstains found in the sitting room and guest bedroom. He listed such details as the number of blood spots on the frame and glass of a picture hanging over the sofa and said that the bloodstains on the wall began 4 feet 10 inches from the floor and the highest were 6 feet 1 inch from the floor. He gave similar statistics for the guest bedroom.

Under cross-examination Seaver testified that all the dresses he and Fleet examined on Saturday had been turned inside out in their thorough inspection of each garment. Asked if he had made a memorandum listing the dresses, Seaver said he had. This would have shown if the Bedford cord dress had been inspected. Robinson promptly asked:

Q: Where is it?

A: But unfortunately I mislaid it or lost it, so I haven't seen it since I was at Fall River at the time the hearing was.

Questioned further by Robinson as to how it happened that he had lost or mislaid the dress list but not the list of blood spots, Seaver answered that he had also lost that list but he had made up a new list of the more than one hundred blood spots and their measurements entirely from memory!

Seaver said he had examined the handleless hatchet and described the broken portion as a "fresh break." Robinson brought out that Seaver had been a carpenter before he joined the state agency. Asked by Robinson to give his opinion as to how recently the hatchet handle had been broken, he replied that he could not tell within three months as to when the handle had been broken.

Before court adjourned, Knowlton indicated that on Monday he would offer into evidence the testimony Lizzie Borden gave at the three-day inquest. The defense stated it would oppose it. Both sides then filed a statement with the court in which they agreed on the following points:

1. The defendant was not under arrest at the time of the inquest but she had been informed that she was a suspect, and police officers had been stationed around the house to keep her under constant observation.

2. She had been subpoenaed to testify at the inquest.

3. Her request to be represented by counsel had been refused by the district attorney and the judge.

4. When her testimony was completed she was not allowed to leave and was placed under arrest two hours later on a warrant that was issued after she finished testifying.

5. A similar warrant was issued even before the inquest but was not served and she was not told about the existence of the first warrant for her arrest.

6. Neither the court nor the prosecutor gave her the customary warning that she did not have to testify or that anything she said might be used against her.

When the court met again on Monday morning for the seventh day of the trial, the jury retired while a long legal argument was held over the admissibility of Lizzie's three-day inquest testimony. The court finally excluded it, ruling that Lizzie had been under virtual arrest while being questioned.

Dr. Dolan, the medical examiner, was the next important witness. He described in great detail each of the ten wounds Borden had received and the nineteen wounds found on Mrs. Borden. A plaster cast of a head, with the position of each wound marked in blue, was used by the witness so that the jurors could follow his testimony. Both skulls had been badly crushed. Dr. Dolan testified that the blows could have been inflicted by a woman of ordinary strength, although in cross-examination he conceded that the blows might have been two-handed ones. The physician stated that a flap wound in Mrs. Borden's forehead showed that she had been facing her killer.

The testimony of Dr. Edward S. Wood, the noted medico-legal expert, contained a number of unhappy surprises for the prosecution. Knowlton had hinted that the illness of the two older Bordens on Tuesday night had been due to a poison attempt. It was for this reason that he had resisted any testimony that Lizzie also had been ill that night. Dr. Wood stated that he had examined the stomachs of both victims and "I found no evidence of poison of any kind."

"Of any kind whatever?" Knowlton asked.

"In either case," was Dr. Wood's discouraging answer.

The toxicologist estimated that Mrs. Borden had died ninety minutes "more or less" before her husband. His testimony that he had found no trace of blood on any of the various axes and hatchets which had been submitted to him indicated that none had been used as a murder weapon. He said he had removed the broken handle piece from the eye of the handleless hatchet and placed it in iodide of potassium which removes blood pigment. He allowed it to soak for several days before making his tests. He did not find the slightest trace of blood. There were several varnish stains on the broken hatchet.

Asked by Knowlton if blood could have been washed from the hatchet so that it could not be detected, the witness replied, "It couldn't have been done by a quick washing."

Q: Why not?

A: It would cling in those angles there and couldn't be thoroughly removed. The coagula would cling. It would have to be very thoroughly washed in order to remove it. It could be done by cold water, no question about that. But it couldn't be done by a careless washing.

He also testified that he had examined the clothing Lizzie had turned over to police. "The blue skirt has, near the pocket, a brownish smooch, which resembled blood, but a test showed it was not. Another lower down, proved not to be blood. The waist had not even a suspicion of bloodstain." He reported he had found no blood on Lizzie's shoes or her stockings.

Adams, during cross-examination, held up the handleless hatchet.

Q: This slot on the inner edge of the head furnishes a good refuge for any blood to gather?

A: Yes, sir, on its face.

Q: And it would be quite a place to clean, assuming that any blood got on it?

A: It would, and there is white dirt in there, and there is dirt there now.

The presence of dirt indicated that the handleless hatchet had not been washed.

Dr. Wood also left no doubt that the killer could not have avoided being bloodstained. "I don't see how he could avoid being spattered," he said. In Borden's case he said the blood-stains would have been from the waist up while the killer, in the case of Mrs. Borden, would have been spattered "from the lower portions of the body and upward."

Dr. Frank W. Draper, medical examiner of Boston, testified that he believed the assailant of Mrs. Borden inflicted all the wounds while standing astride her prostrate form as she lay face down on the floor—except the forehead flap wound. "I think that that was given while Mrs. Borden was standing and facing her assailant," he stated. He also agreed that the killer would have been stained with blood in each murder. It was while Dr. Draper was on the stand that the fleshless skulls of both victims were produced in the courtroom.

Lizzie Borden fainted and later had to be led out of the chamber.

The final medical expert was Dr. David W. Cheever, a professor of surgery at Harvard. Like the others, he agreed that Mrs. Borden had been murdered first and placed the time between one and two hours before her husband's death. He also stated that the killer had to be stained with blood after each murder. He went even further: "I should think the amount of blood would be a great deal."

Marshal Hilliard and Mayor Coughlin testified how they went to the Borden house on Saturday night where Dr. Coughlin admitted to Lizzie that she was suspected. Hilliard, in cross-examination, said that he visited the barn loft on the day of the

COURT HOUSE

LIZZIE BORDEN

THE LIZZIE BORDEN CASE

"Lizzie Borden Faints Away" during trial, as imagined by *Police Gazette* artist

Police Gazette

murders and saw the basket in which Lizzie said she had been searching for lead. "It sat on top of some boards," he stated. In her inquest testimony Lizzie said she moved some boards to reach it.

Mrs. Hannah H. Gifford, a dressmaker, testified that in March 1892 she used the word "Mother" in speaking of Mrs. Borden to Lizzie. "She says: 'Don't say that to me, for she is a mean, good-for-nothing thing.' I said: 'Oh, Lizzie, you don't mean that?' And she said: 'Yes, I don't have much to do with her; I stay in my room most of the time,' and I said: 'You come down to your meals, don't you?' And she said: 'Yes, but we don't eat with them if we can help it.' "

To further buttress its contention of family discord, the prosecution also offered the testimony of Miss Anna H. Borden of Fall River, no relation to Lizzie. Miss Borden had been Lizzie's cabin mate during their tour of Europe two years before the murders. She testified that on the trip home Lizzie had remarked that she was not happy to be returning. The defense asked that her testimony be stricken from the record as too remote. After conferring with his colleagues, Judge Mason said: "The Court are of the opinion that the character of the testimony, the expressions used, are too ambiguous. If the expressions were distinct of personal ill will to either the father or stepmother, it might not be too remote. We think the evidence should be excluded."

Bridget Sullivan made a third, but brief, appearance on the stand. A large colored handkerchief had been found near Mrs. Borden's body. Police thought she had been wearing it as a dusting cap but it showed no cut marks from the murder weapon. Bridget explained that it was one of Mr. Borden's old handkerchiefs and Mrs. Borden liked to use it as a dusting cloth.

There was a gasp of surprise from the press table when the prosecution summoned its next witness, Mrs. Hannah Reagan, the police matron. She testified to the story told here earlier that Lizzie had accused Emma of giving her away.

Jennings, who cross-examined her, read a list of names, including those of Mrs. Brigham and Mrs. Holmes.

Q: Did you tell any of them that there wasn't anything to it, nothing in it?

A: No, sir, I didn't.

Q: Did you tell any reporters that it was all a lie?

A: No, sir, I didn't.

Q: To no reporters?

A: No, sir.

Q: Did you then express willingness to sign [a document prepared by City Missionary Buck which stated the story was untrue] if Marshal Hilliard was willing that you should?

A: No, sir.

Mrs. Reagan also denied that Marshal Hilliard had told her that if she signed the paper it would be against his express order. She identified the reporter to whom she had given the story as Porter of the Fall River *Globe*.

Knowlton then summoned Eli Bence, the drug clerk, to the stand. When Robinson objected to the witness being called as having no bearing on the charge, another long legal argument was held in the jury's absence. The court excluded the witness from testifying and on the morning of the tenth day of the trial, the prosecution rested.

The first important defense witness was Walter P. Stevens, a reporter for the Fall River *News*. He testified that he was at the station house when Officer Allen returned with the news that Borden was dead. He left at once for the house with Officer Mullaly. He entered the house, then looked around the yard and finally went into the barn. Although he did not go up into the loft, he heard somebody walking around up there and then saw three others go up and heard them walking about. Stevens said Medley first arrived at the scene while he was entering the barn. Medley had testified that he did not go to the barn until some ten or fifteen minutes after Fleet arrived, which would place him up in the loft about noon, since Fleet first came at 11:45. Stevens testified that he already was on his way back to the office when the City Hall clock struck the noon hour.

Stevens was followed to the stand by Alfred C. Clarkson, a steam engineer, who arrived at the Borden place almost as soon as Sawyer and waited around in the yard watching police arrive. He saw two young men enter the barn and go upstairs, and he also went up to the loft. He said they walked around up there for three or four minutes and then came down. It was after he was out of the barn that Fleet first arrived. He knew him and recognized him.

Under cross-examination he said he had entered the barn with Deputy Sheriff Wixon, who had previously testified that he was one of the earliest arrivals on the scene.

With these two witnesses the defense began to discredit Medley's testimony that there were no footprints in the loft.

The defense then exploded the first bombshell of its own when it placed Hyman Lubinsky on the stand. A Russian immigrant who spoke English with difficulty, Lubinsky said that he drove a wagon, peddling ice cream for a Main Street merchant. He testified he had picked up his horse and wagon at Gardner's stable on Second Street, between Rodman and Morgan, shortly after 11 A.M. on the morning of the murders. He was on his way to the store to get his ice cream when he passed the Borden home.

"I saw a lady come out of the way from the barn right to the stairs back of the house," he testified. "The north-side stairs, from the back of the house."

Q: Can you tell how she was dressed?

A: She had on a dark-colored dress. She was walking toward the steps.

He said that he had made a delivery of ice cream to the

Borden home several weeks earlier and knew Bridget Sullivan. He was certain it was not the maid he saw.

Cross-examined by Knowlton, Lubinsky said he had told his story to Mr. Wilkinson, his boss, and to many other people. Reporters heard about it and published it. Officer Mullaly saw him about it two days after the murders. He said it was several weeks later when a member of Jennings' staff sought him out. Asked how he remembered that particular day, he said it was because he had been so late in getting out of the stable.

Several times during his cross-examination he said to Knowlton, "You ask me too fast." The printed record of the trial contains just the questions and answers; it does not indicate how questions are asked, what tone of voice is used. In commenting on Knowlton's questioning of Lubinsky, Julian Ralph wrote in the New York *Sun:* "Never did a lawyer try harder to confuse a witness than did Mr. Knowlton on this occasion. He walked up and down between the witness and his desk, prodding him with rapid questions. He was nervous, querulous and scolding in his tone." He added that Knowlton had failed to make a dent in Lubinsky's testimony.

The time element in Lubinsky's testimony was of prime importance and the defense had two witnesses for corroboration. Charles M. Gardner, owner of the stables, testified that Lubinsky left between 11:05 and 11:10. He said that when the peddler had called for his horse he would not let him take it because it was feeding. Lubinsky was late and kept yelling to him to hurry up. He said he had been keeping a sharp eye on the time because he had been hired by a traveling salesman to drive him to several places and then get him to the railroad station on time to catch the 11:50 train for New Bedford. Gardner testified that he left the stables about ten minutes after Lubinsky and while passing the Borden house he heard some people outside shouting about "some trouble, a fight or something." He saw John Manning, a reporter for the Fall River *Globe,* running up

Second Street toward the Borden home and pointed him out to the salesman.

During cross-examination, Knowlton tried to get Gardner to say that Lubinsky might have left before eleven o'clock, but the stableman said he was certain of the time because Lubinsky was late and kept pestering him to hurry up.

Charles V. Newhall, the traveling salesman, backed up both Lubinsky and Gardner as to the times they left. He had been keeping a nervous eye on his watch because he wanted to change a hundred-dollar bill at a bank, call at a harness shop to get an order and then get to the station to make his train. He testified that as they were driving by a house on Second Street, which he learned later was the Borden home, he heard somebody say that a man had been stabbed. He confirmed that Manning, who was the first reporter on the scene, came running up Second Street just as they were turning the corner a few houses beyond the Borden home.

Knowlton did not even attempt to cross-examine this witness and let him step from the stand without a single question.

Two boys, Everett Brown and Thomas E. Barlow, said they were walking by the Borden house when they saw an officer come out of the front gate and run across the street. They hurried into the yard and tried to get into the house but Sawyer refused to let them in. "We dared each other," Brown testified, "so we went upstairs into the barn and looked out of the window." Both said they had been in the barn before Fleet arrived, which would also place them up in the loft before Medley. Later they were put out of the yard.

In cross-examination, Brown was unable to tell the time he had arrived at the Borden home, but Barlow was more definite. He testified that he looked at the clock in Brown's house just before they left and it was 11:08. It was only a three-block walk to the Borden house but they had been "playing" while walking, taking turns at pushing each other off the sidewalk. He estimated the walk took about ten or fifteen minutes and his testimony was punctuated by the phrase "Brownie and me." Both youths said they had their dinner about 10:45 that morning.

The defense put on additional witnesses to dispute Medley's story about the absence of footprints in the barn loft. Charles S. Sawyer, who described himself as an ornamental, fancy painter, stated he had been across the street in a store when he saw Officer Allen run up. He came out to see what was happening and Allen pressed him into doing guard duty at the side door. He testified he saw Lizzie, spoke to her, and said she looked distressed. He saw no bloodstains on her clothing or person. He stated that Officer Doherty was the first to arrive after Allen left.

Q: Before Assistant Marshal Fleet got there, were or were not other people in the yard passing by your door?

A: Oh, yes, a great many.

Asked if any of them had entered the barn, he replied, "I saw them in the door going in and around the barn." Clarkson was one of those he saw enter the barn. "He was there almost as soon as I was, I think. He was there early; he was one of the first." Asked whether Clarkson was there before Fleet arrived, he said, "I should say before Officer Fleet came, quite a time."

Q: Were there any boys in the yard?

A: Yes, sir, lots of them.

Knowlton, at first, said he had no questions to ask the witness, but as Sawyer was preparing to step down, the prosecutor asked him if he knew there had been a murder in the house when Allen posted him at the side door. Sawyer replied he thought it was a stabbing. Asked if he had been nervous when he learned that it was a murder, Sawyer said yes.

Manning, the reporter, became a double-barreled witness for the defense. When the murders occurred he had been working for the Fall River *Globe,* transferring some time later to the

Herald. He was also the local correspondent for the Associated Press. He was the first reporter on the scene and testified that he entered the barn and looked around, and he saw many others, including Clarkson, go up into the loft of the barn long before Fleet arrived.

Asked if he had spoken to Matron Reagan after Porter's story of the quarrel between Lizzie and Emma appeared, Manning said he went to her home that night. "I told her I didn't want the story as it already had been published, but I wanted to know whether or not it was true. She said there was nothing to it."

Under cross-examination he said that Stevens, the reporter from the Fall River *News,* had gone into the barn with him.

He was followed by Thomas F. Hickey, a reporter for the Fall River *Globe,* who testified he saw Mrs. Reagan the day after the quarrel story appeared. "I see you are getting yourself in the papers, Mrs. Reagan," he said he remarked to her. "She laughed and said, 'Yes, but they have to take it all back.' I asked her if there had been a quarrel, and she said, 'No.' I asked her if she had repeated any of the words which had appeared in the paper that 'You gave me away, Emma,' and she said she did not. 'Then,' I said, 'Mrs. Reagan, there is absolutely no truth in the story that was printed?' and she said, 'No, sir, no truth at all.'"

Mrs. Marianna Holmes, wife of a Fall River banker, testified that she had questioned Mrs. Reagan about the story at the Fall River station house and the matron told her, "No, Mrs. Holmes, it isn't so." She said she heard Mrs. Reagan tell the Reverend Buck that she would sign the statement repudiating the story, "if Marshal Hilliard was willing." Mrs. Holmes also testified that Lizzie was on friendly terms with her stepmother for several years before the murder and they frequently attended church services together.

The parade of witnesses against Mrs. Reagan continued.

These included Charles J. Holmes, an official of two Fall River banks, John R. Caldwell, a reporter, and Mrs. Mary E. Brigham, all of whom testified that Mrs. Reagan admitted to them that the quarrel story was a lie. Later, when Marshal Hilliard took the stand during rebuttal, he admitted he had forbidden Mrs. Reagan to sign the document, although she had denied this, along with her other denials during her appearance on the witness stand. Rarely has a single witness in any trial been so contradicted by reputable witnesses.

Women spectators jammed the courtroom when they learned that Emma Borden was to take the stand. The quiet-spoken older sister presented a list of Lizzie's bank accounts to show that her sister had saved regularly at two different banks. She also said Lizzie owned two shares of stock in the Fall River National Bank, and nine shares of stock in a mill. All of these shares had been in Lizzie's possession for at least nine years before the murders. Emma told the story of Lizzie's giving her father a ring which he never removed. She testified that Medical Examiner Dolan told her after the search that it "had been as thorough as the search could be made unless the paper was torn from the walls and the carpets taken from the floor."

Q: Now, then, Miss Emma, I will ask you if you know of a Bedford cord dress which your sister had at the time?

A: I do.

Q: Won't you describe the dress, tell what kind of a dress it was?

A: It was a blue cotton Bedford cord, very light-blue ground with a darker figure about an inch long and I think about three quarters of an inch wide.

Q: And do you know when she had that dress made?

A: She had it made the first week in May.

Q: Who made it?

A: Mrs. Raymond the dressmaker.

Q: Where was it made?

A: At our home.

Emma said that it had been a cheap dress, the material cost-
ing no more than fifteen cents a yard, with eight to ten yards
used. She said the dress took about two days to make and she,
Lizzie, and her stepmother all worked together with the dressmaker. The sewing machine was kept in the guest bedroom. The
dress became paint-stained shortly after it was made "along
the front and on one side toward the bottom and some on the
wrong side of the skirt."

Q: Now where was that dress, if you know, on Saturday, the
day of the search?

A: I saw it hanging in the clothes press over the front entry.

Q: At what time?

A: I don't know exactly; I think about nine o'clock in the
evening.

Q: How came you to see it at the time?

A: I went in to hang up the dress that I had been wearing
during the day, and there was no vacant nail, and I searched
around to find a nail and I noticed this dress.

Q: Did you say anything to your sister about that dress in
consequence of your not finding a nail to hang your dress on?

A: I did.

Q: What did you say to her?

A: I said, "You have not destroyed that old dress yet; why
don't you?"

Knowlton objected to the question and then to the answer
and was overruled.

Q: What was the condition of the dress at that time?

A: It was very dirty, very much soiled and badly faded.

Q: Do you know whether she had been wearing it for some
little time prior to the day of the murder?

A: I don't remember seeing her have it on for several weeks
before I went away.

Jennings then led the witness to the dress-burning incident:

Q: Now will you tell the Court and Jury all that you saw or heard that morning in the kitchen?

A: I was washing dishes, and I heard my sister's voice and I turned around and saw she was standing at the foot of the stove, between the foot of the stove and the dining-room door. This dress was hanging on her arm and she says, "I think I shall burn this old dress up." I said, "Why don't you," or "You had better," or "I would if I were you," or something like that, I can't tell the exact words, but it meant, Do it. And I turned my back and continued washing the dishes, and did not pay any more attention to her at that time.

Q: What was the condition of the kitchen doors and windows at that time?

A: They were all wide open, screens in and blinds open.

Q: Were the officers all about at that time?

A: They were all about the yard.

Q: Was Miss Russell there?

A: Yes, sir.

The defense now tried to show that the family usually disposed of old rags and clothes by burning them in the kitchen stove, but Knowlton objected each time and the questions were excluded.

Q: Was anything said by Miss Russell in the presence of Miss Lizzie, in regard to this dress?

A: Miss Russell came to us in the dining room and said Mr. Hanscom asked her if all the dresses were there that were there the day of the tragedy, and she told him, "Yes." "And of course," she said, "it is a falsehood." No—I am ahead of my story. She came in and said she told Mr. Hanscom a falsehood, and I asked her what there was to tell a falsehood about, and then she said that Mr. Hanscom had asked her if all the dresses were there that were there the day of the tragedy and she told him "Yes." There was other conversation, but I don't know what it was.

That frightened me so thoroughly, I cannot recall it. I know the carriage was waiting for her to go on some errand, and when she came back we had some conversation and it was decided to have her go and tell Mr. Hanscom that she had told a falsehood, and to tell him that we told her to do so. She went into the parlor and told him, and in a few minutes she returned from the parlor and she said she had told him.

Q: Now at the time when Miss Russell said, "It was the worst thing that could be done—"

A: Oh, yes, sir; she said that Monday morning. When she came into the dining room and said she had told Mr. Hanscom that she had told him a falsehood, we asked what she told it for, and [she] said, "The burning of the dress was the worst thing Lizzie could have done," and my sister said to her, "Why didn't you tell me? Why did you let me do it?"

When Jennings brought the questioning around to Mrs. Reagan, Emma categorically denied each and every incident related by the police matron.

District Attorney Knowlton moved gingerly at first in his cross-examination, bringing out that Emma had been visiting friends at Fairhaven at the time of the murders. He asked her about relatives, and Emma said they had an aunt named Mrs. Morse who lived in Fall River and whom they seldom saw. Her father had many cousins, no brothers and one sister, Mrs. Harrington.

Q: Did you go there?

A: Yes.

Q: Much last year?

A: Yes.

Q: Did he come to the house?

A: Mr. Harrington?

Q: Yes.

A: No, sir.

Q: Did Mrs. Harrington come to the house?

A: Sometimes.

Q: Mr. Harrington did not come?

A: No, sir, once or twice, perhaps three or four times he came to the door to inquire for either my sister or I.

Knowlton then led to Borden's purchase of the half-interest in the house, which he gave to his wife.

Q: Did you find fault with it?

A: Yes, sir.

Q: And did Lizzie find fault with it?

A: Yes, sir.

Q: And in consequence of your faultfinding did your father also make a purchase for you or give you some money?

A: Not—I don't think because of our faultfinding.

Q: Did he, after the faultfinding, give you some money?

A: Yes, sir.

Q: How much?

A: Grandfather's house on Ferry Street.

Q: And was there some complaint that that was no equivalent?

A: No, sir, it was more than equivalent.

Q: That it wasn't so productive of rent as the other?

A: I don't know what the other house rented for, but I should think that ours rented for more than hers.

When Emma had testified that relations between Lizzie and Mrs. Borden had been cordial after that episode, Knowlton apparently turned to Emma's testimony at the inquest.

Q: You testified at the inquest, did you not?

A: I did.

Q: Were you asked questions in relation to that matter?

A: I don't remember what you asked me.

Q: Do you remember the answers that you gave?

A: Only two.

Q: Do you remember that I asked you if your relations were cordial between you and your mother?

A: I think you did either then or before the Grand Jury. I don't remember which.

Q: Do you remember you said that they were not?

A: I don't know whether I did or not.

Q: And do you remember that I then asked you if the relations between your sister and your mother were also cordial?

A: I do not.

Q: Do you still say that the relations between your stepmother and your sister Lizzie were cordial?

A: The last two or three years they were very.

Q: Notwithstanding that she never used the term "Mother"?

A: Yes, sir.

Q: They remained cordial?

A: For the last three years they were.

Knowlton then appeared to be reading from the inquest minutes when he asked the following questions:

Q: Now, I want to ask you if you didn't say this: "Were the relations between you and your stepmother cordial?" Answer: "I don't know how to answer that. We always spoke."

A: That was myself and my stepmother.

Q: Do you remember that answer?

A: I do now.

Q: "That might be, and not be at all cordial." Answer: "Well, perhaps I should say no then." Do you remember that, talking about yourself?

A: No, sir. I don't remember it.

Q: "Were the relations between your sister and your mother what you would call cordial?" Answer: "I think more than they were with me." Do you remember that answer?

A: Yes, sir.

Q: The next question is pretty long, "Somewhat more than they were with you, but not entirely so, you mean perhaps? I do not want to lead you at all. I judged from your answer you mean that, or don't you mean that? You say something more than your relations were. Do you mean they were entirely cordial between your stepmother and your sister Lizzie?" Answer: "No."

A: Well, I shall have to recall it, for I think they were.

Q: That is, do you remember giving that answer?

A: No, sir.

Q: How does it happen that you remember the answer in which you did not explicitly state whether they were cordial or not, but don't remember an answer, if one was given, in which you said they were not cordial, which was the following question?

A: I don't understand.

Q: This is a little involved perhaps. You do recall the question next preceding that in which you said "Somewhat more than they were with me"?

A: Not until you read it, I did not.

Q: You did recall it then?

A: Yes, I think I did.

Q: But when the next question, if I may assume to say so, was put to you, if it was put, and such an answer was given by you, you don't now recall that answer?

A: I don't seem to remember it.

Q: Will you say you didn't say that?

A: No, sir, not if you say I did. I don't remember saying it.

At this point, Knowlton, who had qualified very carefully as to whether some of these questions actually were asked, backed off from saying that they had been asked when he remarked:

Q: Do you understand me saying I do? Now, I do not say you did, and have no right to say you did. I haven't said anything about it. I am asking whether you gave that answer to such a question as that: "Do you mean they were entirely cordial

Mr. Knowlton cross-examines Emma Borden

between your stepmother and your sister Lizzie?" Answer: "No"?

A: I can only say I don't remember giving it.

Q: Whether you said it or not, do you say that is true, that the relations were not entirely cordial between your sister Lizzie and your stepmother?

A: I think they were for the last three years.

Q: So that whatever you said then you say so now; you say that is so now?

Robinson immediately arose to object to Knowlton's assumption. He said, "Well, I submit—" and before he could speak further Knowlton interrupted and remarked, "I don't press that question."

Q: Now I will read you this question and answer: "Can you

tell me the cause of the lack of cordiality between you and your mother, or was it not any specific thing?" Answer: "Well, we felt that she was not interested in us, and at one time Father gave her some property, and we felt that we ought to have some too; and he afterwards gave us some." Do you remember that?

A: No, sir.

Q: Is that true?

A: It was true at the time that he gave us the house.

Q: I will read another question: "That, however, did not heal the breach, whatever breach there was? The giving of the property to you did not entirely heal the feeling?" Answer: "No, sir."

A: It didn't, not with me, but it did with my sister after.

Q: Do you remember making any such distinction in your answer to that question?

A: I don't remember the question nor the answer.

Q: Neither one?

A: No, sir.

Knowlton did not read any more from what might have been the inquest minutes. Under the rules of cross-examination, an attorney has the right to read something in order to test the credibility of a witness. Knowlton seemed to be reading from the inquest minutes. Yet, when Emma stated she would accept it as being so if he said so, he made it very plain that he was not making any such claim. The defense attorneys, in questioning Bridget and other witnesses, stated openly that they were reading from the inquest minutes or the District Court hearing and left no doubt about it. Under the rules, where there is a dispute as to whether certain questions were asked and certain answers given, the stenographer can be placed on the stand in rebuttal.

As Knowlton continued his cross-examination, Emma testified that her stepmother had no enemies. She said that she had searched for the note by looking in a little bag that her stepmother carried and also in her workbasket. She had placed a notice in the Fall River *News* asking the writer of the note or the messenger to come forward. She said she never saw the handleless hatchet.

Knowlton introduced a new element in the case when he asked these questions:

Q: Did any of the members of your family have waterproofs?
A: Yes, we all had them.
Q: What kind were they?
A: Mrs. Borden's was a gossamer, rubber.
Q: That is, you mean rubber on the outside?
A: Yes, sir.
Q: Where was that hanging?
A: I think she kept it in the little press at the foot of the front stairs in the front hall.
Q: Did Miss Lizzie have one, too?
A: Yes, sir.
Q: Where did she keep hers?
A: In the clothes press at the top of the stairs.
Q: What kind of one was that?
A: Blue-and-brown plaid, an American cloth.
Q: And you had one too?
A: Mine was gossamer.
Q: Did you have yours with you in Fairhaven?
A: I did.

Knowlton questioned Emma about the incident described by Mrs. Reagan. "I mean to say there was nothing of that kind said," she testified. She also firmly denied some details of Miss Russell's version of the burning of the dress, and the prosecutor asked surprisingly few questions about it, making no further attempt to shake her testimony. At one point he remarked, "That is what I thought you would say." He soon ended his cross-examination.

Jennings promptly picked up Knowlton's inference about the waterproofs and in re-direct examination asked these questions:

Q: Do you know where this waterproof of Miss Lizzie's was on the day of the search?

A: Hanging in the clothes press that has been spoken of so often.

Q: Do you know where it is now?

A: It is there now.

Q: Been there ever since?

A: Every day since.

Emma's testimony had not been shaken on the stand, even though she was often called "the weaker sister."

Mrs. Mary A. Raymond, the dressmaker who had made the Bedford cord dress, testified that it had become paint-stained almost immediately after she had made it and while she was still in the house working on other dresses. In cross-examination she said that when Bedford cord fades it can be described as looking drab.

Mrs. Phoebe Bowen, the physician's wife, testified that when she first came to the house shortly after the murders and saw Lizzie being attended to by the other women, she thought Lizzie had fainted. "It wasn't until I saw her lips or chin quiver and then I knew she hadn't fainted," she said. Shown the dark-blue dress Lizzie had turned over to police, she identified it as the one Lizzie had been wearing the morning of the murders. She was the only witness to identify this dress while Mrs. Churchill was the only witness who said it was not the dress.

The final defense witness was Mrs. Annie M. White, the official court stenographer who had taken the minutes at the inquest and at the District Court hearing in Fall River. She produced her notes and said that Bridget had testified at the inquest that Lizzie had been crying. She also said that Fleet, at the preliminary hearing, had not testified to the disputed sentence: "She saw her father was feeble and went to him and advised and assisted him to lie down upon the sofa."

At this point, without calling Lizzie Borden to the stand, the defense rested its case.

Although called to the stand as a rebuttal witness by the prosecution, Marshal Hilliard admitted telling Mrs. Reagan not to sign a statement saying that her story of the quarrel was a lie. Patrolman Mullaly was summoned to show that police had investigated Lubinsky's story and had discarded it. This also boomeranged when Mullaly testified he had made no investigation at all. He had simply turned in a report as to what Lubinsky had told him. He did not question Gardner or anybody else. He had learned from Wilkinson that Lubinsky normally started work at 10:30 but did not ask Lubinsky what time he left the stable that day.

The prosecutor also called the court stenographer, Mrs. White, to the stand to show that when Mrs. Bowen was asked at the District Court hearing to describe Lizzie's dress, she had remarked, "I was not looking for fashions then." Mrs. Bowen did state that it was a dark-blue dress. Knowlton did not ask Mrs. White about Emma's testimony at the inquest and so did not dispute her denials of the questions and answers read. Although Porter, the Fall River *Globe* reporter, was in the press section along with many of his colleagues who had been called to the stand to refute Mrs. Reagan's testimony, Knowlton did not place Porter on the stand to support Mrs. Reagan's story.

The summations by Robinson for the defense, and by Knowlton for the prosecution, took a day and a half. Under Massachusetts law at that time, a defendant had the privilege of addressing a jury. Lizzie Borden said exactly thirteen words: "I am innocent. I leave it to my counsel to speak for me."

The charge to the jury by the three-man bench was delivered by Justice Dewey, who was fifty-seven years old, the youngest of the three judges. The case entered its final phase at 3:24 on the afternoon of June 20, the thirteenth day of the trial, when the jury retired for deliberation. Fourteen exhibits, including the skulls of the victims and Lizzie's blue blouse and skirt, which she said she had worn on the morning of the murders, were taken into the jury room. The jury stayed out for little over an hour and upon its return the foreman announced its verdict of Not Guilty.

The official minutes noted that the verdict was marked by applause from the spectators in the courtroom. Attendants restored order. Lizzie sat down immediately after the verdict. Knowlton then requested that the remaining two indictments be nol-prossed. "Now, congratulating the defendant and the counsel for the defendant upon the result of the trial, I believe the duties are concluded," he informed the court.

Lizzie's ordeal was over.

Or was it?

IX

The Case Against Pearson

*. . . it is impossible for anyone to begin to
learn what he thinks he already knows.*
—EPICTETUS

This is a difficult chapter for me to write. For years I have been
one of the many warm admirers of Edmund Pearson's works on
the Borden murders. In addition to his original essay in *Studies
in Murder,* and his even longer one in his trial book, Pearson
also discussed the case in print on at least three other occasions.
He wrote an article, "Legends of Lizzie," published in *The New
Yorker,* which later became a chapter in his book *More Studies
in Murder,* and after the deaths of the Borden sisters he wrote
"End of the Borden Case" for *Forum* magazine, which he ex-
panded into a chapter in still another book, *Five Murders.* All
of these are fairly well known and readily obtainable. I also
have in my collection still another essay by Pearson on the
Borden case, one that appeared in a true-crime magazine and
is known to only a few collectors of Americana.

Since my early knowledge of the Borden case came from
Pearson's various works, I was convinced, along with his other
readers, that Lizzie was guilty and had literally got away with
murder.

But I was troubled by two noticeable errors in his accounts.
Pearson always stated that the dress Lizzie Borden had turned
over to police, after they belatedly asked her for it, was a silk

dress. He considered this point so important that he usually italicized it for emphasis, remarking that it was absurd to think that a New England girl would wear a silk dress while doing her morning chores. Yet Lizzie's inquest testimony, printed in Pearson's trial book, proves that it was *not* a silk dress.

This information was brought out during the third day of the inquest, almost at the close, while Knowlton was questioning Lizzie with what might be termed relentless energy. The District Attorney at this point asked her:

Q: Was the dress that was given to the officers the same dress that you wore that morning?

A: Yes, sir.

Q: The India silk?

A: No; it is not an India silk, it is silk and linen; some call it bengaline silk.

Q: Something like that dress there? (pongee)

A: No, it was not like that.

The textile industry, like all the others that cater to the whims and pocketbooks of style-conscious women, has long used fancy-sounding names to describe some rather ordinary items. A certain fur, for example, is labeled "lapin" rather than common rabbit. Similarly, despite its name, bengaline silk is not a true silk fabric like the pongee dress that Knowlton had so thoughtfully provided. In the 1890s, bengaline silk was the name applied by mills to a cotton or wool fabric into which some silk threads had been woven, because, they claimed, it improved the sheen of the cloth. To a woman, it sounded so much better to have a dress that could be called bengaline silk rather than cotton. The mills made no attempt to fool the public. The fabric was not sold as silk, or even as a silk substitute, and the price was much less than for silk, but the impressive name helped the mills get a somewhat higher price than for ordinary cotton. A somewhat better than average cotton was just what a person in Lizzie Borden's social position would wear for daytime use.

I assumed that Pearson either did not recognize the significance of the phrase "bengaline silk," although it is described in the dictionary, or else that he had been misled by Knowlton's clever misdirection. Knowlton must have been familiar with the dress Lizzie had turned over to the police, because he had by then taken over the active direction of the case. He seems to have gone to the trouble of obtaining a pure silk dress, which he tried to get Lizzie Borden to say was similar to the one she had turned over to police. One may wonder at his purpose. Lizzie's descriptive phrase "bengaline silk" seemed to satisfy him at the inquest. At the trial he simply dropped the identifying word "bengaline" and thereafter called it a silk dress. He did this sparingly, and, unlike Pearson, did not emphasize it. He may have succeeded in misleading Pearson, but the jury did request the dress when it retired for its deliberations.

The second obvious error that disturbed me was Pearson's discussion of Miss Russell's testimony with its implication that she had offered clinching proof that Lizzie had been wearing the Bedford cord dress when seen on the morning of the murders. The trial minutes he printed did not bear this out. Miss Russell, as I have shown, testified very definitely that she had seen the Bedford cord dress exactly twice, and she named both occasions. She was most certain of this point. Her testimony destroyed the prosecution's attempts to show, through Dr. Bowen and Mrs. Churchill, that Lizzie had been wearing the Bedford cord dress when they came to the house.

While I was troubled by these errors, I did not doubt, from Pearson's accounts, that Lizzie was guilty—after all there was the attempt to buy poison, which the court did not admit into evidence; there was the story told by Hiram Harrington of bitter family disputes; there was the mystery of the note; there was Medley's testimony of the absence of Lizzie's footprints in

the hayloft; there was Officer Harrington's story of the cylindrical roll of burned paper that fitted the missing hatchet handle
so well; there was Lizzie's failure to see the body as she went up
and down the stairs. Pearson presented all this as incontro-
vertible fact. When you add up such factors you have a strong
case of circumstantial evidence, and I might add that I am a
firm believer in circumstantial evidence when each fact clearly
adds to a chain of evidence. Good circumstantial evidence is
better than dependence on eyewitnesses. Court records are
filled with examples of eyewitnesses who were tragically wrong
in their identifications.

Wondering if these two errors might not provide an interesting footnote for a possible magazine article, I did some preliminary research but quickly backed away. When I consulted
the files of several New York newspapers I found so many
episodes that Pearson had not mentioned that I seemed to be
reading about some other case. I recalled that Pearson said that
most of the big-city newspapers, particularly in New York and
Boston, were highly prejudiced in Lizzie's favor. The more I
thought about this, the uneasier I became. I had been a newspaper reporter for some years and had covered a great many
murders and murder trials. While it is true that there are occasional instances of bias by an individual reporter, it is unlikely
that an entire group of reporters would show bias, all slanted in
one direction, particularly in an out-of-town murder case. I
knew from personal experience that reporters are so busy during a trial jotting down the testimony and writing and filing
copy in a hurry to meet deadlines that they hardly have time to
invent testimony. Even if they did, their inventions would not
be identical.

I was, by now, definitely curious; I still believed that Lizzie
Borden must be guilty, but I decided to follow the path once
traveled by Pearson and go to Fall River to see the records for

myself. It was easier said than done. The search for the official trial minutes took months. They were not in Fall River where the crime occurred, nor in New Bedford where the trial was held, nor in Taunton, the county seat where records are kept. The district attorney's office for the Southern District did not have them, nor did the attorney general's office in Boston. But I eventually found them. The official minutes of the District Court hearing, in which Eli Bence had testified about the poison incident and had been cross-examined, were equally elusive—until a chance remark by Judge Cook led me in the right direction, and I found the only copy. Meanwhile, I interviewed many people and read various documents.

A study of both sets of the court proceedings made it painfully clear that Pearson's trial book and his essays were a distorted, one-sided version of what had actually occurred. Pearson had taken the prosecution's case and presented all the testimony upholding it. But he hacked out from the trial minutes almost all the testimony and information that discredited the prosecution's theory and case. It is true that Pearson had to condense the minutes, because his trial book otherwise would have been too large and unwieldy, but it is difficult to believe that these deletions just by chance eliminated the testimony unfavorable to the prosecution's case and seldom touched any statements made against Lizzie.

A line-by-line study of the official trial minutes and Pearson's version of the trial minutes was an excursion into a never-never land. But his book was not published as a fairy tale; it claimed to deal with the life and reputation of an actual person. To put it bluntly, Pearson presented such a biased version of the case that it might be considered a literary hoax.

Even before the end of the trial, the New York *Sun,* relying upon the dispatches from Julian Ralph, whom Pearson called one of the most distinguished correspondents in the country, wrote this editorial:

> *A chain of circumstantial evidence is strong only if it*
> *is strong in every necessary link. A single weak point, and it*
> *breaks and is useless. The chain tested at New Bedford dur-*
> *ing the past twelve days was proved fragile indeed, not*
> *merely at one place, but in almost every link. . . . Sur-*
> *prise at the weakness of the case against Miss Borden grew*
> *steadily to amazement that upon such slender evidence the*
> *life of a man or woman could have been deliberately at-*
> *tempted by means of a judicial procedure.*

No reader of Pearson ever got the impression that any link
was weak or that the case was anything but a triumph for the
prosecution witnesses. Pearson condemned with equal fervor
the judges, the defense counsel, the jury, and the press for being
prejudiced in Lizzie's favor. This was an amazing performance
on his part.

Knowlton, in his summation, pretended that some things
didn't happen during the trial. He offered weak explanations
of others and then hurried on. Pearson went Knowlton one
better. Since he had carefully deleted testimony embarrassing
to the prosecution in his version, he also carefully erased from
Knowlton's summation all references to such testimony. His
editorial blue pencil was busy with the testimony of almost
every witness. He not only shaped the facts of the trial to suit
himself, he even changed the picture of Lizzie's actions immediately after the murders.

The legend portrays Lizzie as an emotionless, almost inhuman
person, seemingly unaffected by the murders. With a firm
stroke of his pencil, Pearson made certain that the minutes did
not contradict this portrait. What if Bridget Sullivan did testify
at the inquest that Lizzie was crying when she came down from
her room in the attic? Simply eliminate it. What if Mrs. Churchill, the next-door neighbor, testified that only minutes later
Lizzie appeared "excited or agitated"? Take it out. What if

Mrs. Bowen, a good ten or more minutes later, found Lizzie so pale she thought she had fainted? Wave the magic pencil and her sworn testimony vanishes. Instead, present Officer Philip Harrington's testimony in great detail and his statements that he found Lizzie cool and steady and that she was not crying. Ignore the fact that he had arrived at the house more than an hour after the first call to headquarters and that Lizzie had had time to regain her composure.

Pearson had to work hard editing the minutes to make them fit his version of the trial. He had to start with the very first witness. During the cross-examination of Kieran, the civil engineer, it was shown how false was the prosecution's claim that Lizzie Borden could have seen her stepmother's body in the guest room. Pearson summarized this testimony in these exact words: "On cross-examination Mr. Kieran described an experiment made by counsel for the defense to show that a man might be hidden in the closet in the front hall without being observed by anyone in the hall, and another experiment as to the probability of a man, lying where Mrs. Borden's body was found, being seen by a person ascending the stairs." Pearson told his readers that an experiment was conducted, *and then did not state the results of the experiment!*

He completely omitted Kieran's testimony that Mrs. Borden's body could not be seen from the landing. You could consider this an oversight until you read Pearson's trial book essay on this point. He still carefully avoided giving Kieran's testimony. He wrote: "The significance of Miss Borden's presence at that precise place at that moment has been investigated with great care; whether anybody descending or ascending the stairs would necessarily see all that was in the guest chamber. Leaving this question, it may be said that one thing is not seriously disputed; anyone on that landing stood within fifteen or twenty feet of Mrs. Borden's dead body as it lay on the floor of the guest chamber." How true, but also how utterly meaningless in view of Kieran's testimony saying that the body could not be seen from the landing, a fact Pearson deleted from the testimony. This is sophistry and innuendo in its starkest form.

Pearson indicated in his writings that he had visited the Second Street house. If so, he may have been curious enough to conduct a similar experiment to find out for himself. I did. Through the courtesy of the present owners, I was allowed to climb up and down the steps, open the door to the guest bedroom and peer into it from all conceivable angles from the landing. Kieran was so right—you could not see that portion of the room where the body had lain. Knowlton was so right when he did not dare cross-examine Kieran on these points. Pearson accomplished what Knowlton could not. He eliminated this in his version of the trial minutes.

Let us see how Pearson handled one of the key issues of the entire case. The prosecution claimed that Lizzie Borden never went up to the loft of the barn. If she had, she simply would not have had enough time to murder her father. At best, she had ten to twelve minutes from the time Bridget went up to her attic room until she called the maid down. Bridget testified she reached her room at eleven o'clock. Police were notified at 11:15. In those fifteen minutes the murder had to be committed, Lizzie had to wash off bloodstains from her clothes and person, wash off the weapon and hide it; Bridget had to come down from the attic, go back and forth across the street for Dr. Bowen, leave again for Miss Russell; Mrs. Churchill had to come over, talk to Lizzie, go across the street and search for her yardman, talk to him; Cunningham, after overhearing her, had to cross the street to a telephone where he called police. The barn was about twenty feet in back of the house. Considering this time schedule, if Lizzie did go up into the barn loft, it is a safe conclusion that she was innocent.

During the inquest, Knowlton questioned Lizzie closely about her visit to the loft. She said a box, partly covered with boards, had been on a workbench, and it was this box that she had searched for lead. She stated that it had been almost completely full and had contained some nails, old locks, a doorknob and some pieces of thin sheet lead doubled over. Prosecutors like to get such details into the record, because they can often be used to trip up a witness who is lying.

Knowlton asked Lizzie three questions which implied that no such box had been in the loft: "Where was that box you say was upstairs, containing lead?" "Is it there now?" "How long since have you seen it there?" Knowlton must have known that the box was in the station house, in the very building where he was questioning Lizzie. Pearson published this section of the inquest minutes in his trial book without comment and let Knowlton's inference stand.

In addition to insinuating that no such box existed the prosecution, during the trial, also offered two points to prove that Lizzie could not have been upstairs in the barn. The first was that it was too hot up in the loft for anybody to remain there as long as Lizzie claimed she had. A group of officers were placed on the stand and all solemnly testified that it had been very hot up in the loft, as if it had not been very hot everywhere in Fall River that steaming morning. Officer Harrington was overly anxious to show how hot it was. He said that a loft window was closed when it had really been open, and then had to retract his testimony. With an open window and an open barn door, it was not quite as close up there as the prosecution tried to make out.

Officer Medley introduced a new angle when he said he found the barn door locked, thus hinting that Lizzie could not even have entered the barn. Bridget, however, had testified that she saw Mr. Borden open the barn door that morning and she testified further that she made several trips into the barn for water while washing the outside windows; there can be no doubt that the barn door was open before the murders. It is possible that somebody closed the door after the murders and before Medley arrived; he was not among the first at the scene.

The prosecution's strongest point was Medley's testimony about the absence of footprints in the loft.

Let us see how, in his trial minutes, Pearson presented the testimony relating to the box in the loft and to the fact that many people testified they had been up there before Medley.

The defense scored heavily twice about the box while cross-examining police witnesses. Lieutenant Edson testified that he had found a box on the loft workbench and examined it. His description of the contents was similar to that given by Lizzie, particularly of the way in which the thin sheet lead was folded over. This corroborated that there was such a box and that Lizzie had examined it. How did Pearson get around this? Quite simply. His condensed trial minutes at this point listed Edson's name, among others, but did not give a word of his testimony. The reader's natural assumption is that these witnesses, including Edson, simply buttressed previous testimony, and that nothing important was brought out in cross-examination.

The defense scored again when Marshal Hilliard testified he saw the box on the day of the murders and said it was resting on top of some loose lumber. Lizzie said at the inquest that she had to move some boards to reach the box. Hilliard's testimony was even stronger corroboration that she had been up in the loft of the barn. Was it Pearson's anxiety to save space that made him eliminate this portion of Hilliard's brief testimony?

Next, it was the turn of the defense to try to refute Medley's story about the lack of footprints. They began with Walter P. Stevens, a reporter, and Alfred Clarkson, a steam engineer. Both men had arrived at the scene well before Medley. Stevens testified he entered the barn, heard somebody walking about in the loft and then saw three more men go up, one of whom was Clarkson. Clarkson stated that he had gone up into the loft and that two other men went up just ahead of him. In cross-examination, the prosecution asked each man to fix the time he had been in the barn. Neither could do it precisely.

This is how Pearson presented their testimony in his version of the trial minutes:

"Walter P. Stevens and Alfred Clarkson, reporters. [Pearson erred in calling Clarkson a reporter.] Their testimony was offered in refutation of that of Officer Medley as to the visit to the barn loft; the contention of the defense being that others had visited the loft of the barn before Medley made his inspection and found no footprints in the dust. All of these witnesses, on both sides, were rather vague as to time, and consequently inconclusive."

Few people walk about with stop watches in their hands, but both of these witnesses and Medley had placed the time very well. Medley stated he went up into the loft some ten or fifteen minutes after Assistant Marshal Fleet arrived. Fleet testified he arrived at 11:45. This fixes the time Medley went up into the loft. Both Stevens and Clarkson testified they had entered the barn and come out again before Fleet arrived. This definitely placed both men in the barn before Medley. Knowlton, in his cross-examination, had refrained from asking either anything about seeing Fleet arrive. But witnesses placed themselves in the barn well before Medley went up. Pearson to the contrary, there was nothing vague or inconclusive about their testimony on this point.

Still on the incident of the barn, the defense had three block-busting witnesses: Lubinsky, the ice-cream peddler; Gardner, the stable owner; and Newhall, the traveling salesman. Lubinsky's testimony placed him in front of the Borden house at just about the time Lizzie claimed to have emerged from the barn, and he testified he saw a woman, wearing a dark dress, walking from the barn toward the side steps. Gardner and Newhall corroborated the time; and their testimony, as to people shouting that something had happened at the Borden

house as they drove by a short time later, leaves little doubt that
Lubinsky had to pass just before Mr. Borden's murder had been
discovered. Pearson very briefly summarized Lubinsky's direct
testimony and gave some of Knowlton's cross-examination
which emphasized the peddler's difficulty with the language.
By itself, Lubinsky's testimony was not too damaging to the
prosecution without corroboration. It needed the testimony of
the other two witnesses for the full force of his testimony to be
understood. Pearson had this to say about their corroborating
testimony in his trial minutes:

"Mr. Lubinsky was followed on the witness stand by Charles
E. Gardner and Charles V. Newhall. Mr. Gardner, the stableman where Lubinsky kept his horse, testified as to the ice-cream
salesman's movements." This summary, if it can be called that,
told the reader exactly nothing about Gardner's corroborating
testimony. Newhall was mentioned by name and that was all.

Pearson wrote in his original essay that Lubinsky's testimony
was "discarded testimony" because he had been examined by
the government and his idea of time shown to be faulty. The
trial record clearly shows that Mullaly, who questioned Lubinsky, never asked him the time he started out that day and that
the police had not investigated his statement. In his trial-book
essay, Pearson made no errors concerning Lubinsky, Gardner or
Newhall; he neither mentioned them nor discussed their interesting testimony, which is one way to avoid an awkward situation.

There were still other witnesses on this same point and all received similar treatment from Pearson. Perhaps one man should
be mentioned—Sawyer, the painter who had been guarding the
side door. His testimony was damaging to the prosecution because he said he saw many people, including Clarkson, enter the
barn before Medley or Fleet arrived. It will be recalled that
Knowlton, at first, did not even attempt to cross-examine him
and then finally asked him if he had been frightened when he

learned that a murder had occurred. Trying to ridicule a damaging witness is a familiar trick of trial lawyers whose only objective is to win cases. Pearson also summarized Sawyer's testimony. His complete version read:

"Charles S. Sawyer described himself as an 'ornamental painter, a fancy painter.' He was the guard, posted at the door by Officer Allen. He testified that he was nervous as he stood at the door, and apprehensive lest the murderer might attack him by way of the cellar door."

Mr. Sawyer, an honest, law-abiding citizen, stood guard duty from the time Officer Allen left the house until 6 P.M. He deserved better than this from Pearson.

The state failed in its attempt through Medley to show that Lizzie had not been up in the barn, and two of its own witnesses even furnished evidence that she could have been, particularly when this was coupled with the testimony of Lubinsky, supported as to the corroborating time element by Gardner and Newhall. Almost all of this information was omitted from Pearson's version of the trial of Lizzie Borden.

Pearson's acts in compressing out of existence testimony harmful to the prosecution's case were equaled by his omissions of similar testimony.

Assistant Marshal Fleet's performance on the witness stand, during which the second highest police official of a city was exposed time after time during cross-examination as being most reluctant to tell the truth about the search of the house, was appalling. Reputable newspaper correspondents left little doubt as to what they thought of his conduct. Pearson had no difficulty in preserving Fleet's reputation; he merely eliminated the entire cross-examination. In his original essay Pearson made this comment: "The cross-examination of Mr. Fleet was long and severe; it was part of the policy of the defense to impeach all the police testimony as incorrect, sometimes deliberately malicious." If anybody had been malicious, it was Fleet on the witness stand.

When Pearson reached Mullaly's testimony, he wiped out all mention of the handle to the handleless hatchet as though it had never happened, but he managed somehow to find space in his trial book for Officer Harrington's detailed testimony about the cylindrical roll of paper in the stove, from which it might be inferred that the handle to the handleless hatchet had been burned. Pearson was not really being malicious; after all, Lizzie Borden was dead when the trial book was published.

The contradictory testimony in which both Medley and Captain Desmond claimed to have picked up the handleless hatchet, and each demonstrated to a popeyed jury and a stunned courtroom how he had wrapped it, also vanished in Pearson's version of the trial minutes. And when he came to the testimony of State Detective Seaver and Captain Desmond, in which both testified that the search had been thorough, in direct contradiction of Fleet, Pearson simply added their names to the list of "other witnesses today," and let his readers infer that what they had said was too unimportant to be included.

Pearson scored a number of triumphs in editing Bridget Sullivan's testimony. Nowhere in his version of the trial minutes is there any indication that she was recalled to the stand or that Robinson brought out that she had testified at the inquest that Lizzie had been crying. Pearson simply erased this second appearance from his record of the trial. He also eliminated any reference to her excited denial that she had handed the hatchets in the box to Officer Mullaly.

The purpose of cross-examination is to ascertain the complete story. A witness, questioned by a lawyer from one side, is asked questions designed to bring out only what one side wants known. It is up to the opposing counsel to dig out the rest of the information during his examination. Robinson succeeded remarkably well with his cross-examination of Bridget. Courtroom spectators chuckled at the way he had to drag out, a word at a time, how police had so thoughtfully provided Bridget with a job at the jailer's house, after managing to get her released into their custody. And Bridget's solemn statement that all those officers who kept traveling from Fall River to New Bedford to see her had never discussed the case with her should be good for at least a smile of disbelief. But Pearson seemingly was not interested in humor, at least not at the prosecution's expense. All of that testimony was also deleted.

Although Pearson did not mention Bridget's return to the witness stand, he did note that Mrs. Churchill was recalled. That was exactly all he said—that she was recalled. He said nothing about her testimony that she had never seen Lizzie wearing the Bedford cord dress.

Pearson did a distinct disservice to the reputation of a brilliant lawyer when, in his trial-book essay, he accused Robinson of slipping in the word "together" during his examination of Bridget. Robinson did not slip it in, he literally forced Bridget to admit the truth of her testimony at the inquest. The official trial minutes show clearly that Robinson was quoting directly from Bridget's inquest testimony in which she had stated that the members of the family ate together. This testimony had been given one week after the murders. Ten months later at the trial, and after those visits from various officials, who, of course, did not discuss the case with her, the maid indulged in some interesting evasions and changes in her testimony. She tried to avoid acknowledging her inquest testimony. Robinson was too experienced a lawyer to let her get away with this and she finally had to admit the truth. Since Robinson was quoting directly from the inquest minutes and was using the exact language Bridget and Knowlton had used, it is difficult to understand how he could be accused of slipping in anything. It may be possible that Pearson was not familiar enough with the techniques used by court stenographers to understand that the quotation marks in the official trial minutes showed that Robinson was quoting directly from the inquest.

As the trial progressed, it became obvious that the prosecution was twisting every word Lizzie said and everything she did to give a sinister interpretation. Pearson added twists of his own.

In discussing Lizzie's visit to Miss Russell the night before the murders, Pearson, in his trial-book essay, quoted Lizzie as telling Miss Russell, "I am going to take your advice and go to Marion . . ." To this Pearson added a footnote which read: "Despite the roll call of the coming Sunday!" The implication is clear. Lizzie had been stating that she was remaining in Fall River because of the roll call, but here she was telling Miss Russell that she was going up to Marion, so her story about waiting around in Fall River for this roll call was false. But the three dots Pearson put in at the end of this quotation indicate that he had omitted something. What was it? Here is the complete sentence. Lizzie had told Miss Russell: "I am going to take your advice and go to Marion on Monday." Monday was the day *after* the roll call. Pearson omitted the two most important words of that sentence, and then added a footnote that gives a completely false impression.

He performed a similar contortion with the will. In this same trial-book essay he wrote: "It has been conjectured that at some time during this hot season Mr. Borden took a step which suggested he was making his will. This rests on no evidence but is the surmise of many. Whether he consulted his lawyer, or whether a conversation was overheard, we do not know. . . . That within a fortnight afterwards he talked of making a will is unproven, but it has been the belief of well-informed persons." This remarkable paragraph, filled with surmise, conjecture and the lack of evidence, also had a footnote which read: "For example, the late John W. Cummings, Esq., an attorney of Fall River, who was well acquainted with the counsel at the trial." In his footnote, Pearson can only be referring to Jennings, who was Borden's lawyer. The other two defense lawyers did not know Borden. But Pearson had deleted from his version of the trial record statements by Jennings saying that Borden had left no will and that he never discussed making a will. After this deletion, the surmise might sound plausible, but not with the facts placed by Jennings in the official trial record. Borden was a shrewd banker and businessman, well aware of the necessity for making a will if he wanted to distribute his fortune in any particular way. He knew that if he died without a will, his wife would get dower rights and the remainder would be divided between his daughters. Obviously, Borden was well satisfied with this and saw no necessity for spending money to draw up a will to say the same thing. He certainly never showed any inclination to donate money to charity, and his only close relative, besides his wife and daughters, was his sister. It is highly doubtful that he would leave her any money as long as her husband, Hiram Harrington, would benefit. To suggest that he would disinherit his favorite daughter, or leave a major share of his money to his wife, completely contradicts everything Borden did in his lifetime. Mrs. Borden was an elderly woman and after her death his money would go to strangers.

One of Lizzie's most sinister acts, in the eyes of Pearson and the prosecution, occurred shortly after noon on the day of the murders, when she finally went up to her room. Despite Pearson's cutting of the minutes, evidence does show that Lizzie had been displaying many signs of distress. She was not feeling well and became ill after she reached her room, and Miss Russell hurried down to get Dr. Bowen. When she returned to the room, Lizzie had changed into a dressing gown and said she wanted to stretch out on a chaise longue.

To the prosecution and to Pearson, the fact that Lizzie had changed into a dressing gown and removed her dress was highly suspect, and virtual proof of her guilt. She was asked about this at the inquest and replied "they" told her to change, referring to the many people who had been hovering over her after the discovery of the murders. Porter gives an imposing list of names, outside of police officials, who had rushed to Lizzie's side within a short time after the murders. These people took turns at fanning her, rubbing her hands, clucking over her, and expressing their sympathy. During the trial Knowlton asked Miss Russell if she had told Lizzie to change her dress. She replied she had not. This same question was not put to other witnesses who had come to Lizzie's side that morning. Many were not even witnesses at the trial. Yet, with nothing more than this, the prosecution charged that the change of clothes was a deliberate act by Lizzie to hide her bloodstained dress, despite the fact that witness after witness had said there were no bloodstains on the dress. Pearson followed this line in his trial book.

The rule of common sense and customary behavior applies in murder cases as well as in ordinary living. When Lizzie Borden, after what surely must have been a trying morning for anyone, killer or not, went up to her room, not feeling well and expecting the doctor to examine her, and changed into a dressing gown to lie down on a chaise, were her actions suspicious, or normal for the circumstances?

Pearson made much of Lizzie's differing stories concerning her visit to the barn. She told several people she went there to get a piece of iron or tin, and she told the police that she had gone to find lead to make sinkers. No one can seriously dispute that Lizzie Borden, very much the daughter of her father, was not above saving a few pennies if she could find lead she could use for sinkers on her trip to Marion. After Mrs. Holmes, the banker's wife, had seen Lizzie on the first day of the murders, she was interviewed by reporters. In relating to them the story Lizzie told her, she said that Lizzie had gone to the barn to get a piece of metal to wedge a loose screen, but mainly, with the Marion trip on her mind, to see if she could find lead for sinkers. This story appeared before Lizzie was considered a suspect by anyone, with the possible exception of Officer Harrington, so it cannot be considered a belated alibi story. It is possible that the Fall River *Globe* did not carry it since it was not interested in news about Lizzie that did not fit in with its theory. Pearson seems to have spent considerable time digging out items in the *Globe* that were unfavorable to Lizzie. It is significant that Knowlton did not bother to ask Lizzie Borden a single question at the inquest about her so-called differing stories.

Actually, it was not the differing stories that the prosecution used against Lizzie Borden in its opening statement, it was the interpretation it placed on these stories, an interpretation that shows how the prosecution tried to bend facts to fit a theory. When Lizzie spoke to Bridget, she told her she had heard a groan. When Mrs. Churchill asked Lizzie if she had heard anything, Lizzie said she heard "a sound like a distressed noise." When Officer Doherty questioned Lizzie as to whether she heard anything while in the barn, she said she heard a scraping noise. The prosecution added these statements and came up with a theory that Lizzie, alarmed by the noise, had rushed into the house. It then cited her inquest testimony saying that when she came in from the barn, she inspected the fire in the kitchen stove, and when she saw that it was almost out and that she could not continue her ironing of handkerchiefs, she decided to go up to her room. To do this, she had to go through the sitting room. It was only when she came to the door of the sitting room that she discovered her father's body. It was this difference in her stories—first rushing into the house, and then taking her time, which the prosecution said was important because it showed that she was lying. It is a nice theory, but nowhere in any statement that Lizzie made to any witness is there anything indicating that the sound she heard had alarmed her and caused her to rush into the house. This was the prosecution's interpretation, and not evidence.

Another example of twisting facts so that they would take on sinister connotations was the treatment given to Lizzie's remarks to Bridget about the sale of dress goods.

At the trial Bridget testified that after she had washed the windows, Lizzie said to her, "There is a cheap sale of dress goods at Sargent's this afternoon at eight cents a yard." Then Bridget made another of her sudden changes in testimony when she added, "I don't know that she said 'this afternoon,' but 'today.'" She testified further, "And I said, 'I am going to have one.' Then I went upstairs to my room."

In a strange footnote, which will be discussed shortly, Pearson stated that in the lower court Bridget had said nothing about "afternoon" in relating this episode. Pearson does not cite his authority for this statement and he did not indicate in his book that he read the official minutes of the District Court hearing. He may have been relying here on Porter or the Fall River *Globe,* and both were very inaccurate in reporting testimony. The official minutes of the lower court hearing state that Bridget used the word "afternoon" in her testimony there. In addition, while still searching for those particular minutes, I learned that the Fall River *News,* in a splendid example of responsible journalism, had hired a group of skilled stenographers to take down the testimony at that hearing in order to make certain that it was presenting accurate reports to its readers. I made notes on these accounts but was reluctant to use them because they were not the official minutes. When I did find the official minutes, out of curiosity I checked them against the reports that appeared in the *News* and found the latter remarkably accurate. These reports also show that Bridget said "this afternoon" in her lower court testimony. Since both agree, I believe that Pearson was in error.

Now let us look at the footnote Pearson used in his trial book on Bridget's testimony on this point:

"In this conversation, and in the one preceding, it is far more likely that Miss Lizzie said *morning,* rather than afternoon. In the lower court, Bridget said nothing about 'afternoon.' If Miss Lizzie said 'afternoon' the significance of the remark about Sargent fails. But in the previous inquiry, as to whether Bridget was going out, the word 'afternoon' would make the inquiry almost meaningless. It is probable that to Bridget as to many people, both afternoon and evening were very indefinite words. It is possible that Miss Borden used the word 'forenoon'—a word perhaps unfamiliar to Bridget."

This footnote is composed of guesses and surmises instead of the evidence. The preceding conversation Pearson referred to occurred only a few minutes earlier when Lizzie said to Bridget, "Maggie, are you going out this afternoon?" Bridget replied, "I don't know; I might and I might not; I don't feel very well." Lizzie then said to her, "If you go out be sure and lock the door, Mrs. Borden has gone out on a sick call and I might go out too." Why Pearson claims the use of the word "afternoon" in this conversation is meaningless, is something I'll never know.

In both courts Bridget testified to making the same reply about the sale at Sargent's. "And I said, 'I am going to have one.' Then I went upstairs to my room." Her words, "I am going to have one," is as definite a phrase of future action by the speaker as the English language can supply. She indicated very plainly that she now was planning to go out that afternoon to take advantage of the sale. Her action in going up to her room to rest, coupled with her words that she was going to have one, shows that she was not planning to do so that morning, that the reference was to the afternoon. There is other proof as well. The Bordens ate their dinner each day at noon. Bridget cooked this meal. Even if dinner that day was to have been the inevitable mutton and mutton soup, it still needed preparation and

Bridget always did some baking for the dinner meal. This meant that she could rest only a short time before preparing the meal. It is equally obvious that she would have had only a short time to go to a store and examine the material on sale before she would have to hurry home to get dinner. Women do not market for dress goods on the run.

To return to Pearson's footnote—when he said, "It is probable that to Bridget, as to many people, both afternoon and evening were very indefinite words," he seems here to be clutching at straws. Anyone should be able to distinguish between the daylight of afternoon and the dusk of evening. Still trying desperately, Pearson also offered the unhappy suggestion that possibly Lizzie used the word "forenoon" which perhaps might be unfamiliar to Bridget. In this country we have Americanized forenoon to morning, although forenoon was still in use in the 1890s. But forenoon is a British word, Bridget was born in Ireland where they did speak British English, if with a brogue. There is little reason to doubt her ability to understand the use of the word. As Pearson said, "If Miss Lizzie said 'afternoon' the significance of the remark about Sargent fails." All the facts, instead of such vague expressions as "most likely," "probable" and "possible," indicate that Lizzie said afternoon and meant afternoon and the significance of the remark about Sargent did fail. It failed despite Bridget's change in testimony that the prosecution needed so desperately.

There are many other illustrations of Pearson's curious treatment of the trial minutes, but enough examples have been given here to show that he presented a one-sided version that is not a fair representation of the actual trial testimony. Any reader interested in further examples can compare the testimony in Pearson's trial book with the actual testimony from the official minutes given in the trial chapter in this book.

Pearson made four points against Lizzie which the trial minutes do not answer. These are: Lizzie's supposed attempt to buy poison the day before the murders; the story of Hiram Harrington; Lizzie's failure to take the stand in her own defense; and the note the prosecution said never existed.

Pearson followed the lead of the prosecution and has stated, without any qualifications, that Lizzie was positively identified as the woman who had tried to buy prussic acid from Eli Bence. In his trial-book essay Pearson wrote: "Mr. Bence was taken to the Borden house that evening and placed where he could see Miss Borden. He repeated his statement that this was the person to whom he had refused prussic acid. Of course, this was not the best method of identification, but even had it been possible to place her in a line-up, it would have been superfluous to do so, since Mr. Bence for years had seen Miss Borden passing on the street, and recognized her when she made her request."

Although Pearson mentions the District Court hearing in Fall River at which Bence testified, he does not quote from those minutes in his trial book. Even in his original essay on the case in *Studies in Murder,* where he gave summaries of what some of the witnesses said, he also failed to mention any of Bence's testimony. Instead, he quoted from Porter's book that Bence's appearance "in the judgment of many spectators . . . produced evidence of uneasiness on the part of Lizzie Borden." This, of course, is insinuation, not testimony.

What did Bence say? Why should Pearson be so hesitant about giving his testimony? After all, Pearson did say he made an absolute identification and recognized her.

Bence testified in direct examination that he was in the pharmacy when a young woman entered and asked to buy ten cents' worth of prussic acid and he refused to sell it to her without a doctor's prescription. Asked if he had identified the woman, he replied that it was Lizzie Borden.

Bence was cross-examined by Jennings. The clerk said that up to that day Lizzie Borden had never been in that drugstore. Asked if he ever had waited upon her before in his business career, he replied that he might have done so once or twice some six years earlier when he was working at another pharmacy. He could not remember whether the woman who asked for prussic acid was carrying a fur cape over her arm, and he was not certain whether she carried a purse or wore a veil. He could not recall any other woman customer who had been in the store that day except his sister. Asked where and how he had identified Lizzie, Bence testified that he was taken to her home that night by Officers Harrington and Doherty. He waited outside the kitchen door while Harrington pretended he was checking up on a report that a man had been seen in the yard. The purpose was to get Lizzie talking so that he could listen to her voice. *Bence testified that he had identified Lizzie Borden by her voice.*

Jennings then asked:

Q: What was there peculiar about the voice?

A: It was tremulous.

The next witness was Frank H. Kilroy, a student, who said he was sitting in the store when a woman came in and he heard her say something about prussic acid. He stated she was carrying a fur cape. He said he had identified Lizzie at the inquest as the woman. He had never met her but knew who she was from seeing her around town.

Jennings then asked these questions:

Q: How did she speak?

A: Quite loud.

Q: Did you notice any tremulous tones?

A: No, sir.

The third witness from the drugstore was Frederick E. Hart, also employed there as a clerk. He said the woman had been carrying a fur garment over her arm. She was dressed in black. He testified that he did not know Lizzie Borden but identified her along with Kilroy when he was shown a woman seated in a room in the station house where the inquest was held.

This was the "positive" identification of Lizzie Borden as the woman who had tried to buy the prussic acid. Bence could only recognize her by voice, which he described as tremulous; a young student who had never met her but who said he recognized her from seeing her around town disagreed with Bence about her voice, and the third witness recognized her when shown a woman sitting alone in a room more than one week later!

At the end of their testimony Jennings offered to put Lizzie Borden on the stand to deny under oath that she ever had entered that drugstore in her life. She did so testify at the inquest.

It must be remembered that it was Officer Harrington, whom Porter credits as the first officer to suspect Lizzie, who brought Bence to the Borden house and staged the voice identification with Bence outside the room. Even the Fall River *Globe* did not dare go so far as Pearson, who stated so flatly that Bence had seen her often in the street and promptly recognized Lizzie Borden when she asked for the poison. The strongest the *Globe* would go was, "The young man [Eli Bence] was not previously well acquainted with the young woman but he told them [Harrington and Doherty] that he could identify her at sight." The "sight" turned out to be Lizzie's voice and the great confrontation scene that the *Globe* described so well, as mentioned earlier in this book, never took place since Bence remained out of sight near the door.

Pearson also quoted from Porter to indicate that the other newspapers largely ignored the identification of Lizzie Borden as the woman who had tried to buy the poison. Porter's exact words were somewhat different. He wrote: "The Fall River *Daily Globe* published the particulars of this incident the next day. But almost every newspaper in the country failed to accept it as authentic." The other papers may have had good reason for this. As soon as the story appeared in the *Globe*, other reporters questioned Bence, Kilroy and Hart. They reported that none of these men knew Lizzie Borden, and the description they offered of the woman in the store was so vague as to be meaningless; the reporters stated bluntly that it was an obvious case of mistaken identity. Nowhere does Pearson mention any of this information in telling his readers that Bence had made a positive identification.

As has been pointed out, Fall River then was an important gateway to New England for travelers using the steamship line. At that time many railroad lines did not have direct through service from New York City. A woman carrying a fur cape and dressed in black could very well have been on her way to or from one of New England's mountain resorts where women do wear fur jackets on cool evenings. The prosecution contended that prussic acid is not used to kill moths in fur garments. They produced several furriers to say so during a preliminary hearing as to whether Bence would be allowed to testify at the trial. It is no trade secret that prussic acid vapors were for many years an important ingredient in commercial preparations used to destroy insect pests of various kinds.

Significantly, police were unable to locate a single witness who saw Lizzie Borden walking on the street that hot Wednesday morning when she was supposed to have gone to the drugstore with a fur garment over her arm. They did find witnesses who saw her on the street that evening when she left the house and called upon Miss Russell. The sight of Lizzie Borden walking on the street with a fur garment over her arm on a blistering hot day is not one that is likely to pass unnoticed or be easily forgotten.

Pearson also added some touches to the poison legend. He has written, and apparently seriously, that when an official entered the Borden home he happened to pick up a book that contained recipes, or perhaps household hints, and the book immediately opened to a page discussing prussic acid! If anybody in the Bor-

den house, or elsewhere, ever thought of committing murder
with prussic acid and took the trouble to read about it first, he or
she would change his mind fast. It is always described as one of
the quickest-acting poisons known, one which can kill in twenty
seconds to a minute. The least astute investigator would
promptly suspect murder if he found that a person ate or
drank something and then dropped dead almost immediately.
Prussic acid is also known for the distinctive odor that makes it
one of the few poisons which can be detected at once without an
autopsy. It advertises its presence so readily that it is almost
never used in actual murders.

Pearson quotes a New Bedford paper as saying that Lizzie
Borden also attempted to buy poison in that city during the
summer of 1892. This story appeared only after Lizzie Borden
had died in 1927 and the legend was being accepted as true.
Balanced against this is the fact that at the time of the murders
two Fall River police inspectors checked every drugstore in New
Bedford, and even the Fall River *Globe* had to report there had
been no attempts by Lizzie to buy any poison on this visit, her
only trip to New Bedford in several years.

Pearson went even further in his attempt to link Lizzie Borden with poison. In his trial-book essay he discussed the sudden
illness on Tuesday night, spoke about the hot weather and in-
judicious diet, and then added, "Except for later events and
fuller knowledge, this might be a satisfactory explanation."
What later events and fuller knowledge he referred to is lost in
the mists of his innuendo; the trial record contains the positive
testimony by Dr. Wood that there wasn't the slightest trace of
any poison in the stomachs of Mr. and Mrs. Borden.

The story of family dissension told by Hiram C. Harrington,
Borden's blacksmith brother-in-law, needs little explanation
because it is just that—a wild and woolly story. One of the Fall
River *Globe* reporters, who was local correspondent for the
New York *World,* telegraphed Harrington's story to the New

York paper but added an important qualifying sentence: "Mr. Harrington is embittered against the family and does not hesitate to make startling statements." Even Knowlton doesn't seem to have been very impressed with Harrington's story. After he questioned Harrington at the secret inquest, he never called him as a witness at the trial.

In trying to prove family dissension, Knowlton offered two witnesses. One was a dressmaker to whom Lizzie had said that her stepmother was "a mean old thing," hardly an expression that prophesies murder. The other was her shipmate who said that Lizzie was unhappy at the thought of returning home after some three enjoyable months of touring Europe; and this was two years before the murders! Bridget did change her testimony from that which she had given under oath at the inquest and said at the trial that the daughters did not often eat with their elders, but she also testified that she never heard any quarrels or saw any signs of unpleasantness.

Knowlton certainly could have used a witness with the information Harrington claimed to possess about family dissensions, and he did not hesitate to place Mrs. Reagan on the stand, knowing that she would be under severe attack by a long list of reputable witnesses, but he drew the line at Hiram Harrington. Yet Pearson presented extracts from Harrington's statements without indicating to his readers the history of the long and notorious family feud and, in his essay, used some of Harrington's blatantly false statements as uncontested facts.

Pearson implied that Lizzie's failure to testify was a sign of her guilt. He backed up this strange attack on a fundamental right in our law by quoting the advice a judge once gave to a young lawyer: "If the attorney believes his client innocent, put him on the witness stand without hesitation, if however, he believes him guilty, never put him on the witness stand." What the circumstances were in the particular case that led to this aphorism is not given, but I doubt that any lawyer or any judge would expect such advice to apply in every case. To bolster his insinuation, Pearson pointed out that in the Hall-Mills murder trial Mrs. Hall took the witness stand and was acquitted. He then added, "The bearing of all three did much to convince the jury of the fact of their innocence."

Pearson is quite correct on one point. There is little doubt that if the defendants in the Hall-Mills case had not taken the stand they would have been convicted. They had to take the stand; but there was no reason for Lizzie Borden to do so. The state's own witnesses, under cross-examination, made the weakness of the prosecution's case so obvious that several reporters asked Robinson after the trial why he had not moved for a directed verdict of acquittal at the end of the people's case. They quoted him as replying that lawyers seldom did that in Massachusetts because they feared the jury would react unfavorably if the routine motion should be denied.

I have covered many trials in which a defendant without a criminal record did not take the stand. A lawyer must not only size up the case against his client, he must also understand his client. Lizzie was blunt and forthright in her statements. She had reason to dislike Knowlton. Such a combination could lead to explosive moments on the witness stand, particularly if Knowlton could goad Lizzie into becoming angry, and Robinson had every reason to believe that he would try. Her behavior on the stand under such conditions could affect a jury adversely.

This is not farfetched. Juries do react strongly to impressions rather than facts. During a trial in New York, a lawyer with a weak case once deliberately baited a judge, hoping for some judicial error which would give him grounds for an appeal. He objected at one point to the judge's banging his hand on the bench. The judge, probably unaware of the action, denied that he had done so. His act had nothing to do with the evidence in the case. The jury acquitted the defendant. A curious court attendant asked several jurors why they voted for an acquittal.

"He did, too, bang the bench," one of them replied. There are many good reasons beyond guilt or innocence why lawyers sometimes do not put clients on the stand.

In every murder case there are loose ends, gaps, unexplained incidents. The reason is obvious: often the only person who knows the answer is the victim—who is dead. District attorneys always seize upon these unexplained facts and, in summation, dramatically challenge the other side to produce an answer or admit guilt. Whether it works or not, it is a good tactic. In the Borden case, the unexplained note was the loose end and Knowlton was not above using it to try to force a Guilty verdict.

In his summation to the jury, he said: "No note came; no note was written; nobody brought a note; nobody was sick. . . . I will stake the case on your belief or disbelief in the truth or falsity of that proposition."

Was there a note? Nobody can say. But there are certain facts that should be considered. First, here is the portion of Lizzie's inquest testimony that deals with the note:

Q: Did she [Mrs. Borden] say she had done the work?

A: She said she had made the bed, and was going to put on the pillowcases, about nine o'clock.

Q: I ask you now again, remembering that—

A: I told you that yesterday.

Q: Never mind about yesterday. Tell me all the talk you had with your mother when you came down in the morning?

A: She asked me how I felt. I said I felt better, but did not want any breakfast. She said what kind of meat did I want for dinner. I said I did not want any. She said she was going out; somebody was sick and she would get the dinner, get the meat, order the meat. And I think she said something about the weather being hotter, or something; and I don't remember that she said anything else. I said to her: "Won't you change your dress before you go out?" She had on an old one. She said, "No, this is good enough." That is all I can remember.

Q: In this narrative you have not again said anything about her having said that she made the bed?

A: I told you that she said she made the bed.

Q: In this time saying you did not put that in. I want that conversation that you had with her that morning. I beg your pardon again, in this time of telling me, you did not say anything about her having received a note.

A: I told you that before.

Q: Miss Borden, I want you now to tell me all the talk you had with your mother, when you came down, and all the talk she had with you. Please begin again.

A: She asked me how I felt. I told her. She asked me what I wanted for dinner. I told her not anything; what kind of meat I wanted for dinner. I told her not any. She said she had been up and made the spare bed, and was going to take up some linen pillowcases for the small pillows at the foot, and then the room was done. She says: "I have had a note from somebody that is sick, and I am going out, and I will get the dinner at the same time." I think she said something about the weather; I don't know. She also asked me if I would direct some paper wrappers for her, which I did.

Q: She said she had had a note?

A: Yes, sir.

Q: You told me yesterday you never saw the note?

A: No, sir; I never did.

Q: You looked for it?

A: No, sir; but the rest have.

Q: Does she usually tell you where she is going?

A: She does not generally tell me.

Q: Did she say when she was coming back?

A: No, sir.

We do have some information which makes it possible to draw a few conclusions about the note. The prosecution claimed that it was impossible for a note to have been delivered because Bridget was around and she saw nobody. But Bridget, according to her own testimony, had been vomiting in the back yard for ten to fifteen minutes and was, during this time, hardly in a position to keep a constant eye on the house. It is quite possible that a note or a messenger could have arrived during that interval.

There are additional facts to be considered. Lizzie testified at the inquest that when her father came home she told him that Mrs. Borden was out, that she had received a note saying that somebody was sick. She said her father made no reply. Bridget, who overheard the conversation, gave the same account. Borden was seventy years old, an age where the ranks of his friends and acquaintances were thinning fast. His silence was significant. It would have been normal for him to ask who was ill; after all, it might be a close friend or a relative. He was a former undertaker with more than the usual interest in such matters. Yet he kept silent. Why? The answer could be that he knew about the note or message. We know that Borden first appeared in town that morning at 9:30. He left the house later than usual, so he was still at home when Bridget was being sick in the back yard, and when the note could have arrived. Since he knew about it, he asked no questions and made no comment. In view of this, it is very possible that a note was delivered.

Why then didn't the person who wrote it or the messenger who delivered it come forward and say so?

Again we have several facts that offer a possible explanation. Fall River, as has been pointed out, had a large immigrant population. Some of these people spoke English with difficulty. It is well known that many aliens of that era had an unreasonable fear of police and did not want to get involved with the law no matter how innocent they were. Police in all cities are familiar with this pattern of behavior. Why can we assume that the note may have come from such a foreigner? Again the reason is based on testimony. Lizzie stated at the inquest that, when asked if she would change her dress, her stepmother said, "No, this is good enough." Although Mrs. Borden was a person who would probably respond to an appeal for assistance from a foreigner, she was also a member of an old Fall River family who regarded these aliens as socially unimportant. Her reply, "No, this is good enough," would be characteristic of her if she were planning to make a brief call at the home of such a family.

Borden's lack of curiosity is a strong indication of prior knowledge, and Mrs. Borden's indifference to her clothes is an equally strong indication that the message did not come from a friend or a social equal. And if it was a written note which was received, its disappearance can be easily explained by the fact that Mrs. Borden was cleaning the downstairs rooms after breakfast and the Bordens did use their kitchen stove for the disposal of waste.

One thing is certain. Note or not, Mrs. Borden never left the house that morning. When she went upstairs to put on the pillowcases, somebody followed her and committed murder. The jury, which heard *all* the evidence, not merely the portions carefully selected by Pearson, agreed that it was not Lizzie Borden.

It is time now to see if we can discover who did use the ax.

X

The Big Question

Some two weeks after the trial many people thought the Borden murders had been solved. A letter was found on a street in Rome, New York, addressed to Joseph W. Carpenter, Jr., at Albany. The curious finder read the letter and then hurried to police. It was dated June 22, 1893, and read:

My dear Husband:

Lizzie has been acquitted, and I don't think they can do anything with you now. I want you to come home to spend the Fourth. The papers give a description of the man seen over the fence on the morning of the murder. Can you prove where you were on the morning of the murder?

Annie

There was immediate excitement. Fall River police had no difficulty in recognizing Carpenter's name. He was the former Borden & Almy bookkeeper who had stolen $6,000 but had escaped prosecution when he returned the money.

The reference in the letter to the man seen over the fence had been one of the early false clues in the Borden murders. A neighbor had reported seeing a man clambering over the six-foot-high back fence that separated the Borden property from a stonemason's yard on Third Street. Police had finally located a stoneyard employee who said he had climbed some material piled up near the barbed-wire-topped fence and reached over to snag a pear or two from one of Borden's trees. Knowlton, careful not to give the defense any opportunity to claim that the man on the fence was the killer, made the unfortunate man appear at the trial and publicly confess his pear-snatching.

As soon as the story of the letter broke, Fall River reporters interviewed Pete Driscoll, a barber who originally claimed he saw Carpenter in Fall River shortly before the murders in his shop at the Wilber House. Although police had investigated at that time and said Driscoll was mistaken, he still insisted it had been Carpenter whom he had shaved.

After Carpenter left Fall River in disgrace, he went to Buffalo where he began to manufacture ink. He later moved to Albany. His wife, meanwhile, quietly returned to Fall River and lived with relatives.

Spurred on by the letter, Fall River police again investigated Carpenter's alibi. They reported that he had been on a sales trip at that time and had not been near Fall River, once more clearing him as a suspect.

The police refused to discuss Carpenter's alibi with reporters, but the ninety minutes or more between the murders makes it extremely doubtful that he, or any passing thief, escaped lunatic, or other stranger from the outside could have murdered the Bordens.

With Lizzie eliminated, this leaves only three logical suspects for the Borden murders: Emma Borden, Uncle John Vinnicum Morse and Bridget Sullivan.

Here is the case against each and the reader's opportunity to solve for himself one of the most baffling murder cases in the history of crime.

It is true that Emma Borden was in Fairhaven the day of the murders, but this town, on the outskirts of New Bedford, is only fifteen miles away from Fall River. There was frequent train service between the two communities.

Emma arrived home toward evening of the day of the murders

in response to the telegram from Dr. Bowen. The police quickly cleared her as a suspect to their own satisfaction, if they suspected her at all. Pearson indicated that her alibi had been checked, but my careful study of the local newspapers, including the Fall River *Globe,* failed to disclose that any officers actually went to Fairhaven to make direct inquiries. The fact that Emma had received the telegram Dr. Bowen sent her appears to be the only evidence Fall River police thought necessary. In fact, by the time she did return home, some of the officers were concentrating solely on Lizzie.

Emma, who seldom left the house unless she was calling on one of her small circle of friends, was the least-known member of the family. She could have slipped into town unnoticed. During the trial she admitted frankly that she never had been too cordial to her stepmother after the house incident. Her behavior when she was a girl of fourteen, and refused to call the second wife by anything but her first name, shows that her resentment of Mrs. Borden was deep and of long standing. There are no indications of any affectionate bond between Emma and her father to match that between Lizzie and her father. Most commentators on the Borden case portray Emma as weak-willed, self-effacing and ineffectual. But, as has been shown, she was as strong-willed as Lizzie and her father when she wanted to be, and Knowlton learned quickly enough during the trial that she was a match for him in his attempts to shake her testimony. Emma, of course, knew the house well enough to have been able to conceal herself between the murders.

Although Pearson clung to the prosecution's belief that the handleless hatchet was the murder weapon, Dr. Wood's testimony was quite conclusive that it was not. I had the good fortune to locate the handleless hatchet during my research and I examined it. I am no stranger to medico-legal technique and have written a book largely devoted to it. There is a popular belief that bloodstains can be washed from metal surfaces. Dr.

Wood said at the trial that it was possible but indicated that a thorough job was required. He did not explain that what a scientist considers "thorough" goes far beyond what a layman would consider thorough. There are minute imperfections and blemishes on virtually any piece of metal. The handleless hatchet was a cheap one. The face had deteriorated badly over the years, but even when new there must have been many imperfections in so inexpensive a hatchet. The sides of the weapon used by the killer in the Borden murders had to be saturated with blood since some twenty-nine blows had been struck. Blood seeps into these tiny, almost microscopic imperfections, and no ordinary scrubbing can remove all traces. Long and repeated floodings are needed and sometimes chemicals also must be used if every trace of blood is to be removed.

There have been tremendous improvements in techniques, particularly in blood-grouping identification, since the days of Dr. Wood, but the basic method of determining the presence of blood still remains pretty much the same. The suspected weapon is treated with a specially prepared liquid which penetrates all the tiny imperfections. A chemical change in color occurs the instant the preparation comes into contact with even the slightest trace of blood; it does not matter how old or dried-out the trace may be. As Dr. Wood pointed out in his cross-examination, there was a recess in the face of the handleless hatchet in which dirt was still encrusted. Had there been any blood on that hatchet, it would have come in contact with this dirt. Since his test showed no trace, the handleless hatchet could not have been the murder weapon. This means that the actual weapon never has been found; it disappeared from the house.

Emma could have taken the weapon with her and disposed of it somewhere in the waters of Buzzards Bay where she was vacationing. She could have changed into another dress before leaving the house, taken the bloodstained garment with her, and disposed of it on the way back to Fairhaven. A horse and buggy was parked for an hour or more in front of the Borden home on the morning of the murders. The person who left the buggy there has never been identified. It was a busy street, conveniently near the shopping center, and unattended horses and wagons were often left at the curbside.

There are, of course, many weaknesses in any case against Emma. She didn't like her stepmother, but nothing is known to have occurred shortly before the crime that could have caused such a murderous rage. She had no way of knowing in advance whether an opportunity for murder existed. She would have been taking more than a fair risk of being seen and recognized during her travels. If she avoided the train and hired a buggy, the stableman might have recognized her. If police had checked on her more thoroughly than is indicated, she would be completely eliminated as a suspect.

Uncle John Vinnicum Morse was the immediate popular suspect. His sudden unannounced appearance at the Borden home was strange in that he did not carry an iota of baggage with him, although he clearly intended to stay overnight, if not longer.

Lizzie stated during the inquest that while her father and uncle were in the sitting room the afternoon before the murders, she had been disturbed by their voices and had closed her door, even though it was a very hot day.

It is evident that Lizzie did not tell everything she overheard between her father and her Uncle Morse. At that time Jennings had a young law associate named Arthur S. Phillips. A few years ago, not too long before his death, Phillips revealed in a newspaper story that he had always suspected Morse of the murders. He said Morse and Borden had quarreled violently in the house that day, information which must have come from Lizzie. It was obviously the sound of this argument that caused Lizzie to close her door.

The New Bedford *Standard-Times* has reported Knowlton as saying, long after the trial, that if he only knew what Borden said during his conversation with Morse, he would have convicted "somebody." Notice, Knowlton did not say that he would have obtained a conviction in the trial of Lizzie Borden. He said he would have convicted "somebody."

It is known that Morse did associate with a group of itinerant horse traders who made their headquarters at Westport, a town not far from Fall River. They were a vagabond lot and considered to be shady and undesirable characters. Fall River police did go to Westport to see if they could get any information against Morse and possibly find an accomplice whom he might have hired from among these men. The officers found no incriminating information.

Morse's alibi was not as solid as it seemed. He said he returned from the visit to his niece on the 11:20 streetcar. The woman in the house where the niece was staying backed up his story and said she left when he did to shop for her dinner. Fall River is not a fashionable town. The dinner hour there was twelve noon. If this woman had delayed until after 11:20 to start her shopping, she would have had little time in which to prepare the substantial meal that was eaten at dinner in those days. It is possible that Morse told the woman it was 11:20, but it could have been earlier, since she did serve dinner on time. Police did make an attempt to check on Morse's alibi. They interviewed the conductor of the streetcar Morse said he had taken, but the man did not remember Morse as a passenger. Questioned further, Morse said that there had been four or five priests riding on the same car with him. The conductor did recall having priests as passengers and this satisfied police, although the conductor also pointed out that in heavily Catholic Fall River there were priests riding on almost every trip the streetcar made, so Morse's statement really proved nothing.

We do know that Morse left the house before nine o'clock.

Bridget testified she saw him leave through the side door. Morse said Borden let him out and locked the screen door. From that point on he said he went to the post office and then walked leisurely to where his niece was staying, more than a mile away. He met nobody he knew on this walk. There is no accounting of his movements in this long gap of time which covers the early hours when Mrs. Borden was killed.

Morse testified that while he was having breakfast in the dining room, Mrs. Borden told the servant, "Bridget, I want you to wash these windows today." Bridget's testimony was in direct contradiction. She said it was after she returned from her vomiting spell in the back yard that Mrs. Borden told her to wash the windows. This was long after Morse had left the house.

Morse's knowledge of what Mrs. Borden told Bridget could indicate that he had returned secretly to the house and was hidden there. He knew the house fairly well, he had been there on two previous visits during the past three or four months alone. And despite Knowlton's attempts to show that the house was locked up tighter than a drum, this was not true. The screen door was unlocked for some ten or fifteen minutes while Bridget was sick in the back. It was unlocked all the time she was washing windows. Morse could have returned openly while Bridget was sick in the back yard and gone up to the room he had occupied. Mrs. Borden would not have been alarmed if she saw Morse with an ax or hatchet in his hand. He had been to the farm the previous day and he could have said they needed the ax or hatchet at the farm. Mrs. Borden would have had no reason to disbelieve him and he could have approached close enough to her to swing before she could cry out. He could have left for Weybosset Street after her murder and made it in plenty of time by using the streetcar.

If he took an earlier streetcar than the 11:20 on his return, he could have arrived at the Borden house shortly after Mr. Borden came home. With Lizzie in the barn, the screen door unlocked and Bridget upstairs in her attic room, he would have had free and easy access to the house. With the second murder over, he could have left, hidden the weapon in some vacant lot or an abandoned cistern in the neighborhood. His unconcerned stroll down the side of the house to a pear tree, with crowds already gathering in front of the building and Sawyer guarding the side door, was odd. There was no close examination of his clothes for bloodstains, and certainly no scientific test was made of them. And for a man who traveled around without any change of clothing, a few more stains on his dark suit may very well have gone unnoticed.

The motive may have been the mysterious quarrel; there was no financial gain for Morse in the murders.

On the other side of the ledger is the fact that he did see his niece and the woman with whom she was staying. The time would have been shortly after the murder of Mrs. Borden and they noticed nothing unusual in his behavior. He said he had promised Mrs. Borden to return in time for dinner and that was close to the time when he did turn up at the Borden house.

What did Pearson say about Bridget Sullivan as a possible suspect in his trial-book essay? He wrote:

"The police soon ceased to look upon either Bridget or Mr. Morse as in possession of guilty knowledge. Neither had any interest in the deaths; indeed, it was probably to Mr. Morse's advantage to have Mr. and Mrs. Borden alive. Both he and Bridget were exonerated by Lizzie herself." That was his complete discussion of Bridget Sullivan as a possible suspect.

Although Pearson disbelieved almost everything Lizzie said, and read a sinister purpose into almost everything she did, he happily accepted her statement about Bridget as the whole truth. He felt nothing further need be said about the servant girl.

The exoneration Pearson speaks of is not an exoneration, but

Lizzie's expression of her opinion, as reported in the testimony of Assistant Marshal Fleet. This officer had asked Lizzie if she suspected her Uncle Morse, and she replied she didn't think he did it because he left the house before the murders and returned after them. Fleet asked the same question about Bridget, and Lizzie pointed out that as far as she knew Bridget had gone up to her room before her father's murder and came down when she called her.

Lizzie, actually, never named any suspect. She told police about the prospective tenant she had heard quarreling with her father some weeks before the murders, but she said she thought he was from out of town because she heard him mention something about talking to his partner. And, much as she detested Hiram Harrington, she also did not accuse him. At the inquest she was asked specifically whether she knew anybody her father had bad feelings toward, or who had bad feelings toward her father. She replied, "I know of one man that has not been friendly with him. They have not been friendly for years." Asked who this was, she named Harrington. Her statement certainly was true; the press reported the same facts in using Harrington's interview, but Lizzie did not suggest at the inquest that Harrington was the killer.

When I interviewed Kirby, who as a boy picked up pears in the Borden yard, I asked if anybody else in the household besides Lizzie and Morse had been under any suspicion at the time of the murders. He said he had not heard of anybody else. "How about Bridget Sullivan?" I inquired. "Oh, she was just the maid there," he replied, waving a hand to indicate how completely unimportant she was. Kirby was, of course, reflecting the opinion that existed at the time of the murders.

Everyone somehow manages to overlook completely the fact that, as far as we know, there were exactly two people in and about the house at the time of both murders: Lizzie Borden and Bridget Sullivan.

All the officials on the case seem to have been afflicted with a similar myopia as far as Bridget was concerned, although records in police files contain many reports of servants who have murdered their employers.* True, it is no longer cricket for the butler to be the killer in mystery fiction, but we are dealing here with actual people in real life and not imaginary characters and situations.

The actions of Bridget should be examined, since she was there and opportunity did exist, if only to establish her innocence. There are also other factors that require closer examination.

The legend as it exists in Fall River today always includes the solemn assurance that Bridget returned to Ireland after the trial with a "big bundle" of cash which Lizzie gave her for keeping her mouth shut. The people who believe and retell the legend have apparently never troubled to read the trial testimony and do not know that the maid changed her testimony on several key points, always to the detriment of Lizzie. If Bridget did get any bundles of cash, the last person who would have rewarded her for services rendered would have been Lizzie Borden.

Bridget was born in Ireland, one of fourteen children. She was apparently the pioneer in her family because she had no close relatives in this country at that time. She worked as a domestic, first in Newport for a year, and then in South Bethle-

---

*This writer, a few years ago, investigated a case in the Bronx. A doctor's wife had been bludgeoned to death with a baseball bat as well as slashed seventeen times with a knife. The maid seemed to have a perfect alibi. She said her mistress had been resting when she left the apartment to go marketing. The maid had gone directly to two stores where she placed orders to be delivered, and then met the victim's daughter after school and took her to her weekly dancing lesson. The servant "discovered" the body when she returned home with the child several hours later. New York police, who do not exclude anybody as a suspect without thorough investigation, finally gathered information pointing to the maid, who then confessed. Her motive? The doctor's wife had scolded her for not cleaning a room properly.

hem, Pennsylvania, for another year. She finally settled in Fall River and, after being employed for a time by a Mrs. Reed, was hired by the Bordens.

I have previously described how, during the week of the murder, Bridget spent the first few hot days scrubbing and ironing clothes. On Thursday, the morning of the murders, Bridget testified that when she got up she had a headache and did not feel well. She came down about 6:15 A.M., busied herself with her chores, got the stove fire going, and then when Mrs. Borden had come down and told her what to prepare for breakfast, she did the cooking.

We now come to the first discrepancy in her story. Morse testified that during breakfast between 7:00 and 7:30, he heard Mrs. Borden say to the servant, "Bridget, I want you to wash these windows today." They were then in the dining room. Notice the words Mrs. Borden used. Since there was no discussion of just what windows Mrs. Borden wanted washed, and we know, from later events, that she was referring to the downstairs windows, this would indicate some prior discussion with Bridget.

Bridget gave an entirely different version. She testified that Lizzie came down about nine o'clock, entered the kitchen, "left down" the slop pail, and discussed breakfast with her. Bridget then became ill and dashed out for some ten to fifteen minutes. It was only after her return, when, as Bridget put it, "As I was fixing my dining-room table," that Mrs. Borden asked her if she had anything to do that morning. Her exact testimony then was: "I said, no, not particular, if she had anything for me to do. She said she wanted the windows washed. I asked her how and she said inside and outside both, they are awful dirty." There is quite a lot of difference between Morse's testimony on the window washing and that given by Bridget.

Can we determine who was telling the truth? Let us examine the testimony and Bridget's story so far. Breakfast, which started at seven o'clock, was over for the elderly Bordens and Morse by 7:30; Morse and Bridget both stated this on the stand. Bridget testified she then ate her breakfast. Give her a half hour to eat, which brings the time to eight o'clock that morning when she was ready for her regular after-breakfast chores of washing the dishes and clearing up the dining-room table.

An hour passes and Lizzie comes down. It is now about nine o'clock.

Bridget said she talked to Lizzie briefly, became ill and went outside. Upon her return, what did she do? According to her own testimony, she still had dishes to wash and the stove to clean. It was only after she finished these tasks, went into the dining room and began fixing the table there that she said she received instructions for the first time from Mrs. Borden to wash the windows. One wonders why Bridget would not have completed her simple after-breakfast chores in that hour between eight and nine o'clock.

Let us look now at a second discrepancy in Bridget's same story. Here is Lizzie's inquest testimony covering her movements just after she had come downstairs.

Q: Where was Maggie?

A: Just came in the back door with the long pole, brush, and put the brush on the handle, and getting her pail of water; she was going to wash the windows around the house. She said Mrs. Borden wanted her to.

Q: Did you get your breakfast that morning?

A: I did not eat any breakfast; I did not feel as though I wanted any.

Q: Were the breakfast things put away when you got down?

A: Everything except the coffeepot; I am not sure whether that was on the stove or not.

Q: What was the next thing that happened after you got down?

A: Maggie went out-of-doors to wash the windows, and

Father came out into the kitchen and said he did not know whether he would go down to the post office or not. And then I sprinkled some handkerchiefs to iron.

Once again this is a direct contradiction of Bridget's story. Lizzie said when she came down Bridget already had her cleaning equipment and was drawing a pail of water to start washing the windows. But Bridget said that she did not even get instructions to wash the windows until *after* Lizzie had come down, *after* she had gone outside and was sick, and *after* she had come back and was fixing the dining-room table. Which story is more logical—that Bridget had completed her after-breakfast chores in the hour between eight and nine o'clock and had already gathered her equipment for cleaning windows as Lizzie said, or that she still had not completed those chores as Bridget said? Add to this Morse's testimony that during breakfast he heard Mrs. Borden instruct Bridget to wash those windows. Which story is more believable? It is to be regretted that Pearson, for reasons known only to himself, eliminated the window-washing episode from Morse's testimony in his trial book, so that the contradictory statement by Bridget was never presented to the serious students of the crime.

Think whatever you wish of Lizzie Borden, think that she is the killer of her father and stepmother, but can you produce a single reason why she should have lied about what Bridget was doing when Lizzie came down that morning? Lizzie had absolutely nothing to gain by lying about this, and it would have been pointless for her to make up so involved a story about the brushes and pail of water. In fact, Lizzie's story made the case against her even stronger by placing Bridget outside even earlier.

What did Bridget have to gain by lying? Here we have something. Bridget was asked at the trial what time she had started to wash the windows and she replied, "Nine-thirty." Lizzie placed this at about nine o'clock. Bridget's story gave her a half hour of unexplained time on the morning of the murders—a half-hour covering the very time during which doctors said Mrs. Borden might have been murdered!

Dr. Wood, the toxicologist who examined the stomach contents, estimated that Mrs. Borden had been murdered about an hour and a half before her husband, which would place it about 9:30. Asked if he were fixing a limited time, he said the murder could have occurred within a half-hour either way of this statement. Mrs. Borden's murder, then, could have taken place shortly after 9:00 A.M. Dr. Cheever testified that Mrs. Borden might have been murdered about two hours before her husband. This again placed the possible time of the murder not long after nine o'clock. Lizzie, at the inquest, stated that the last time she saw her stepmother alive was when she came down about nine o'clock. *It was Bridget, and Bridget alone, who said Mrs. Borden was still alive about 9:30, and then placed herself outside the house.*

Bridget's own testimony was that she washed the exterior of the sitting-room, parlor and dining-room windows, a total of seven in all. Curiously, she ignored the first-floor kitchen, pantry and sinkroom windows.

Those seven windows she cleaned, ordinary house-size double-hung windows, took her, by her own testimony, at least an hour or more to wash, with a few minutes out to chat with the Kelly girl over the south-side fence. Bridget's outside washing consisted of scrubbing the windows down with a long-handled brush and then rinsing them off. She said she entered the house only shortly before Borden came home, and, again by her own testimony, had washed only the top half of her first inside window when she stopped to admit him. In washing the inside windows, Bridget used a hand basin, rags and a stepladder. She had to be more careful about not spilling water. The washing of the inside windows should take as long, if not longer than

those on the outside, where she was not burdened with moving
and setting up a stepladder in front of each window. Mr. Borden
came home about 10:45; Bridget testified she was up in her room
at eleven o'clock. In those fifteen minutes Bridget had not only
washed the inside of the same windows that took her more than
an hour outside, but she also had washed out the rags she had
used and was already upstairs in her attic room!

Why did it take Bridget so much longer to wash the windows
outside than it did to wash the same windows inside? Bridget
could have taken time off from her outside window-washing
chores to enter the house when she saw Lizzie go down to the
water closet in the cellar. Bridget's vomiting spell could have
been a reaction after the murder of Mrs. Borden.

The behavior of a person after a murder is a relevant and
legitimate subject of inquiry. The prosecution and Pearson
made much of Lizzie Borden's conduct after the murders.

The trial testimony presented a picture of a scared and quiv-
ering servant girl, who, when Dr. Bowen asked for a sheet to
cover the body of Mr. Borden, was too frightened to go alone to
the Borden bedroom to get it. Mrs. Churchill volunteered to go
up with her, and when they reached the bedroom, the trembling
Bridget, still too fearful to enter, told Mrs. Churchill in which
drawer the sheets were kept. The neighbor entered the room
alone, got a sheet and both of them came back down together.

Then, a short time later, when Lizzie said she thought she had
heard Mrs. Borden come in the house and asked Bridget to look
for her, the testimony again presented the picture of a frightened
maid, unwilling to go alone, and once more Mrs. Churchill
volunteered to accompany her.

The logical place to have started the search for Mrs. Borden
was in her bedroom. Only the rear staircase led there. True, Mrs.
Churchill had already gone into the Borden bedroom, but the
elder Bordens occupied a two-room suite. Mrs. Churchill had
not searched the bedroom, nor had she entered the smaller

adjacent room. Mrs. Churchill testified that when they went to look for Mrs. Borden, "Bridget was just ahead of me; *she led the way.*"

Where did Bridget lead?

Not up the back staircase to Mrs. Borden's suite. Without hesitation, Bridget went immediately into the sitting room where the sheet-covered body of Borden lay, out into the front entry and up the front stairs. Bridget was not too familiar with the front stairs leading to the second floor. She seldom had duties taking her to the front bedroom. Kieran, the civil engineer, testified he could not see a body on the guest-room floor on the far side of the bed, when he walked up the stairs in a normal fashion. There was exactly one spot on the stairs where you could see a body, and you had to pause at that precise spot in order to see it. As he explained in his testimony, a person walking up the stairs would normally have no reason to pause there. Yet Bridget did just that.

What happened when this badly frightened servant girl saw

TIME TABLE THE DAY OF THE MURDERS

A.M.

6:00	Morse wakes up, comes downstairs to sitting room.
6:15	Bridget comes down to kitchen.
6:30	Mrs. Borden comes down.
6:35	Mr. Borden comes down, empties slop pitcher in back yard; opens barn door, picks basket of pears, washes in kitchen.
7:00	Morse, Mr. and Mrs. Borden start breakfast. During breakfast Mrs. Borden tells Bridget to "wash these windows today." (Morse's testimony.)
7:30	Breakfast finished. Mrs. Borden starts dusting first floor. Bridget starts her own breakfast.
8:00	Bridget, having eaten, clears table, starts washing dishes.
8:40	Morse leaves the house. Note or message may have arrived between then and 9:00.
8:45	Mr. Borden goes upstairs; last time he is seen by Bridget until he returns home shortly before his murder.
9:00	Lizzie comes downstairs.

(*Continued overleaf*)

	LIZZIE'S STORY	BRIDGET'S STORY	COMMENT
9:00	Mrs. Borden in dining room, tells her about note; asks her to address paper wrappers. *Last time she sees Mrs. Borden alive.* Kitchen clean, dishes washed. Does not eat breakfast. Bridget has pole, brush, tells her Mrs. Borden wants windows washed.	Hears Lizzie and Mrs. Borden talking in dining room. Is washing dishes when Lizzie enters kitchen. Lizzie says she will get her own breakfast.	Bridget, according to her own testimony, cleared table and began washing dishes after her breakfast, so she has been washing dishes now for at least an hour, since 8:00 A.M.
9:03 } 9:05	Bridget fills pail with water, leaves by side door to wash outside windows.	Becomes ill and hurries out to back yard.	
9:05	Speaks to father in kitchen about mailing letter to Emma. Sprinkles handkerchiefs to iron. Sets up board on dining-room table. Eats a pear. (Uncertain whether she ate a cookie or two. May have addressed paper wrappers while waiting for iron to heat.) Irons several handkerchiefs until iron cools.	Is sick in back yard from 10 to 15 minutes.	Mr. Borden did mail Lizzie's letter to Emma. It was returned from Fairhaven. Bridget must have been very ill to vomit all that time.
9:20	(Mr. Borden probably leaves the house about this time. Neither Bridget nor Lizzie sees him leave.)		
9:20 to 9:30	Is still occupied as above.	Returns from yard, resumes washing dishes, cleans stove, goes to dining room to fix table.	Would Bridget still be working on after-breakfast chores? Lizzie said kitchen cleaned up by 9:00.

————— BRIDGET'S UNEXPLAINED HALF HOUR —————

————— SOMETIME DURING THIS PERIOD —————

Mrs. Borden began feather-dusting sitting room, dining room, and front entry right after breakfast at 7:30. The rooms and hall are small. Would she still be doing this two hours later?

Morse testified that Bridget received orders between 7:00 and 7:30 to wash windows. Lizzie said Bridget was preparing to wash windows when she came down at 9:00.

These 7 windows took Bridget over an hour. She did not wash the kitchen and back windows on first floor.

Mrs. Borden is feather-dusting between sitting room and dining room.

Mrs. Borden instructs her to wash windows. She closes windows, gets pail and other equipment. *Last time she sees Mrs. Borden alive.*

Goes outside to wash windows. Lizzie comes to side door. She tells Lizzie she can lock screen door, that she will get water in barn. Screen door is not locked. Washes 7 outside windows.

Enters house, locks screen door. Does not see Lizzie. Prepares to wash inside of windows.

Used basin, rags and stepladder for inside washing.

Lizzie subsequently said that she did this earlier.

(Continued overleaf)

9:30 to 10:35 Fire almost out in stove, puts in stick of wood and, while waiting for iron to reheat, begins reading a magazine. May have visited cellar water closet during part of this period; time she went to cellar not fixed at inquest.

10:35 to 10:40 Is occupied as above.

10:40 Goes up to her room with clean clothes. Sews a loop on a dress. Is there not longer than 5 minutes. Does not see Bridget.

LIZZIE'S STORY	BRIDGET'S STORY	COMMENT
10:45 (Mr. Borden comes home, finds doors locked.)		
First testified she was on her way down the steps when she heard father ring bell. Later said she was in kitchen when he arrived home.	She is washing top half of first inside window when she hears Mr. Borden trying to get in. Does not hear bell. Goes to door, has difficulty with locks, makes exclamation. Hears Lizzie laugh out loud on stairs behind her.	I believe Lizzie was on her way down the steps at the time.
(Mr. Borden enters house.)	They are overheard by Bridget, who confirmed this conversation.	
Speaks to father, tells him Mrs. Borden received note saying that somebody was ill.		
Father lies down on sofa.		
10:50 Leaves house, picks pears in back yard, then up into loft of barn. Stands at window eating pears, straightens shade, then searches box on workbench for lead for sinkers.	Lizzie sets up board in dining room, begins ironing, and tells Bridget that Mrs. Borden had received a note.	Lizzie said she did ironing much earlier, shortly after 9:00.
	Finishes inside windows, washes out rags.	Washing windows on the inside was more complicated because she had to be more careful not to spill water

WITHIN THIS PERIOD

and had to use stepladder and basin. But Bridget says that she finished in 15 minutes the same windows it took her an hour to do outside.

Time		
11:00	Is occupied as above.	Goes to her attic room to rest; hears City Hall clock strike 11 as she lies down on bed.
11:10 } 11:12 }	Returns to house, finds father, calls Bridget down.	Hears no sound until called down by Lizzie.

11:12 — Bridget goes across street for Dr. Bowen, finds he is not there, comes back. Mrs. Churchill sees her returning.

Lizzie sends Bridget for Miss Russell. Mrs. Churchill comes over to Borden house, then goes to stable, asks her yardman to get a doctor, is overheard by Cunningham.

11:15 — Cunningham phones police and newspapers. Mrs. Churchill returns to Borden house, followed by Dr. Bowen, Bridget and Miss Russell.

11:20 — First police officer arrives.

11:30 — Mrs. Borden's body found.

11:40 — Morse returns to the house.

Noon — Lizzie goes up to her room with Miss Russell, changes dress. Harrington and Fleet question her there. Tells both she has been up in loft of barn.

12:30 — Police begin search of house, barn and yard which continues all afternoon.

4:30 } 5:00 } — Emma arrives by train from Fairhaven. Testimony merely says "late afternoon."

Night — Bridget leaves house with bundle, stays away overnight. Returns Friday morning, leaves again either Friday or Saturday and is away for entire weekend.

a body on the floor? Did she rush back down the steps in terror? No. Mrs. Churchill testified that Bridget ran up the stairs into the guest room and *opened a shutter for a better light* before looking at the body. Mrs. Churchill, who had bravely volunteered twice, stopped on the steps where Bridget had paused, saw the body through the guest-room door, and did not dare go farther. Pearson gave only Mrs. Churchill's testimony about finding the body; he omitted all reference to the fact that it was Bridget who saw it first.

If, on Thursday night, anybody believed that a murdering maniac was loose in Fall River, then the safest haven was in the Borden house which was guarded by police officers. Alice Russell was not afraid to stay there overnight. Emma and Lizzie slept in the house. Yet Bridget Sullivan left with an unexamined bundle to stay the night at the home of a cousin. Could the bundle have contained her bloodstained dress and the missing murder weapon?

Bridget returned the next day during the first really intensive search of the house and, after serving supper, fled again, staying away over the weekend. While she was in the house she refused to enter the sitting room and she wept frequently. Police officials had meanwhile issued a statement saying that anybody who tried to leave the Borden house would be arrested on the spot. It was some of the reporters who saw Bridget returning with a bundle of her things and learned of her unauthorized absences.

Trial testimony shows that Bridget not only stayed away Thursday night and then the weekend; she also left the house four times during the morning of the murders. It was during one of these trips that Bridget may have been seen by Dwight Waring. When I interviewed Mr. Waring he recalled vividly the excitement of that morning. One incident was still fresh in his mind, so many years later, because it had always puzzled him. As he stood outside he saw a woman wearing a shawl come out of the Borden house and go across the street. Bridget, testify-

ing about her four trips, mentioned that she had put on her
shawl before leaving the house. Three of her four trips that
morning were to houses across the street. Waring said he
thought the woman he saw going across the street was Bridget
Sullivan, but this woman was limping somewhat as she walked
and he knew Bridget had no limp. As pointed out earlier, neither
the murder weapon nor a bloodstained dress has ever been
found. If Bridget did have the murder weapon concealed under
her skirt, it might account for Bridget's unusual manner of walking. If Bridget murdered the Bordens, she had more opportunities than any other suspect to destroy the evidence against her.

There are other instances of curious behavior by Bridget after
the murders. Porter wrote in his book that when Officer Doherty
went to pick up Bridget on the first day of the inquest, the maid
began weeping because she thought police had come to arrest
her. The officer was a strangely incurious man. He neglected
to ask Bridget why such a thought should have entered her head,
particularly since the police had indicated the very first day of
the investigation that they had no interest in Bridget as a possible suspect. And then several weeks later, when the preliminary
hearing was held in Fall River, Bridget came to court accompanied by her own lawyer, James T. Cummings. This was duly
reported by the press and Porter. In all the murder cases I have
studied, and there have been many, this is the first instance I
have ever come across in which an unsuspected witness in a case
is attended by a lawyer.

Some of Bridget's many changes in her trial testimony from
her earlier testimony at the inquest and the District Court hearing have been noted in previous chapters. All of these changes
helped the prosecution's case against Lizzie Borden.

During the trial, Mrs. Churchill testified that Bridget told
her, "Mrs. Borden had a note to go to see someone that was
sick, and she was dusting the sitting room, and she hurried off,

and says, 'She didn't tell me where she was going; she generally does.' "

There was much to-do later about this particular bit of testimony. Pearson, in his trial-book essay, claimed that Robinson misused this testimony in his summation to the jury in an attempt to show falsely that Bridget knew about the note from Mrs. Borden, whereas Bridget had testified that she heard about the note only from Lizzie. Despite Pearson's indignation, there was no attempt by Robinson to fool the jury. What he did was to read directly from the minutes to show that the information Bridget gave to Mrs. Churchill certainly went further than anything Lizzie ever said about the note, particularly that little detail, *"and she was dusting the sitting room."* How did Bridget know about that? Lizzie testified at the inquest that she never saw the note, never saw the messenger, and that her stepmother told her about it when she came down for the first time that morning. Her stepmother then was in the dining room. Yet Bridget told Mrs. Churchill that Mrs. Borden had been dusting the sitting room when the note arrived. Bridget either had to know about the note, or else she embroidered upon her testimony. If she did embroider upon the story, how much reliance can be placed on anything she said?

Another unexplained discrepancy in Bridget's testimony was her most emphatic and excited denials that she had removed the hatchets from the box in the cellar and handed them to Officer Mullaly. Mullaly was certain she had done so and he testified so at both the District Court hearing and at the trial. He would have been happy to grab the credit the way Medley and Desmond both claimed credit, simply for picking up the handleless hatchet on Monday, days after Fleet had seen it there. Here is Mullaly's examination at trial on this point:

Q: Did she go searching for them, trying to find where they were?

A: No, she seemed to know. She went right where they were, and I followed along.

He then added that she reached up into the box and took out two hatchets.

Q: And did she hand them into your hands?

A: She did.

Bridget did not deny leading Mullaly to the box, but she denied *touching* the hatchets in that box.

The various medical experts at the trial all agreed on one point: the wound on Mrs. Borden's forehead had been delivered when the killer faced the victim. Since Mrs. Borden's body had been found lying face down on the floor, and the first blow had to be powerful enough to stun, if not kill, there can be little doubt that this blow on the forehead was the first one. Mrs. Borden had to be facing her killer at the instant of the attack. If, as the prosecution contended, Lizzie had been on such bad terms with her stepmother, the sight of Lizzie with an ax or hatchet in her hands should have been enough to alarm Mrs. Borden to the extent of making some kind of outcry. The Borden house was quite close to the Churchill home, and only a few feet from the sidewalk. The guest bedroom had windows facing the busy street and the Churchill house. The windows were open. There were usually people walking about on Second Street and Mrs. Churchill, her mother, her son, a boarder, and her yardman, were in the house or the yard at the time Mrs. Borden was murdered. Nobody heard the slightest cry or sound from the Borden house.

In dealing with Morse as a suspect, I said he could have approached Mrs. Borden with an ax or hatchet without alarming her. The same holds true for Bridget Sullivan. Bridget occasionally chopped wood for the kitchen stove. If she had entered the guest bedroom carrying an ax there would be no reason for Mrs. Borden to be alarmed; she knew Bridget used it. Only Lizzie approaching her with an ax would have alarmed her.

The inference has been made repeatedly that only Lizzie Borden had the opportunity to murder her father and step-mother. This does not agree with the facts. One opportunity for Bridget to kill Mrs. Borden came when Lizzie went down to the cellar. By mutual agreement before the trial, with a touch of Victorian delicacy, the opposing counsel agreed not to mention the fact that on the morning of the murders Lizzie was in the final stages of a menstrual period. When Lizzie, at the inquest, stated she thought she had been in the cellar bathroom a few minutes, Knowlton himself hurriedly told her she might have been there longer than she realized. In addition to the time spent in the bathroom, she had to wash out certain cloths, and she also gathered and folded laundered clothes which she brought upstairs. The time she spent in the cellar would have given Bridget opportunity to come inside and murder Mrs. Borden.

But Bridget had an even greater opportunity during most of the morning, particularly during her half hour of unaccounted time. Bridget testified that she had closed the windows in the sitting room, dining room and parlor before going outside to wash the windows. This brought her into the front entry where she could have opened the locks on the front door. After going outside she could have slipped into the house through the front door and walked up the steps to the guestroom without being seen by Lizzie or Mr. Borden, if he was still in the house. Her apron would have protected her dress from bloodstains, and she testified that she had made many trips to the barn to get water. It would have been easy enough for her to wash out the apron while she was in the barn. The murder weapon could have been an old ax or hatchet kept in the barn. Later when Bridget entered the house to wash the inside windows, she could have relocked the front door.

Bridget's chance for Mr. Borden's murder came when Lizzie went to the barn. Lizzie said at the inquest that she left the house right after her father lay down on the sofa and that was within a few minutes after he came home. Lizzie did not see Bridget go upstairs. If Mr. Borden arrived home about 10:45, as evidence indicates, Lizzie would have left for the barn about 10:50. A twenty-minute visit to the barn would have brought her back to the house about 11:10. This part of her story does check since police were notified at 11:15.

It is only Bridget's unsupported story that places her and Lizzie in the house until eleven o'clock, which narrowed down the time of Mr. Borden's murder to the almost impossible ten minutes. If Lizzie told the truth, then Bridget's story gave the servant girl a vital additional ten minutes at the time of Mr. Borden's murder. Bridget then would have had about twenty minutes for the second murder, which would have given her time to clean up. The abandoned water tank in her attic room could have served as an excellent temporary hiding place for the murder weapon. This tank was not searched by police until the following day, and Bridget did leave the house that night with an unsearched bundle.

The question of motive also arises. Pearson pointed out that neither Morse nor Bridget could gain financially by the murders. Actually, few murders are committed for financial gain; most are perpetrated for emotional reasons. The thorough butchering of Mrs. Borden's head indicates that most of the fury of the killer was directed against her. We know that Bridget had undergone a difficult work week in all that heat. Morse's testimony as to Mrs. Borden's orders to "wash these windows today" indicates some friction in connection with the washing of the windows. It was the hottest day of the year. Bridget woke up not feeling well. She reported her conversation with Mrs. Borden as much later than the facts indicate. It is possible that Bridget did have a second conversation with Mrs. Borden, one in which she requested a postponement of washing the windows because of the weather and the way she felt. Mrs. Borden might have refused and thus triggered the emotional explosion that led to murder.* We know Borden left later than usual that morning. He could have heard Mrs. Borden turning down Bridget's request, and therefore Bridget had to eliminate him as a witness against her.

There are strong indications that Jennings suspected Bridget Sullivan and had received reports from the Pinkerton Detective Agency about her. At the Fall River hearing he asked several pointed questions about Bridget's changes in employment in Newport and elsewhere, mentioning the names of her employers. He also remarked to Judge Blaisdell in asking for Lizzie's release that Bridget's story had not been checked by police and said in court: "In the natural order of human nature who would be the party liable to be cross-questioned, her clothing to be examined, to be subjected to suspicion? Which of these two people?"

If his planned strategy was to bring out evidence against Bridget at the trial, this was dropped when Robinson entered the case as chief trial counsel. Robinson was content to shoot holes in the testimony of the prosecution's witnesses and so destroy the case against Lizzie. He refrained from confusing a jury by trying to build up a case against some other particular person.

The facts presented here against the three possible suspects have been taken almost entirely from official records. It is the opinion of this writer that Bridget's story does not stand up when examined closely. She told patent falsehoods on the witness stand. There are too many glaring flaws in her story which indicate that she did not tell the truth about her movements and actions on the morning of the murders. She may have been an uneducated servant girl, but she showed many times that she

---

* In a murder case I covered as a reporter, a young bride was killed by a window washer because she ordered him to use ammonia in the water and he resented being told what to do.

had the ability to think fast and brazen her way out of awkward situations. When she was trapped with her lie about Lizzie's not crying and confronted with her testimony at the inquest, she simply dug in her heels on the witness stand and loudly insisted during a battering examination by Robinson that the minutes had to be wrong. Most witnesses wilt under such a situation, but Bridget stood up to it. Knowlton could not and did not help her, nor did he try to refute the official stenographer who showed that Bridget was lying.

Bridget also put on a performance in the District Court hearing in Fall River when she blandly stated on the witness stand that she could not remember what she had discussed with Knowlton the previous evening. While Bridget demonstrated she knew how to take care of herself, I have little doubt that if the authorities had made a proper investigation of her story at the time of the murders, she would have been arrested instead of Lizzie. While this is the writer's personal opinion, it is based on two decades of writing about and examining crime. The reader can agree with the writer, make his own choice or reject them all. As in a trial, a reader is a juror and a juror is the sole judge of the facts.

XI

The Blight

It is a great American myth that when a jury in a murder trial returns with a verdict of Not Guilty, a defendant walks out of the courtroom a free person, ready to resume his rightful place in society. He is free as far as the courts and law enforcement agencies are concerned, but his reputation has been destroyed permanently in the eyes of some, and as long as the murder remains unsolved he is never free of suspicion. In addition, there will always be some people who will disagree with a verdict of acquittal in a murder trial, not on the basis of the facts or the evidence which can lead to honest disagreement, but on the basis that police must have known something or they would not have made an arrest. Yet those same people would recoil at a suggestion that we abandon jury trials and convict simply because police made an arrest, which is the logical conclusion of their reasoning.

Permanent suspicion is but one of the enduring blights an acquitted person has to face. He has become a public character and is fair game to the press, having lost the precious right of privacy.

When a murder and a trial have aroused such enormous and widespread interest as did the Lizzie Borden case, the public's desire for information does not end with the verdict. A good trial normally increases newspaper circulation; many people want to read about it, and as long as there is public interest no editor is going to sit back and pull off his men.

Lizzie got a foretaste of what her future life was going to be when reporters surrounded her immediately after the verdict and asked for details of her future plans. With the exception of Mrs. McGuirk, who had been successful on the basis of friendship, Lizzie had rebuffed repeated attempts by reporters to interview her, and she made little effort, while awaiting trial, to sway public opinion. She would not talk to reporters, and what was even worse, she never bothered denying stories no matter how patently false they were. She continued this practice throughout her life. She would have been far wiser, and much more intelligent, to have acted otherwise, particularly during the first weeks after the trial. Reporters would have obtained their follow-up stories, the public's curiosity would have been somewhat satisfied, and she would not have been watched so closely.

In the first flush of excitement immediately after the verdict, Lizzie did speak briefly to the newsmen who crowded around her in the courtroom. Julian Ralph of the New York *Sun* quoted her as saying, "A good many persons have talked to me as if they thought I would go and live somewhere else when my trial was over. I don't know what possesses them. I am going home and I am going to stay there. I never thought of doing anything else."

This statement was typical of Lizzie Borden's stiff-necked pride, her stubbornness, and the touch of arrogance she had inherited from her father. She was always blunt and forthright when she did talk, and this is probably one reason why Robinson did not place her on the stand when it was not necessary. Her direct way of speaking, without softening her words, could antagonize people.

Pearson claimed that some newspapers were quite maudlin and sentimental in their editorials praising Lizzie's acquittal, but there was nothing maudlin or sentimental in the way the press went after continuing news about Lizzie. Determined to get their follow-up stories, reporters kept the house on Second

Street under close observation and shouted questions at Lizzie whenever she appeared outside her door. She was unable to resume her normal activities. Some of the reporters who were hard pressed for news were not above inventing a few stories to keep their far-off editors satisfied, and these reports later found their way into the legend. When Lizzie made a trip to Taunton to see Mrs. Wright, some days after the trial, the editor of a local paper there sent out a flash saying that Lizzie had surrendered to Sheriff Wright. He later explained, somewhat lamely, that he had put out a "jocose statement."

This striving for some kind of news resulted in ludicrous situations. When Lizzie returned on the 8:15 P.M. train from New Bedford on the day of her acquittal, she had planned to go directly to Second Street, but was intercepted by friends who reported that a huge crowd had gathered in front of her home awaiting her arrival. Lizzie heeded the advice of Mrs. Holmes and stayed overnight with her. A reporter succeeded in getting inside this house and his paper proudly announced the next morning that it had an exclusive interview with Lizzie Borden. Although I have read the clipping many times, I have been unable to find a single word in the story attributed to Lizzie. Perhaps the paper did not want to mention that its reporter's exclusive interview with Lizzie seems to have consisted of her request that he leave.

Seeking some privacy, Lizzie appealed to a friend, the former Sarah Remington, who turned over to Lizzie an isolated cottage in a wooded point near Newport. Lizzie managed to slip away from watching reporters and spent several weeks there by herself. In appreciation, she later sent her friend a sterling silver pie fork as a gift. A descendant later revealed this incident and wrote that the pie fork was a "treasured possession in the family."

Emma, as the elder daughter, was appointed administratrix of her father's estate. In her first and only accounting to the court, her document stated: "Duly paid all debts and divided and distributed balance between myself and Lizzie A. Borden, the only two heirs." The two sisters shared their father's considerable wealth equally. They sold the old narrow house on Second Street and moved to a fourteen-room home on French Street in the fashionable hill section. Lizzie, separately, purchased some vacant land across the street, possibly to keep curiosity seekers from gathering there. The new home was named Maplecroft, and a cement slab bearing this title was set out at the front.

Legends are easier to start than to stop. The four-line verse about the ax is a catchy one, and it became a great favorite with children in Fall River who sang it while jumping rope and playing other games. Kirby said it was sung to the tune of "Ta-ra-ra-boom-de-ay." The acquittal did not stop the children from using it, and adults laughingly continued to repeat it.

The legend had been building up during the months before the trial, and while the acquittal temporarily halted the stories, Lizzie's continued cold-shouldering of the press resulted in episodes that swelled the legend. Shortly after she had moved, a reporter called at Maplecroft for an interview. Like all the others, he was turned down. He paid Lizzie back in this story which he sent out: "She is a regular attendant at church, where she is a member still, although the church did not extend its support during the trial." The newspapers, and even Pearson, described the many appearances of the Reverend Mr. Jubb at Lizzie's side, showing how strongly the church supported Lizzie. The reporter, having made his false point that Lizzie had been abandoned by her own church people, now poured it on. In the same story he stated that before Lizzie moved into Maplecroft she had asked a next-door neighbor to tear down his fence which separated the two properties. The man replied that if Lizzie Borden was going to be his neighbor, he was going to make his fence even higher. The reporter finished this dispatch off with a flourish, stating that Lizzie was being snubbed by her new neighbors.

The elderly lifelong residents of the area whom I questioned all agree that there never was a fence between Maplecroft and any of its adjacent neighbors while Lizzie lived there. The reporter's story seems to have been made up out of whole cloth, and in a cotton-mill town like Fall River there was plenty of whole cloth on hand. Lizzie, as usual, made the mistake of ignoring the story. With no denial on record, the legend makers seized upon this story and embroidered it. You are assured by many in Fall River today that her neighbors practically barricaded themselves behind high fences so that they would not even have to look at Lizzie Borden, and they forced her to become a virtual recluse. She must have been a somewhat unusual recluse, because so many of the same people who told this story also mentioned how often they had seen Lizzie riding about town in her car. In the early years after the trial, Lizzie maintained a stable with her own coachman to drive her horse and carriage. She also used a pony cart when she wanted to drive about herself.

The Fall River *Globe* was quiet for a while after the trial. Emboldened by her silence, the paper returned to its private war against Lizzie Borden and printed every rumor its busy reporters could gather against her. It also inaugurated the custom of celebrating the anniversary date of the murders with stories filled with innuendo and carrying such a headline as PERHAPS MURDERER OR MURDERESS MAY BE IN THE CITY. WHO CAN TELL? The paper still aimed its editorial appeal at those who had grievances, whether real or imaginary, against the old families, and the *Globe* readers showed no hesitancy in accepting any stories against Lizzie. In his trial-book essay, Pearson mentioned some of these annual stories and added that it finally came to an end when a priest suggested that the paper discontinue the attacks. Pearson did not discuss the background of the *Globe,* or mention the many false stories it published right from the start.

During a period when newspapers were merging and cities lost many papers, the Fall River *Herald* and *News* combined and used the title of both as its new name. The *Globe* continued until 1929 and then sold out to its rivals. The new owners discontinued its publication. Perhaps because they did not consider the *Globe's* name an asset, they did not add its title to the masthead, and so the Fall River *Globe* died.

There are some indications that romance may have entered Lizzie Borden's life about three years after her trial, when she was a woman of thirty-six. The Fall River *News*, which carefully checked its stories before using them, published a brief item that Lizzie's friends were expecting her to announce her engagement to a Swansea schoolteacher. It hinted that the couple had known each other since childhood; he had lived on a farm near where Lizzie had spent her summers. The story was picked up by the wire services and out-of-town reporters soon swarmed into Fall River and Swansea. The schoolteacher went into hiding. Lizzie, of course, maintained her aloofness from the press. If anything ever convinced Lizzie that the blight of the trial had made her public property, it probably was this incident. No engagement was ever announced and Lizzie never married.

One may reasonably ask why Lizzie Borden did not move away from Fall River and lose herself in the anonymity of a large city. The answer lies in her character. She was a stubborn woman and as she said at the end of her trial, "I am going home and I am going to stay there."

The story of the expected engagement appeared on December 10, 1896. I found a letter written by Lizzie dated December 12, two days later, which could indicate that there was no truth to the engagement story, but it may have been referring to some other incident. Lizzie Borden had, from a researcher's viewpoint, an irritating habit of starting all her letters with the salutation, "My dear Friend," thus making it impossible to

identify the person to whom it was written. This letter shows
Lizzie's attitude toward the stories circulating about her.

MY DEAR FRIEND:

*I am more sorry than I can tell you that you have had any
trouble over the false and silly story that has been about the
last week or so. How or when it started I have not the least idea.
But never for a moment did I think you or your girls started it.
Of course I am feeling very badly about it but I must just bear
[it] as I have in the past. I do hope you will not be annoyed
again. Take care of yourself, so you can get well.*

                              Yours sincerely,

                                        L. A. BORDEN

Lizzie was in the news again the following year when the papers reported that the Tilden-Thurber Corporation, Providence
silversmiths, had obtained a warrant charging her with theft.
The stories stated that two paintings on porcelain had disappeared from the store without any recorded sale. Some time later a woman brought in one of them, titled "Love's Dream," to
have it repaired. Asked how she had acquired it, the woman replied that it was a gift from Lizzie Borden. The store then obtained the warrant, but no further news about the incident
ever appeared in newspapers and the warrant was not served.

When Pearson was preparing his original essay on the Borden case in 1924 he wrote to Tilden-Thurber, and an official of
the firm replied that the store had no record of the incident,
but his recollection was that the matter had been "adjusted."
From that Pearson inferred, particularly in his original essay,
that Lizzie had stolen the paintings and settled out of court
with the store.

The action by the firm in obtaining a warrant against a
wealthy client was unusual; such matters are usually handled
quietly. The fact that it did obtain a warrant, with all the attendant publicity, and then did not immediately serve it, al-

though Fall River is only eighteen miles away, is also unusual.
The word "adjusted" is ambiguous. It could mean, as Pearson
inferred, that the adjustment had been made by Lizzie Borden.
It could also mean, if the store had been in error, that the store
had made the adjustment by dropping the charge.

There are many women who are kleptomaniacs. Store records and police files show that these women continue to steal,
even after they are caught. With all the publicity and all the
digging that has been done to find incidents unfavorable to Lizzie Borden, there has never been the slightest hint from any
other source that she had shoplifted any other merchandise. The
absence of any store records, the absence of any evidence to show
that Lizzie Borden followed the customary behavior pattern of
kleptomaniacs, plus the undeniable fact that so many stories
about her have proven to be false when records could be
checked, makes me doubt that the Pearson inference is correct.

Lizzie Borden maintained her customary silence. The incident did not appear to disturb her. In a letter written in August
of that year, she gave this picture of her summer activities at
home.

My dear friend:

*Where are you, how are you and what are you doing? I
dreamed of you the other night, but I do not dare to put my
dreams on paper. Have you been away and has your little niece
been to visit you? We have been here all summer. I spend much
of the time on the piazza in my steamer chair reading and building castles in the air. I hope you have been away and are well
and strong now. Do you expect to work this fall and are you going to New York? Every time we pass your corner the pony wants
to turn down. The weather has been so warm and full of thun-
derstorms I am quite ready for fall. I should be very glad to
hear from you.*

L. A. BORDEN

Lizzie gave an indication of how much she disliked her first name when she changed it to Lizbeth in the Fall River telephone directory. It was not a legal change. She usually signed her letters L. A. Borden and used the name Lizzie on legal documents.

In order to avoid the constant watch on her movements in Fall River, Lizzie made occasional trips to New York or Boston, where she would attend the theater and concerts. In 1904, at a summer resort, Lizzie met Nance O'Neil, a well-known Boston actress of that day, and the two women became friends. The following year the actress appeared in a show on the road and played at a theater in Fall River. To celebrate this event, Lizzie invited Miss O'Neil and the others of the cast to a party at Maplecroft. Emma did not approve of her sister's friendship with an actress, was shocked when Lizzie entertained a theatrical troupe in their own home, and they quarreled about it. It was not long after this that Lizzie and Emma parted company. Emma left the house and lived a while with the sister of the Reverend Mr. Jubb. The break was complete and the two sisters did not see each other again.

Lizzie's party also scandalized some of the old families of Fall River, who clung to their standards that nice people did not associate with "persons of the theater." I interviewed several elderly women in Fall River, members of the old families, and they all mentioned this incident in tones of voice that showed they were still shocked at the thought of having an actress as a friend.

Lizzie proved to be as stubborn about her friendship with Miss O'Neil as she was in her determination to remain in Fall River. There can be little doubt that her friendship did cause some of the old families to snub her after that. But Lizzie continued her trips to New York, Washington, and Boston, returning each time to Maplecroft. She lived well, employing a housekeeper, a maid and a chauffeur, even though she was alone. Her favorite food was not mutton or mutton broth, but a dish that does not find great favor with the general public—tripe with mushrooms.

Despite her experiences, Lizzie showed no signs of bitterness in her dealings with people; those who came in contact with her after the trial said she always was a very kind person. The son of a house painter, whose services were used by Lizzie for many years, quoted his father as saying that Lizzie always supplied his workmen with cold drinks, and if the weather was exceptionally hot, she would ask that they stop work until it became cooler and would pay the bill for their full time. Neighborhood boys, contrary to the legend, found her an easy mark; she always bought church raffle tickets and other things from them. Toddlers who lived in the area were sure of getting cookies whenever they wandered over to see Lizzie. One was Victoria Endicott Lincoln, who later became a noted novelist. Lizzie demonstrated a continuing affection for animals. A bull terrier was seated beside her whenever she went for a ride, and there were always several cats and a litter of kittens around Maplecroft. She purchased peanuts regularly and put them on the lawn for squirrels. When her dogs died they were buried in Pine Ridge Cemetery of the Animal Rescue League, and Lizzie had a marker erected which read, "Sleeping Awhile."

Twenty years after the murders, an enterprising Boston reporter managed to obtain an interview with Emma. "The happenings in the French Street house that caused me to leave I must refuse to talk about," Emma said. "I did not go until conditions became absolutely unbearable." But while Emma no longer spoke to Lizzie and was completely estranged from her, she warmly defended her sister against the murder charge. "Often it has occurred to me how strange is the fact that no one save Lizzie was ever brought to trial . . . as for her being guilty I say, 'No' and decidedly, 'No.' Here is the strongest thing that has impressed me of Lizzie's innocence. The authorities never found the ax or the implement or whatever it was that figured in the killing. If Lizzie had done that deed, she could never have hidden the instrument of death so the police could never find it." In the same interview Emma stated, "Time and again she has avowed her innocence to me and I believe her."

In 1925, Emma, then living in Providence, petitioned the Probate Court at Taunton to make an equal distribution of the A. J. Borden Building. She was, in effect, requesting that the building be sold. Still remembering her father's advice, Lizzie managed to raise sufficient funds to buy out Emma's half and she became the sole owner of the building bearing her father's name. Here Lizzie demonstrated her sound business judgment. The property continued to increase in value and Lizzie's estate at her death was far more valuable than Emma's, even though she lived on a more expensive scale than her sister.

The stories of the legend, confined largely to Fall River, received far wider distribution when Pearson began writing about the case. National interest revived and the literature on the case grew. Alexander Woollcott and many others followed Pearson in writing about Lizzie Borden. Novelists also turned their attention to the crime. Mrs. Belloc Lowndes wrote a strange novel, *Lizzie Borden: A Study in Conjecture*. In it she gave Lizzie a mysterious European lover whom she presumably met during her summer tour two years before the murders. Edward Hale Bierstadt wrote *Satan Was a Man,* a psychological study of a fictional killer who had studied famous murder cases and who, at different times, believed himself to be the various murderers. One of these was Lizzie Borden.

Dramatists seem to have been fascinated by Lizzie. *Nine Pine Street,* by John Colton and Carlton Miles, opened at the Longacre Theatre on April 27, 1933, and ran for three weeks, with Lillian Gish playing the role of Lizzie Borden, known in the play as Effie Holden; her romantic interest was a minister. Another drama, *The Legend of Lizzie,* opened on February 9,

1959, and closed after only two performances. Lizzie probably also inspired *Suspect,* a play starring Pauline Lord in the role of an unconvicted ax murderess seeking anonymity years after the crime. It was no secret that the central character in *The Man Who Came to Dinner,* by Moss Hart and George Kaufman, was a take-off on Woollcott. Playing on Woollcott's fondness for the Lizzie Borden case, the authors introduced a Lizzie type of character in the comedy and used the famous four-line verse about the ax. In a strange coincidence, while the present book was being written, my daughter was selected to play the Lizzie role in a school presentation of the play. When asked what interpretation she was giving to the part, she replied, "Oh, I'm making her a kind of beatnik character."

The ballet *Fall River Legend,* with choreography by Agnes De Mille, was first presented in 1948 by the American Ballet Theatre. It became an immediate hit. I was fortunate enough to attend the premiere performance and have renewed my acquaintance with it since. The ballet, which is performed almost every year, opens with Lizzie before the gallows listening to the reading of the indictment. It does not pretend to tell the actual story. In a series of flashbacks, Lizzie is shown before her mother's death having a happy childhood, then comes her grief at her mother's death, her father's remarriage, and her stepmother's interference with her life, even to the extent of disrupting a blossoming romance, also with a pastor. Finally Lizzie murders her father and stepmother.

Two writers have advanced the possibility that Lizzie Borden was innocent, in each instance somewhat in the spirit of fun. Lillian de la Torre, in a fine one-act play, *Goodbye, Miss Lizzie Borden,* has Emma as the killer, with Lizzie bravely bearing the brunt of suspicion to protect her sister. Emma is portrayed as a rather weak-minded person. The murder weapon was hidden behind some loose bricks in a fireplace. Curiously, just after this play was first published in *Murder: Plain and Fanci-*

ful, edited by James Sandoe, a hatchet was found behind some bricks in a fireplace in the Second Street house. A workman later examined the hatchet and sheepishly identified it as one he had accidentally bricked into the fireplace several years before when working on a remodeling job.

In *The Case for Lizzie,* mystery novelists Richard W. Webb and Hugh C. Wheeler, who write under the pseudonym of Q. Patrick, offered what they called a theoretical reconstruction of the murders. They advanced the interesting thought that it was Mr. Borden who had killed his wife and then was accidentally killed by Lizzie after she discovered the murder. They accounted for the nine additional blows her father received by theorizing that Lizzie struck these after his death so that both murders would seem to have been done by an intruder who was a homicidal maniac. This article first appeared in *The Pocket Book of True Crime Stories* edited by Anthony Boucher.

The house on Second Street, now numbered 230, has gone through many changes of hands since it was sold by Lizzie and Emma. At one time, after Fall River police discovered that it was serving as headquarters for a bookmaker, they raided the place. Its present owners, Mr. and Mrs. John McGinn, have demonstrated how, with a few changes, the first floor could be considerably improved and made attractive. They maintain the second floor as a separate apartment for an elderly relative. McGinn owns a large printing plant which he has built in the south yard of the property, and an ell of this building occupies what was once the back yard and covers the area where the barn once stood.

McGinn's son, in his youth, occupied the attic bedroom once used by Bridget Sullivan. He told me that the attic often became unbearably hot during the summer and he often wondered why Bridget should have gone up there to rest on such a hot morning. He also remembers the barn and said that its loft was cool by comparison.

On the evening of June 1, 1927, shortly before her sixty-seventh birthday, Lizzie Borden died at Maplecroft. She had undergone a serious operation the year before and never fully recovered her strength. A local paper reported that, at private funeral services held at her home, Mrs. Alfred G. Turner sang "My Ain Countree." In addition to relatives, pallbearers included Ernest Perry, her chauffeur for many years; Fred Coggeshall, who had been her coachman; and Norman Hall, identified as another former employee. Lizzie was buried in the family plot with her father, mother and stepmother.

The day before Lizzie died, Emma fell in a house in New-market, New Hampshire, where she had been living with a paid companion, and suffered severe injuries. These injuries, plus the shock of learning about her sister's death, are said to have hastened her decline, and ten days after Lizzie's death, Emma also died. Her last request was that her funeral services be held at a cousin's home in Massachusetts and that her pallbearers be colored. These wishes were carried out and she was buried next to the fresh grave of her sister.

When Lizzie's will was filed for probate, newspapers reported that her estate was valued at over a million dollars; this was considerably more than the entire fortune left by her father. In her will she left twenty-nine numbered bequests. The first is, perhaps, the most interesting of them all.

"1. To the City of Fall River the sum of five hundred dollars, the income derived therefrom to be used for the perpetual care of my father's lot in Oak Grove Cemetery in said Fall River."

In the next to the last bequest, she wrote, "I have not given my sister, Emma L. Borden, anything, as she had her share of her father's estate and is supposed to have enough to make her comfortable."

Lizzie remembered many of her old friends and schoolmates with gifts ranging from $1,000 to $5,000. She left $3,000 to each servant who had been with her for at least five years and gave

$2,000 each to the wife and children of her chauffeur. One of the largest of her gifts, $30,000 in cash plus all her shares in the Stevens Manufacturing Company, went to the Animal Rescue League of Fall River. "I have been fond of animals and their need is great and there are so few who care for them," she wrote in her will. She also left money to the Washington, D.C., branch of the same organization. The remainder of her estate she divided equally between Helen Leighton, an old friend, and Mrs. Grace H. Howe, a cousin. The latter also received many fine sets of books that had been part of Lizzie's personal library.

Mrs. Howe, the widow of Louis Howe, former private secretary to President Franklin Delano Roosevelt, broke her long silence about Lizzie Borden in 1942 when she gave an interview to a reporter for a Boston newspaper. She denied that Lizzie had lived as a recluse. She said Lizzie had continued her charitable work after the trial, but had insisted upon absolute secrecy. Mrs. Howe said that Lizzie had financed the college education of many deserving students.

Emma did not leave Lizzie out of her will. She had moved out of the French Street house, but she still owned an interest in it. She left this share of the house to Lizzie and added that if she should dispose of her interest before her death, then Lizzie was to receive $1,000 instead. Emma also honored the memory of her father and left money to the local high school to establish the Andrew J. Borden scholarship. She left varying sums to relatives, friends and charity, $5,000 to the Providence chapter of the Animal Shelter League, and an additional sum to the Massachusetts Society for the Prevention of Cruelty to Animals. Shortly after Emma's will was filed for probate, with the estate valued at almost $500,000, two cousins living in Illinois contested the will, claiming undue influence and charging that she was "of unsound mind when the will was drawn." The disappointed cousins did not contest Lizzie's will, although they were also omitted in her document.

The story has persisted in Fall River for years that Lizzie gave Bridget a fortune for her testimony and that the servant girl returned to Ireland and lived there in great luxury. Through the help of Miss Mollie O'Meara of the Butte Public Library, this writer can reveal for the first time some of the history of Bridget after the trial, and the story of her strange behavior when she thought she was dying.

Bridget Sullivan never returned to the Borden home after the trial and she disappeared not long afterward from Keeper Hunt's home where she had remained as a domestic. If she did go to Ireland, she returned later to this country because she died in a hospital in Butte, Montana, on Thursday, March 26, 1948, at the age of eighty-two. She is buried in Mt. Olivet Cemetery in Anaconda.

Bridget Sullivan first appeared in Anaconda several years after the murders. There she married a man named Sullivan, so there was no change in her last name. Bridget was closemouthed about her past and apparently told no one in Anaconda about her connection with the Borden case. She lived there for forty-five years and then, after a serious illness, moved to Butte, where she remained until her death.

The strange episode occurred during Bridget's serious illness in Anaconda when she was stricken with pneumonia and thought she was dying. When Bridget first emigrated from Ireland, she came to this country with a girl friend from her own home town. They separated soon after landing; Bridget settled in New England, and her friend went on to Montana. They corresponded irregularly over the years. The friend married and became Mrs. Minnie Green. Bridget never wrote to her friend about the Borden murders and Mrs. Green did not hear of the case at the time it happened.

When Bridget finally came to Montana and settled in Anaconda, she resumed her friendship with Mrs. Green, who was living in Butte, about twenty-seven miles distant. The friends visited each other but Bridget still did not mention the Borden murders to her childhood companion.

In 1942, when they were both about seventy-five years of age, Mrs. Green received an urgent telephone call from Bridget who said that she was dying, wanted to see her friend, and had a secret she wanted to confide to her before she passed away. Mrs. Green had to make arrangements to get to Anaconda and this took her a little time. When she arrived, Bridget had passed the crisis in her illness and she recovered shortly afterward.

Several days after visiting Bridget, Mrs. Green entered the Butte Public Library. Miss O'Meara noticed an elderly woman staring at the stacks of books and in obvious need of assistance. The woman hesitantly asked if the library had any books on real murders, and when she learned there were quite a few, asked if anything had been written on the Lizzie Borden case. She told the librarian how Bridget had sent for her and related what occurred during her visit to Anaconda. While the principals were alive, Miss O'Meara never revealed the story; she did not even tell anybody that Bridget Sullivan was living in the area. Since both Bridget and Mrs. Green were dead, she consented in 1960 to tell me the details.

Mrs. Green told Miss O'Meara that Bridget had informed her old friend for the first time that she had been a witness in the Borden case. Bridget said that her testimony was favorable to Lizzie who, to show her gratitude, had given her money to visit her parents in Ireland, and added that the Borden lawyer had advised her to remain in Ireland and never return to the United States. Bridget said she bought a farm for her parents and stocked it with horses, cows, pigs, chickens and sheep. Later, Bridget said, she became restless, obtained a passport under another name and returned to this country, going to Anaconda. Mrs. Green said that Bridget told her she was fond of Lizzie and frequently took her part in family disputes. Bridget also said she had testified only to the truth at the trial.

Mrs. Green, who had known Bridget since they were children, was frankly skeptical of her friend's story. She failed to find anything in it to account for Bridget's urgent demand that she rush to her bedside because she wanted to confide something to her before she died. Mrs. Green borrowed several books on the case from the library and returned them several days afterward. When Miss O'Meara asked if she had learned anything, the older woman shook her head, looked puzzled, and left. As far as Miss O'Meara knows, she never came to the library again. Bridget recovered and moved to Butte. Whether the two old friends saw each other after this episode is also unknown.

Believers in Lizzie's guilt can seize upon this incident to bolster their claim that Bridget withheld information and was paid off by Lizzie. It also would help substantiate the stories about her return to Ireland with a lot of money. Bridget's statement to Mrs. Green is the only evidence that she may have gone back for a time. Bridget still had relatives living in Fall River after the trial and could have heard from them what was being said about her.

There are many reasons to be skeptical of the story Bridget told Mrs. Green. As Mrs. Green realized, Bridget had really said nothing which could explain why she had asked an elderly friend to hurry to her bedside. Her claim that she interjected herself into family disputes to side with Lizzie is unbelievable. So is her insistence that she told only the truth at the trial. And despite what she told Mrs. Green, her trial testimony, as has been shown, was anything but favorable to Lizzie. There are also serious discrepancies in her testimony concerning that vital half hour of time unaccounted for on the morning of the murders. One can only speculate as to what Bridget might have told Mrs. Green had she still thought she was dying when her friend finally arrived.

Pearson presented District Attorney Knowlton as a David battling a mighty Goliath made up of a prejudiced court, a prej-

udiced press, and a jury unwilling to believe that a woman could
have committed the crime; there is no doubt that a woman could
have committed the crime.

Pearson's regard for Knowlton is seen in the dedication of
his trial book: "This book is dedicated to the honored memory
of a courageous public official, Hosea Morrill Knowlton, District Attorney, 1879–1893, Attorney General of Massachusetts,
1894–1901."

Knowlton was the chief architect in building up the prosecution's trial case against Lizzie Borden. The facts show that Marshal Hilliard was reluctant to act on the basis of the information his men had uncovered. It was only after his conference
with Knowlton on Saturday, as reported by Porter who was on
very close terms with Fall River police, that the Marshal went
to court at noon on Monday and obtained a warrant for Lizzie's arrest. He still had not served the warrant late that afternoon when Knowlton came back from New Bedford. The District Attorney did not mention the warrant to reporters: instead,
a spokesman told the newsmen that Knowlton was planning to
hold some sort of informal hearing to get everybody's final story.
In reality, he was planning to hold the very formal secret inquest, starting the next morning.

Lizzie Borden, kept on the stand for the major part of three
days at this inquest, was forced to give her story over and over
and over, and was prodded with sharp remarks and treated in
a way that would have brought a rebuke from any judge in an
open court. At one point, when he did not like her answer to a
question, Knowlton said: "You did not answer my question, and
you will, if I have to put it all day." Yet at the District Court
hearing, when Jennings protested about the secret inquest,
Knowlton remarked that the inquest had been held against no
one. The record hardly substantiates him. ·

Early on the first day of the inquest, Knowlton was questioning Lizzie as to the number of visits Morse had made to the

Borden house. Her answers had been very full and she seemed to be trying to help, when this exchange took place:

Q: Before that had he been at your house, before he came East?

A: Yes, he has been here, if you remember the winter that the river was frozen over and they went across, he was here that winter, some fourteen years ago, was it not?

Q: I am not answering questions, but asking them.

From that point on, Lizzie's answers became brief and curt. She obviously began to realize that Knowlton was more interested in trapping her than in acquiring information. After three days of constant questioning, of being asked to repeat over and over again each act, each word that had been spoken, Knowlton said he had found variations in her testimony and ordered her arrest. The only discrepancy of any real importance that Pearson singled out for special comment was that Lizzie stated on the first day of the inquest that when her father came home she was upstairs and on her way down the steps. The next day she claimed she was in the kitchen when Bridget opened the front door to let her father in. I believe she was correct the first day when she said she was upstairs. Pearson also believes she was upstairs. He said that she changed her testimony because she realized the danger she had placed herself in when she had admitted being so near that open door through which she could see the body of her stepmother. But Kieran's testimony, deleted by Pearson from the trial minutes, shows that Lizzie could not have seen the body of her stepmother whether she was upstairs or downstairs, so the variation in her testimony is not significant.

Pearson blamed two rulings by the three-judge bench as a virtual death blow to the prosecution's case; the one which kept Bence from testifying, and the other which kept the inquest minutes from being presented to the jury.

I have just shown that the major variation in Lizzie's testimony in the inquest minutes was meaningless in view of Kieran's testimony, and I quoted previously from the official District Court minutes that Bence identified Lizzie Borden only by a tremulous voice, and even here was disputed by his companion. Bence's testimony would have been no more effective than the other discredited testimony of other prosecution witnesses.

Pearson quoted at great length from a series of letters written by a judge and an article by a law-school professor to back up his claim that the court was prejudiced in its rulings. Lawyers love to argue over legal interpretations. How long and assiduously Pearson had to look to find his two examples, I do not know; I do know that scores of communications were sent to newspapers at that time by eminent members of the bar who upheld the rulings of the court.

In his book *The Fall River Tragedy*, Porter wrote, "The Government authorities knew that once the warrant had been issued, Miss Borden's character, which had always been irreproachable, was blotted forever; it must have known that even if she left the Superior Court acquitted, nothing that it could do could lift the blight from her life."

He wrote these words in justification of the arrest of Lizzie Borden. To him, it was inconceivable that Lizzie Borden would be arrested unless the authorities fully believed they had a solid case against her. Did they all believe this? Here is a letter written by Knowlton to Attorney General Pillsbury some months before the trial:

NEW BEDFORD, MASS.
April 24, 1893

Hon. A. E. Pillsbury, Attorney General:
MY DEAR SIR:
I have thought more about the Lizzie Borden case since I talked with you and think perhaps that it may be well to write

you, as I shall not be able to meet you probably until Thursday, possibly Wednesday, afternoon.

Personally, I would like very much to get rid of the trial of the case, and fear my own feelings in that direction may have influenced my better judgment. I feel this all the more upon your not unexpected announcement that the burden of the trial would come upon me.

I confess, however, I cannot see my way clear to any disposition of the case other than a trial. Should it result in disagreement of the jury there would be no difficulty then in disposing of the case by admitting the defendant to bail; but a verdict either way would render such a course unnecessary.

The case has proceeded so far, and an indictment has been found by the Grand Inquest of the county, that it does not seem to me that we ought to take the responsibility of discharging her without trial, even though there is every reasonable expectation of a verdict of Not Guilty. I am unable to concur fully in your views as to the probable result. I think it may well be that the jury might disagree upon the case. But even in my most sanguine moments I have scarcely expected a verdict of guilty.

The situation is this: nothing has developed which satisfies either of us that she is innocent, neither of us can escape the conclusion that she must have had some knowledge of the occurrence. She has been presented for trial by a jury which, to say the least, was not influenced by anything said by the Government in favor of the indictment.

Without discussing the matter more fully in this letter I will only say as above indicated that I cannot see how any other course than setting the case down for trial, and trying it, will satisfy that portion of public sentiment, whether favorable to her or not, which is worthy of being respected.

June seems to be the most satisfactory month, all things con-

sidered. I will write more fully as to the admission of her con-
fession after I have looked the matter up.

Yours truly,

HOSEA M. KNOWLTON

Knowlton's reference in his letter to Lizzie Borden's confession was, of course, an error. More than likely he was referring to
her inquest testimony. The letter plainly indicates that Attorney
General Pillsbury, the highest law official of the state, had his
doubts as to the admissibility of the inquest testimony as evidence. Yet Pearson calls the court prejudiced for doing what the
Attorney General expected.

Whether Pillsbury agreed with Knowlton's assertion in the
letter that both of them were not satisfied that she was innocent,
is not known. Pillsbury's actions certainly indicate he thought
otherwise, since the letter reveals that he did not want Knowlton even to bring her to trial, and he emphasized the point by
announcing months before the trial that because of "ill health"
he would not take part in the prosecution.

But the astonishing part of Knowlton's letter was his sentence, "But even in my most sanguine moments I have scarcely
expected a verdict of guilty."

Knowlton was the man responsible for Lizzie Borden's arrest. He was the man who tried Lizzie Borden. Yet he admitted
in his letter he was trying her without the necessary evidence. He
was willing to blight her life with nothing more than a belief
that she *might* be guilty, without the evidence to back it up.
Anybody can believe anything; that does not make it true, and
it certainly does not justify an arrest on a first-degree murder
charge. Knowlton, of course, did not lose by his belief. A district attorney who can take advantage of a situation so that it
will result in headlines, often does so because the publicity can
have a desirable effect on his political career. That same fall the

"courageous public official" was elected attorney general of Massachusetts to replace the retiring Pillsbury.

The Lizzie Borden legend is still growing. The hints, rumors and innuendoes that served Pearson so well have not satisfied some people; they now make flat, unequivocal statements that she was guilty beyond any doubt. The only thing seemingly lacking in the case against her was a confession. This defect was remedied in 1959 and the blight was now complete.

In that year Edward Rowe Snow, writer and newspaper columnist, the author of thirty-five books dealing mainly with pirates, buried treasure, lighthouses, and sea stories of New England, published *Piracy, Mutiny and Murder*. One chapter concerned the Lizzie Borden case.

Snow tells how, after discussing the Borden case in a radio broadcast in 1952, he received a letter from a man who stated that he possessed a confession signed by Lizzie Borden. Snow went to see the writer of the letter in Providence where he was then living and heard the following story, an outgrowth of the popular belief in the Tilden-Thurber shoplifting episode. Lizzie, Snow's informant said, was summoned to the Tilden-Thurber store in 1897, accused of theft and told that a warrant had been sworn out against her. She denied the charge and said that she had purchased the articles legitimately. She was asked to return again for another conference. This was held a few days later and Lizzie was shown a story which had been prepared for newspaper release, saying that the warrant had been issued.

Her reaction, as described, was dramatic: "Her anger rose at once. 'You wouldn't dare publish that,' she shrieked, her eyes flashing."

The story appeared in the Providence *Journal* the next day, and Detective Parker visited Lizzie in Fall River and told her that service of the warrant might be postponed if she would return to Tilden-Thurber's with him at once. "Blustering and fuming for the next few minutes, Lizzie finally calmed down . . ." She then accompanied Parker to Providence and a final conference took place at the store beginning at six P.M. Present were Henry Tilden and William Thurber of the silversmith firm, Morris House, an employee, Parker, and Stephen O. Metcalf, "who later became an important figure on the Providence *Journal*." She was told that if she confessed to the murders the theft charge would be dropped. She was also promised that none of the five men would ever "reveal to a living soul" that she had confessed.

"Never," Lizzie is said to have replied. "Never, never, never!"

A six-hour conference followed which Snow describes dramatically with verbatim conversations. Lizzie remained adamant. At eight minutes to twelve she was told that unless she signed a confession before midnight the warrant would be served and she would go to jail. Lizzie remained silent. On the stroke of midnight, as Parker started to serve the warrant, Lizzie walked across to a typewriter and began typing. Then she wrote her signature. The undated two-line document is reproduced below.

Unfair means force my signature here admitting
the act of August 4, 1892 as mine alone.

Lizbeth A. Borden

The next day House decided to have a copy of the confession made, in case the original should ever be lost or destroyed. "Going to Boston, to get far enough away," he went to a photographic shop and ordered the copy. He then, according to Snow's account, did a curious thing. "Because of the desire for secrecy, House told him [the photographer] the story in full. . . ."

This man, Snow's informant, "agreed never to reveal what he had been told."

Mr. House was much luckier than some people who confide secrets in others; the photographer's assistant claimed he kept the secret from 1897 until he told it to Snow in 1952, after all five of the men concerned and Lizzie were dead.

House, he said, ordered one print and took it and the negative with him. The photographer did not tell him that he had retained a first print that had not turned out too well. A copy of this print, which he had kept for fifty-five years, he turned over to Snow, who visited the Tilden-Thurber store the same day and was told by a store official that he recalled seeing a sealed envelope in the safe but that "everything in the safe had been reduced to indecipherable pulp by the action of the hurricane of 1938." Snow also says that "no one alive today has any knowledge of what happened to the plate and print which Mr. House had made, but it is believed to have been destroyed in a fire around the year 1913."

Since my researches indicated that Lizzie was innocent I could not believe that she had signed the confession which Snow quoted in his book. I visited Snow on one of my research trips, told him that I doubted that the confession was authentic, and asked if I might have a copy of it.

Snow said that at first he had also been skeptical. The photographer, an elderly man in poor health, had been living on a small pension and had asked $100 for a copy of the confession. Snow offered $50 and bought it for that amount, more as a literary curiosity than because he had any belief in it. The photographer also asked that the confession not be published until after his death. Snow agreed, and even after the man died he did not publish it at once. Snow says that he showed it to the late Joseph Welch and was urged by this noted lawyer to investigate the document further. He learned that the photography shop in which his informant said he had worked had

existed at the Boston address. After traveling through much of
the state, he finally located relatives of the deceased owner of
the shop who told him that his informant had been working
there in 1897, as he had said. Since these statements checked
out and since Snow did not think his informant would have in-
vented such a detailed story in order to obtain such a small sum
of money, Snow concluded that he had been telling the truth,
and he then published the story. Snow gave me a photo copy
of the confession, told me to conduct my own investigation and
then use the confession as I saw fit, with no strings attached.

With my knowledge of scientific crime detection, my in-
vestigative approach differed completely. I noted that the
confession was signed Lizbeth A. Borden. Lizzie began using the
name Lizbeth some time after the trial but she signed most of
her letters simply L. A. Borden. I had seen no letters signed
Lizbeth as early as 1897.

I compared the confession signature with those on letters
written by her in 1897. The latter were firm, clear and flowing;
the confession signature was shaky and ragged. If the confession
story were true, this might have been due to her emotional
stress at the time she wrote it, but since a person's handwriting
changes and deteriorates with age it could also mean that the
signature was written at a later date. I then made another comparison. Samples of Lizzie's signature are not readily available;
most of her letters are in the possession of family friends, a few
collectors, and the Fall River Historical Society. There is one
notable exception. Her will is on file. It is a public document
and anyone can obtain a photostat of it upon payment of a
nominal fee.

I had seen a copy of the will and knew that Lizzie had affixed
two signatures. She had first signed Lizbeth A. Borden and then
her legal signature: Lizzie A. Borden.

I obtained a photostatic copy of the will from the Probate
Court in Taunton and compared the alleged 1897 signature on

the confession with the Lizbeth A. Borden signature on the will, written twenty-nine years later, in 1926. They are remarkably similar. But the similarity is *too* great. Except for the fact that the confession signature had been written with a much broader pen than the fine-pointed one Lizzie used on the will, the signatures were identical. A person's signature always varies. Even in the two signatures which Lizzie had signed on the will, seconds apart, the middle initial and the last name are not identical. She could not have written the confession signature in 1897, at the age of thirty-seven, and then duplicated it so exactly on her will, twenty-nine years later when she was sixty-six, ill, and facing a major operation.

A Simon and Schuster editor, Clayton Rawson, had photostatic copies made of both signatures, enlarging them to the same size. We superimposed one on the other and held them over a light. The two signatures coincide perfectly. Two signatures so alike meant only one thing to me: one must have been traced from the other. The confession signature must have been traced from the will signature.

Since I am not an expert in handwriting analysis I decided to get a professional opinion. There are, in this country, a number of court-recognized specialists popularly called handwriting experts, but known professionally as questioned document examiners. They are qualified to examine paper, ink, and typewriting, as well as handwriting.

One of the outstanding experts is Ordway Hilton of 15 Park Row, New York City. He is president of the American Society of Questioned Document Examiners, whose membership is composed of the recognized experts in this country. He is former president of the American Academy of Forensic Sciences, an organization of the leading medico-legal experts, and he is Police Science Editor of the *Journal of Criminal Law, Criminology and Police Science,* published by Northwestern University Law School. Mr. Hilton is author of the book, *The Scientific Examination of Questioned Documents,* has served for many years as lecturer at a special course given yearly for prosecuting attorneys by Northwestern University and also lectures at the Southern Police Institute held at the University of Louisville. He was one of the experts in the Alger Hiss typewriter investigation; he testified for the New York State Crime Commission during its waterfront investigation; and his private clients include banks and the Vincent Astor estate.

I turned over to Mr. Hilton the copy of the alleged confession given to me by Snow, the photostat of the will containing the Lizbeth A. Borden signature and photographic copies of letters written by Lizzie, including two written in 1897. I asked him to determine whether the signature on the confession was genuine and also to ascertain, if possible, the year and make of the typewriter used.

I later received a detailed, six-page report from Mr. Hilton in which he confirmed that the signature on the alleged confession is actually a very accurate tracing of the will signature. "When the signature to the alleged confession is studied in detail," he wrote, "it is found that there is evidence, particularly in the 'n' of Borden, of the pen having been taken from the paper twice. The very heavy strokes, particularly in the 'A,' suggest a going over of the signature to correct slight defects in form. All in all the slightly greater tremor or uncertainty that appears in several strokes of this signature to the alleged confession compared to the will signature, coincidences in design, spacing, and proportions, established definitely that the signature to the alleged confession is a forgery and that it was prepared by tracing from some reproduction of the will signature in 1926."

In a letter accompanying the report, Mr. Hilton summarized his handwriting findings as follows:

ORDWAY HILTON

ELBRIDGE W. STEIN - ORDWAY HILTON
EXAMINERS OF QUESTIONED DOCUMENTS - HANDWRITING AND TYPEWRITING

15 PARK ROW

NEW YORK 38, NEW YORK

BArclay 7-7095

ast-President
can Academy of
ensic Sciences
President-
rican Society of
ioned Document
Examiners

Laboratory
8 North Star Drive
Morristown, New Jersey
JEfferson 8-3028

December 7, 1960

Dear Mr. Radin:

I am enclosing herewith my report on the so called Lizzie Borden
confession, a typewritten statement which reads: "Unfair means
force my signature here admitting the act of August 4, 1892 as
mine alone," and which bears a signature Lizbeth A. Borden.

I have made a careful study of the signatures of Miss Borden
including those written in 1897 and those written on her will
in 1926. After this study and as a result of the comparison
of these signatures with the signature to the so called
confession, I have reached the definite conclusions set forth
in detail in my report under the heading, Opinion and Reasons.
My findings can be summarized as follows:

1. It is my definite opinion that Miss Borden did not
   sign the so called confession.

2. It is my further opinion that the signature to this
   document is in fact a traced forgery, the signature
   being a very accurate tracing of the signature Lizbeth
   A. Borden which she affixed to her will in 1926.

3. It is impossible to conceive that Lizbeth A. Borden
   could have signed two signatures exactly the same in
   detail and design of letters some 29 years apart and
   to have one exactly proportional to the other in every
   detail.

4. When the document as a whole is considered in the light
   of the findings regarding the signature, it is obvious
   that the confession is fraudulent.

Very truly yours,

Ordway Hilton
OH:gm
Enc.

1. It is my definite opinion that Miss Borden did not sign the so-called confession.

2. It is my further opinion that the signature to this document is in fact a traced forgery, the signature being a very accurate tracing of the signature Lizbeth A. Borden which she affixed to her will in 1926.

3. It is impossible to conceive that Lizbeth A. Borden could have signed two signatures exactly the same in detail and design of letters some 29 years apart and to have one exactly proportional to the other in every detail.

4. When the document as a whole is considered in the light of the findings regarding the signature, it is obvious that the confession is fraudulent.

His complete letter is reproduced here.

Mr. Hilton's report on the typewriting is also extremely interesting. He pointed out that the entire statement consists of only 15 words for a total of 72 typewritten characters and some of these letters were repeated several times. "Their repeated impressions show very great variation. The form of one or two letters is so different from typewriting that they look as though incomplete impressions could have been traced over with pencil or ink. Some of the forms of letters, particularly the 'a,' 'e,' and 't,' vary from one impression to another to such an extent that it is not easy to estimate what the original design was like. The type faces themselves undoubtedly were worn."

Mr. Hilton concluded that the fake confession had probably been typed on a Caligraph, an early machine which is no longer made, with a type face which was first introduced about 1895. The forger had managed to locate a machine of the proper period but had overlooked the fact that the typewriter would have been almost new in 1897. The impression of the typewritten characters in the confession indicates that both the type and

Unfair means force my signature here admitting
the act of August 4, 1892 as mine alone.

Lizbeth A. Borden

L. A. Borden · Miss L. A. Borden

nineteen hundred and twenty-six.   D

August 4, 1892 as mine alone.

Lizbeth A. Borden
Lizzie A. Borden

Lizbeth A. Borden

Lizbeth A. Borden   F

Lizbeth A. Borden

LIZZIE BORDEN "CONFESSION" HANDWRITING EXHIBITS

(a)   The confession which Lizzie Borden is said to have typed and
signed in 1897.

(b)   Two signatures taken from letters which Lizzie Borden wrote on
December 12, 1896, and March 6, 1897, when she was 36. Note easy,
graceful flow of writing; also formation of the "B's."

(c)   The signatures which Lizzie affixed to her will in 1926 at the age
of 66. Note deterioration of writing due to age and how strokes of the
"B" have closed up.

(d)   The "confession" signature in negative form.

(e)   A composite in which the will signature has been superimposed
on the "confession" signature. The black will signature falls neatly
within the heavier white "confession" signature.

(f)   The black upper portion of the will signature lines up exactly
with the lower portion of the "confession" signature and also shows
that the 1897 "confession" signature is a forged tracing of the 1926
signature on the will.

the roller on the machine used were so worn that only many years of use could account for the condition.

The fake confession is another example of how the case against Lizzie Borden crumbles when it is subjected to careful examination.

In his Lizzie Borden chapter Snow also printed another story against Lizzie which he had reported earlier in his 1952 radio broadcast. In April of that year, he said, he had met an elderly man, now deceased, in Fall River, and had recorded on tape the following story. The informant stated that at the time of the murders he had been twelve years old and was working as a Western Union messenger boy. He said that he was passing the Borden house when he saw Bridget run across the street to Dr. Bowen's house. He was there when the first policeman, Officer Allen, arrived. He became curious and waited. Allen, after learning of Mr. Borden's murder, hurried back to the station, made his report, and then returned to the Borden house to find that Mrs. Borden's body had been discovered. At this point the messenger boy said that he overheard Allen question Lizzie and heard her say that she had been up in the barn loft looking for sinkers.

The boy decided to investigate this alibi for himself, obtained a ladder, climbed up and looked into the loft. He saw dust almost a half-inch thick on the floor and undisturbed cobwebs across the head of the stairs. He realized that Lizzie was lying about having been up in the loft and he ran home and told his mother. She advised him not to tell anyone because she did not want him to become involved. He managed to remain uninvolved by withholding this startling information for sixty years!

There are several things in the trial testimony that contradict this story. Allen testified to his actions in detail at the trial and made no mention of Lizzie having told him that she had been up in the loft. The first time she told anyone that she had been up in the loft was after the noon hour when she was questioned in her room by Officer Harrington and later by Assistant Marshal Fleet. Allen had long before returned to more prosaic duties at headquarters. Since the messenger boy says he knew what Lizzie's alibi was before she told anyone he must have been psychic.

The prosecution actually used the fact that Lizzie had not told her story of being up in the loft until later as a point against her. The messenger boy also gave no reason for having gone to the trouble of finding and using a ladder when there were stairs in the barn leading up to the loft. A great many people testified to having gone up into the loft and none of them, including the sharp-eyed Officer Medley, saw anything of a barrier of cobwebs.

The messenger boy's story is like many others that can be heard in Fall River today. I was assured by dozens of people that when Mrs. Churchill, the next-door neighbor, started upstairs to get a sheet so that Dr. Bowen could cover Mr. Borden's body, Lizzie plainly indicated that she knew that another body was yet to be found by saying, "Better get two."

Many of these people said they had heard the story from Mrs. Churchill's son who was a young boy at the time and is no longer living. I have little doubt that the son did tell such a story; whether or not he told it with his tongue in his cheek, I don't know. The trial record clearly shows that Dr. Bowen asked for a sheet, that Lizzie asked Bridget to get it, that the maid said she was afraid to go up alone, and that Mrs. Churchill volunteered to go with her. At that time Bridget, Mrs. Churchill and Miss Russell were all in the kitchen with Lizzie. Neither Miss Russell nor Bridget had any hesitancy in testifying against Lizzie and yet neither they nor Mrs. Churchill reported hearing Lizzie say anything about getting two sheets.

Information comes at times from least expected sources. While I was still searching for the elusive official trial minutes, I visited the clerk's office of the Superior Court in Taunton. Mrs.

Estella Margarido, the head clerk, kindly conducted a long and arduous search through tons of records without success. Before leaving, I chatted with her for a few moments. She was young, had never lived in Fall River, and seemed unlikely to know anything firsthand about Lizzie Borden. I idly remarked that I was trying to find people who had seen and known Lizzie and could tell me things they knew personally.

"Well, I know something about her," she said unexpectedly. "When I was a little girl I went to the Hornbine School. It was a one-room schoolhouse at the edge of Swansea. There was a boy attending the school who you might say was feeble-minded. He never learned anything, but he sat quietly and it was a way of keeping him out of mischief. Every year on the day school opened, a large black car, with a woman in back and a chauffeur in front, would pull up to the school and the boy would run to the car. The woman always had some presents for him: clothes, some simple toys that could keep him amused, and some pocket money. This went on year after year while I was attending the school. The woman was Lizzie Borden. The boy lived on a farm not far from her place in Swansea."

She paused and looked out of a window at the busy stream of traffic beyond the courthouse square. "You know," she said softly, almost as if speaking to herself, "they say so many terrible things about Lizzie Borden. I saw those gifts and I realized how much care and thought went into selecting them to make certain they would be appropriate for a boy like that. I have never believed she could be as bad as they say."

Bibliography

(AUTHOR'S NOTE: *The following are among the more important works on the Borden Case.*)

NONFICTION

Davis, Judge Charles G. *The Conduct of the Law in the Borden Case.* A series of letters published originally in the Boston *Daily Advertiser* in December 1893. A legal discussion in which the letter writer disagreed with some of the rulings by the Court. Quoted extensively by Pearson.

Lunday, Todd. "The Mystery Unveiled: The Truth about the Borden Tragedy." Providence: J. A. & R. A. Reid, 1893. A rare 56-page pamphlet, published immediately after the trial, in which the writer concludes that, with Lizzie Borden acquitted and no other suspect substituted, nobody committed the murders. The only copy known to this writer is at the Harvard University Law School Library.

Patrick, Q. (pseudonym). "The Case for Lizzie" in *The Pocket Book of True Crime Stories,* ed., Anthony Boucher. New York: Pocket Books, Inc., 1943.

Pearson, Edmund. *Studies in Murder.* New York: The Macmillan Co., 1924.
———*Five Murders.* New York: Doubleday, Doran & Co., 1928.

Contains chapter, "End of the Borden Case," a revision of article appearing in *Forum* magazine, March 1928.

———— "The Whole Truth about Lizzie Borden at Last!" in *True Detective Mysteries,* July 1931.

———— *More Studies in Murder.* New York: Harrison Smith and Robert Haas, 1936. Contains chapter, "Legends of Lizzie," which first appeared in *The New Yorker,* April 22, 1933.

———— *Trial of Lizzie Borden.* New York: Doubleday, Doran & Co., 1937.

Porter, Edwin H. *The Fall River Tragedy.* Fall River: George R. H. Buffington, 1893. Written shortly after the trial. Porter was a police reporter for the Fall River *Globe.*

Samuels, Charles and Louise. *The Girl in the House of Hate.* Gold Medal Books. New York: Fawcett Publications, Inc., 1953. The authors went to Fall River and New Bedford to gather material. They did not locate the trial minutes but published, from newspaper accounts, some of the testimony deleted by Pearson.

Snow, Edward Rowe. *Piracy, Mutiny and Murders.* New York: Dodd, Mead & Co., 1959. Contains Lizzie's alleged confession.

Wigmore, John H. "The Borden Case" in *The American Law Review,* November–December 1893. A legal discussion, probably based upon newspaper clippings, since it contains errors of fact. Quoted at length by Pearson.

Fiction

Bierstadt, Edward Hale. *Satan Was a Man.* New York: Doubleday, Doran & Co., 1935.

Lowndes, Marie Belloc. *Lizzie Borden: A Study in Conjecture.* New York: Longmans, Green & Co., Inc., 1930.

DRAMA

Colton, John and Miles, Carlton. *Nine Pine Street* (1934).

De La Torre, Lillian. *Goodbye, Miss Lizzie Borden* (1947). First published in *Murder: Plain and Fanciful*, ed., James Sandoe. New York: Sheridan House, 1948. Has been presented on television.

Denham, Reginald, and Percy, Edward. *Suspect* (1940).

Lawrence, Reginald. *The Legend of Lizzie* (1959). A two-act play; closed after two performances on Broadway.

Reach, James. *Murder Takes the Stage*. New York: Samuel French, Inc., 1957. A three-act play in which a woman known as "Miss Liz," who had been acquitted fifty years earlier for a double-ax murder, becomes a suspect in a new murder. Mr. Reach said his inspiration for the "Miss Liz" character was based upon Lizzie Borden. The play contains a quatrain similar to the famous one.

MISCELLANEOUS

Case and Trial of Lizzie A. Borden. Cambridge: Harvard University Law School Library. A bound volume of clippings from the Boston *Herald* and the Boston *Record* containing news accounts of the murders and the trial.

Fall River Legend, a ballet by Agnes De Mille. Choreography by Miss De Mille. Music by Morton Gould. Presented several times yearly since 1948 by the American Ballet Theatre.

Minutes of preliminary hearing in Second District Court, Fall River, August 25–September 1, 1892.

Official trial minutes, June 5–20, 1893, 2 vol., 1,930 pp.

About the Author

EDWARD D. RADIN *has covered hundreds of murder cases and trials as a reporter. For almost twenty years his work has appeared in nearly every major American magazine, as well as in seven previous books. He is the only writer to have received two Mystery Writers of America "Edgar" awards for fact-crime writing. He lives in Glen Cove, New York, is married and has two daughters, one of whom once appeared in a school play in the role of—Lizzie Borden.*

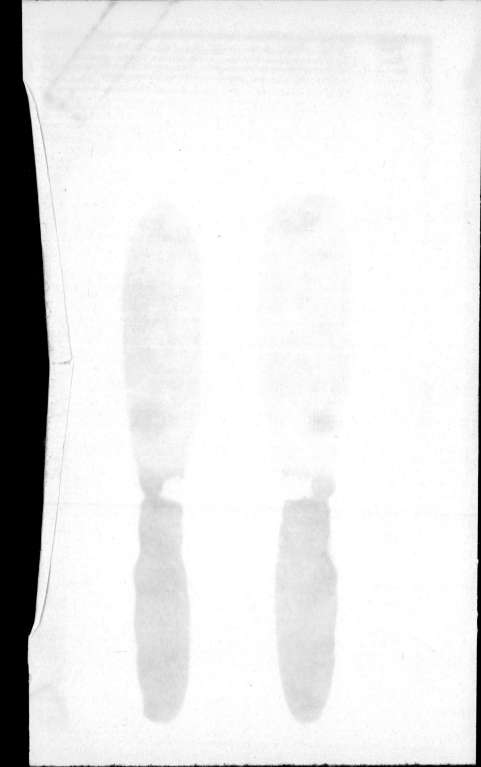